Teacher's Guide

1

A CONVERSATION BOOK
English in Everyday Life

FOURTH EDITION

D1609217

PEARSON
Longman

Sarah Lynn

A Conversation Book 1, Fourth Edition, Teacher's Guide

Pearson Education, 10 Bank Street, White Plains, NY 10606

Staff credits: The people who made up the *A Conversation Book 1, Fourth Edition, Teacher's Guide* team,
representing editorial, production, design, and manufacturing, are: Karen Davy, Nancy Flaggman,
Sasha Kintzler, Laura LeDrean, Melissa Leyva, Amy McCormick, and Patricia Wosczyk

Text design: Patricia Wosczyk
Text composition: Integra
Text font: 11/13 Times Roman
Cover art: Andrew Lange

ISBN: 0-13-150048-1

Printed in the United States of America
3 4 5 6 7 8 9 10–OPM–10 09 08

CONTENTS

Introduction—Welcome to *A Conversation Book 1* v

Scope and Sequence. viii

To the Teacher xiv

Unit-by-Unit Teaching Suggestions 1

UNIT 1   Welcome to Class! 3

UNIT 2   Everyday Life 14

UNIT 3   Your Home. 26

UNIT 4   Food 39

UNIT 5   Your Community 51

UNIT 6   Shopping 62

UNIT 7   Your Calendar. 74

UNIT 8   Your Health. 87

UNIT 9   Your Work. 97

UNIT 10   Your Free Time 108

Unit Tests 1–10. 121

Welcome to A Conversation Book 1

Every unit has a clear and consistent format.

Find out what students already know.

Introduce a conversation strategy and practice it in the unit.

Use Conversation Chants with Carolyn Graham on the CD to practice the rhythms of American speech.

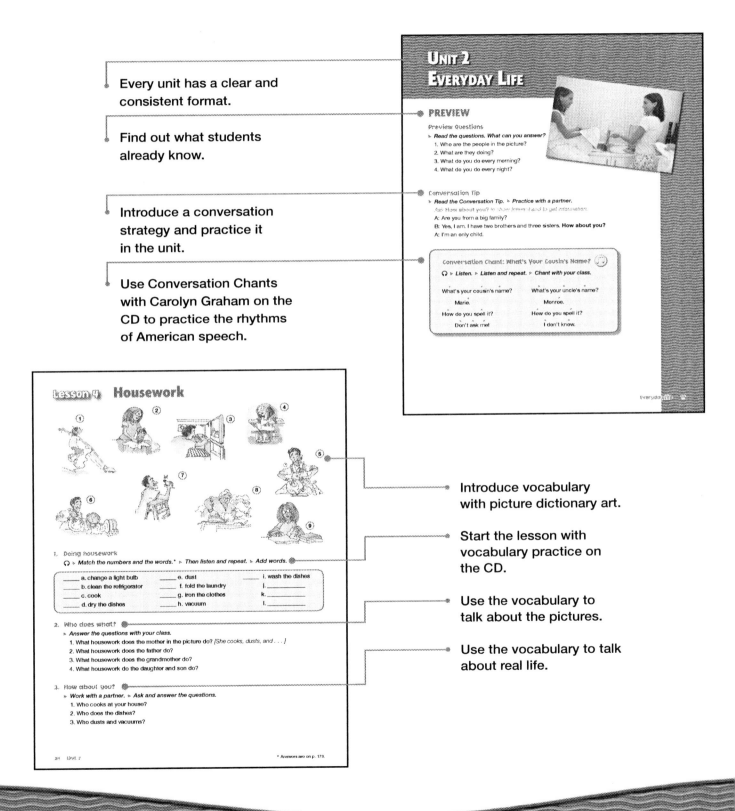

Introduce vocabulary with picture dictionary art.

Start the lesson with vocabulary practice on the CD.

Use the vocabulary to talk about the pictures.

Use the vocabulary to talk about real life.

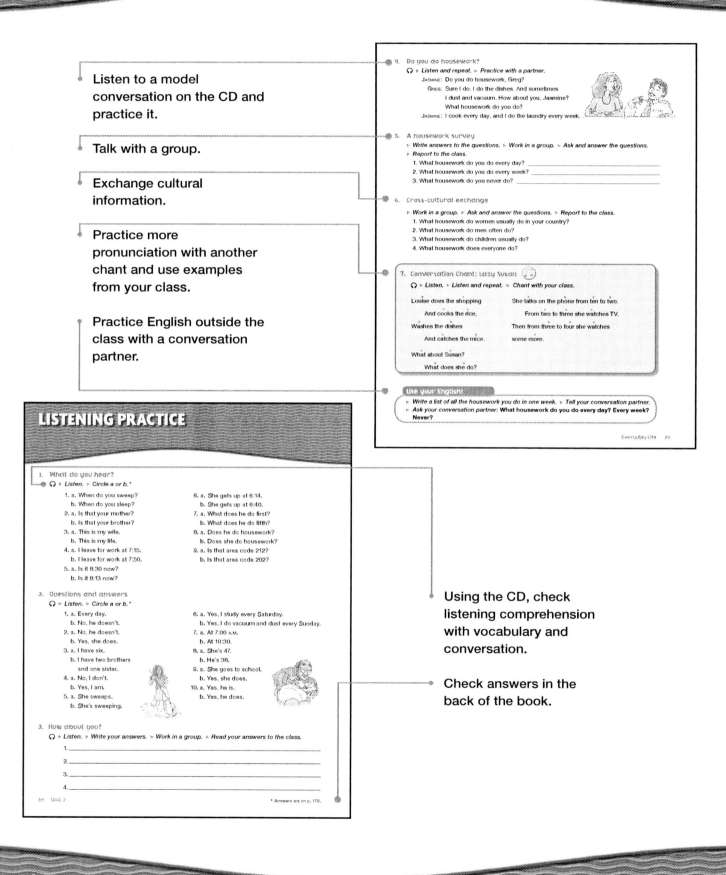

Listen to a model conversation on the CD and practice it.

Talk with a group.

Exchange cultural information.

Practice more pronunciation with another chant and use examples from your class.

Practice English outside the class with a conversation partner.

4. Do you do housework?

🎧 ▸ *Listen and repeat.* ▸ *Practice with a partner.*

JASMINE: Do you do housework, Greg?
GREG: Sure I do. I do the dishes. And sometimes I dust and vacuum. How about you, Jasmine? What housework do you do?
JASMINE: I cook every day, and I do the laundry every week.

5. A housework survey

▸ *Write answers to the questions.* ▸ *Work in a group.* ▸ *Ask and answer the questions.*
▸ *Report to the class.*
1. What housework do you do every day? _____
2. What housework do you do every week? _____
3. What housework do you never do? _____

6. Cross-cultural exchange

▸ *Work in a group.* ▸ *Ask and answer the questions.* ▸ *Report to the class.*
1. What housework do women usually do in your country?
2. What housework do men often do?
3. What housework do children usually do?
4. What housework does everyone do?

7. Conversation Chant: Lazy Susan

🎧 ▸ *Listen.* ▸ *Listen and repeat.* ▸ *Chant with your class.*

Louise does the shopping
And cooks the rice,
Washes the dishes
And catches the mice.
What about Susan?
What does she do?

She talks on the phone from ten to two.
From two to three she watches TV.
Then from three to four she watches some more.

Use your English!

▸ *Write a list of all the housework you do in one week.* ▸ *Tell your conversation partner.*
▸ *Ask your conversation partner: What housework do you do every day? Every week? Never?*

LISTENING PRACTICE

1. What do you hear?

🎧 ▸ *Listen.* ▸ *Circle a or b.* *

1. a. When do you sweep?
   b. When do you sleep?
2. a. Is that your mother?
   b. Is that your brother?
3. a. This is my wife.
   b. This is my life.
4. a. I leave for work at 7:15.
   b. I leave for work at 7:50.
5. a. Is it 8:30 now?
   b. Is it 8:13 now?

6. a. She gets up at 6:14.
   b. She gets up at 6:40.
7. a. What does he do first?
   b. What does he do fifth?
8. a. Does he do housework?
   b. Does she do housework?
9. a. Is that area code 212?
   b. Is that area code 202?

2. Questions and answers

🎧 ▸ *Listen.* ▸ *Circle a or b.* *

1. a. Every day.
   b. No, he doesn't.
2. a. No, he doesn't.
   b. Yes, she does.
3. a. I have six.
   b. I have two brothers and one sister.
4. a. No, I don't.
   b. Yes, I am.
5. a. She sweeps.
   b. She's sweeping.

6. a. Yes, I study every Saturday.
   b. Yes, I do vacuum and dust every Sunday.
7. a. At 7:00 A.M.
   b. At 10:30.
8. a. She's 47.
   b. He's 38.
9. a. She goes to school.
   b. Yes, she does.
10. a. Yes, he is.
    b. Yes, he does.

3. How about you?

🎧 ▸ *Listen.* ▸ *Write your answers.* ▸ *Work in a group.* ▸ *Read your answers to the class.*

1. _____
2. _____
3. _____
4. _____

* Answers are on p. 179.

Using the CD, check listening comprehension with vocabulary and conversation.

Check answers in the back of the book.

Review the unit with your class.

Play a game—have fun!

1. Get to know your partner.
   ▸ Work with a partner. ▸ Ask and answer questions about your families. ▸ Take notes.
   ▸ Tell the class about your partner.

2. What time . . . ?
   ▸ Complete the two questions. ▸ Write a third question. ▸ Walk around your classroom.
   ▸ Ask three students your questions. ▸ Then answer their questions.
   1. What time is _____?
   2. What time do _____?
   3. _____?

3. Housework: Who am I?
   ▸ On a piece of paper, write one kind of housework and how often you do it (every day, every
     week, always, often, sometimes, never). ▸ Fold your paper. ▸ Make a pile. ▸ Open one.
   ▸ Read it to the class. ▸ Guess who it is.

4. What do you do?
   ▸ Work with a partner. ▸ Ask and answer the questions.
   1. What do you do first in the morning? Second? Third? Last?
   2. What do you usually do each day of the week?

5. Favorite day
   ▸ Work with a group. ▸ Ask and answer the questions.
   1. What's your favorite day of the week?
   2. Why?

Everyday Life   31

ASSESSMENT

PART 1: Questions
▸ Write questions to ask a classmate.
   1. Family: _____
   2. Time: _____
   3. Morning routine: _____
   4. Housework: _____
   5. Telephone: _____

PART 2: Speaking
▸ Work with a partner. ▸ Ask and answer your questions from Part 1.

PART 3: Listening
🎧 ▸ Listen. ▸ Circle a or b. *
   1. a. Yes, she is.
      b. Yes, she does.
   2. a. He watches TV.
      b. They practice their English.
   3. a. She's 18.
      b. She's fine, thanks.
   4. a. It's 6:30. He's getting up.
      b. He gets up and takes a shower.
   5. a. Every day.
      b. Yes, I do the dishes.
   6. a. I go to work.
      b. I leave for class.

Find out what you have learned.

PART 4: Writing
▸ Write conversations for these pictures.

   HARRY: What a cute baby!
   GRANDFATHER: Thanks. She's my _____
   HARRY: What's her name? How old is she?
   GRANDFATHER: _____

   GREG: _____
   JASMINE: _____
   GREG: _____
   JASMINE: _____

32   Unit 2   * Answers are on p. 179.

SCOPE AND SEQUENCE

Units	Life Skills	Social Language	Conversation Tip	Conversation Chants
UNIT 1 **Welcome to Class!**	• Making introductions • Spelling names • Practicing cardinal numbers • Talking about countries and continents • Asking and answering questions about colors and clothing • Discussing feelings • Talking about classroom objects, rules, and activities • Giving and following instructions	• Nice to meet you. • Oh, sorry. • Where are you from? • How are you today? • You look good in red. • Where is it? • What's this in English? • Bye. • See you later.	Ask *Is that...?* to confirm new information	• *I'm Worried* • *What's Your First Name?* • *How's Brad?* • *Look at Ted!*
UNIT 2 **Everyday Life**	• Describing your family • Telling time • Describing daily routines • Talking about housework • Describing your everyday life • Using the telephone	• Are you married? • How many brothers and sisters do you have? • How old are they? • How about you? • What do you do every day? • What time do you get up? • What do you do after class? • Who's calling please? • I'm sorry, you have the wrong number. • Do you have a cell phone?	Ask *How about you?* to show interest and to get information.	• *What's Your Cousin's name?* • *My Dog's a Night Owl!* • *Lazy Susan*
UNIT 3 **Your Home**	• Describing your home • Talking about kitchens • Talking about dining areas and living rooms • Talking about bedrooms • Talking about bathrooms • Talking about problems at home	• What street do you live on? • What's your apartment number? • What's your ZIP code? • What's your area code? • What's your e-mail address? • What's wrong? • What's the problem? • What do you want to do today? • What do you have to do today?	Ask *How do you say this in English?* and *How do you spell that?* to learn new words.	• *Kathy's Dog Moved to Paris* • *A House Is Not a Home* • *Where's My Toothbrush?*

Listening	CASAS	LAUSD	LCPs
• Answering questions on conversations about greetings, introductions, countries and languages and feelings • Answering questions about classroom items and activities	0.1.1, 0.1.2, 0.1.3, 0.1.4, 0.1.5, 0.1.6, 0.2.1, 0.2.2, 0.2.4, 1.1.9, 1.3.9, 2.2.1, 4.6.1, 5.2.5, 7.4.1, 7.4.7	I.1, I.2, I.4, I.5, I.7, II, II.9 a–d, II.10, II.11.a–c, II.12, II.14. a & b, II.12, II.13, III.A.15, III.A.18, IV.33, IV.34, VIII.58.a–c, VIII.59.a & b	36.04, 39.01, 39.02, 39.03, 39.04, 41.02, 43.02, 45.04, 48.03, 49.01, 49.02, 49.03, 49.17, (56.02)
• Understanding questions and statements about time and everyday life • Understanding and answering questions about everyday life	0.1.1, 0.1.2, 0.1.4, 0.1.5, 0.1.6, 0.2.1, 0.2.2, 0.2.4, 1.4.1, 1.4.7, 1.7.4, 2.1.7, 2.1.8, 2.2.1, 4.6.1, 7.4.1, 7.4.7, 8.1.1, 8.1.2, 8.2.3, 8.2.6	I.3, I.4, I.5, I.6, I.7, II.9.a–d, II.10, II.11.a–c, II.14.a & b, III.B.19 & 20, III.D.25 & 26 & 27, IV.C.38, VII.55, VIII.58.a–c, VIII.59.a & b	36.04, 39.01, 39.02, 39.01, 40.01, 40.02, 42.01, 43.02, 45.08, 49.01, 49.02, 49.03, 49.17
• Listening to questions and answers about addresses and life at home • Answering questions about life at home	0.1.1, 0.1.2, 0.1.4, 0.1.5, 0.1.6, 0.2.1, 0.2.2, 0.2.4, 1.4.1, 1.4.7, 2.2.1, 4.6.1, 7.4.1, 7.4.7, 7.5.5, 8.1.1, 8.1.2, 8.2.2, 8.2.3, 8.2.6	I.7, II.9.a–d, II.10, II.11.a–c, II.14.a & b, IV. C. 38 & 39, VIII. 58. a–c, VIII.59.a & b	36.04, 39.01, 39.02, 41.02, 43.02, 45.08, 49.01, 49.02, 49.03, 49.17

CASAS: Comprehensive Adult Student Assessment System
LAUSD: Los Angeles Unified School District (ESL Beginning Low content standards)
LCPs: Literacy Completion Points (Florida & Texas: Level B Workforce Development Skills & Life Skills)

Units	Life Skills	Social Language	Conversation Tip	Conversation Chants
UNIT 4 Food	• Talking about vegetables • Talking about fruit • Shopping at the supermarket • Talking about breakfast • Talking about lunch • Talking about dinner	• Would you like some more? • Please pass me the bread. • Let's make a salad. • What vegetables do you like? • What's your favorite fruit? • Excuse me, where can I find the milk? • Where do you usually eat lunch? • Who cooks dinner at your house?	Say *please* and *thank you* or *thanks* to be polite.	• *It's Time To Eat!* • *He Likes Cucumbers* • *Let's Eat In*
UNIT 5 Your Community	• Describing your neighborhood and neighbors • Asking directions around town • Using the post office • Using the bank • Calling 911, describing a fire • Calling the police, describing an emergency	• How do you like your neighborhood? • Do you have any problems with your neighbors? • Where's the laundromat? • How do I get to the florist? • Can I help you? • Anything else? • How often do you write letters? • I'd like a stamp. • What do you need to cash a check? • I'm calling to report a fire.	Repeat information to be sure you understand.	• *Nice Neighborhood* • *Lots of Mail* • *Firefighters Climbing*
UNIT 6 Shopping	• Shopping at a mall • Buying shoes • Shopping for clothing • Shopping for jewelry • Understanding sales and advertisements • Shopping in the 21st century	• Where can I get some pencils? • Where do you shop for shoes? • What stores do you recommend? • What size do you wear? • How do they fit? • Can I try it on? • How much is it? • No, thanks. I'm just looking. • What stores have good sales? • Do you like to shop online?	Repeat the question words when you don't understand what someone says.	• *At the Shopping Mall* • *Buying Shoes*
UNIT 7 Your Calendar	• Talking about months, years, and birthdays • Talking about dates and holidays • Understanding weather reports • Talking about good and bad weather • Describing seasons • Taking a trip	• Where were you yesterday? • Will you be home tonight? • When's your birthday? • What do you like to do on your birthday? • What's your favorite holiday? • What's the temperature? • What's the weather like today? • What was it like yesterday? • What kind of weather do you like the most? • Where do you want to go on a trip?	Give extra information when you answer a question.	• *A Surprise Party* • *Sailors Love the Wind* • *Taking a Trip*

Listening	CASAS	LAUSD	LCPs
• Listening to supermarket conversations and completing signs. • Answering questions about meal conversations	0.1.1, 0.1.2, 0.1.4, 0.1.5, 0.1.6, 0.2.1, 0.2.2, 0.2.4, 1.1.3, 1.1.7, 1.2.1, 1.3.1, 1.3.7, 2.2.1, 2.6.4, 4.6.1, 7.4.1, 7.4.7, 8.1.3, 8.2.1	I.7, II.9 a–d, II.10, II.11.a–c, II.14.a & b, VIII.58.a–c, IV.A.31 & 32, IV.B.35 & 36 & 37, VIII.59.a & b	(28.01, 28.03), 39.01, 39.02, 36.04, 41.06, 43.02, 45.03, 49.01, 49.02, 49.03, 49.17
• Answering questions about a post office conversation, an emergency conversation, and a conversation asking directions	0.1.1, 0.1.2, 0.1.4, 0.1.5, 0.1.6, 0.2.1, 0.2.2, 0.2.4, 1.8.1, 1.8.2, 1.9.4, 2.2.1, 2.2.5, 2.5.1, 2.5.2, 2.5.4, 2.6.1, 2.6.3, 4.6.1, 5.6.1, 7.4.1, 7.4.7, 8.3.2	I.7, II.9 a–d, II.10, II.11.a–c, II.14.a & b, III.B.21, III.C.22, III.C.23.a & b, IV.30, VIII.58.a–c, VIII.59.a & b	36.04, 39.01, 39.02, 40.03, 41.09, 42.04, 42.05, 43.02, 43.03, 46.01, 46.02, 49.01, 49.02, 49.03, 49.17
• Choosing answers to shopping questions • Answering questions to place an order	0.1.1, 0.1.2, 0.1.4, 0.1.5, 0.1.6, 0.2.1, 0.2.2, 0.2.4, 1.2.1, 1.2.2, 1.3.1, 1.3.3, 1.3.4, 1.3.5, 1.3.7, 1.3.9, 2.2.1, 2.5.4, 4.6.1, 5.1.6, 7.4.1, 7.4.4, 7.4.7, 8.1.4	I.7, II.9 a–d, II.10, II.11.a–c, II.14.a & b, IV.A.31 & 32 & 33 & 34, VIII.58.a–c, VIII.59.a & b	36.04, 39.01, 39.02, 43.02, 45.01, 45.04, 45.09, 45.10, 49.01, 49.02, 49.03, 49.17
• Choosing answers to holiday questions. • Answering questions about a weather report. • Matching conversations with pictures.	0.1.1, 0.1.2, 0.1.4, 0.1.5, 0.1.6, 0.2.1, 0.2.2, 0.2.4, 1.9.4, 2.2.1, 2.2.3, 2.2.4, 2.2.5, 2.3.2, 2.3.3, 2.6.1, 2.6.3, 2.7.1, 4.6.1, 7.4.1, 7.4.7	I.7, II.9 a–d, II.10, II.11.a–c, II.14.a & b, III.C.23.a & b, III.C.24, III.D.26, III. D.28 & 29, V.40, V.42, VIII.58.a–c, VIII.59.a & b	36.04, 39.01, 39.02, 42.01, 43.01, 43.02, 43.03, 46.04, 47.01, 47.02, 49.01, 49.02, 49.03, 49.17

Units	Life Skills	Social Language	Conversation Tip	Conversation Chants
UNIT 8 **Your Health**	• Staying healthy • Getting sick • Getting medicine at a drugstore • Going to the doctor • Going to the dentist • Going to the hospital	• How are you doing? • What's the matter? • I'm sorry to hear that. • I'm glad to hear that. • I don't feel very well. • What medicine do you recommend? • You should go to the doctor. • Do you like your dentist? • What are the visiting hours? • Where do I check in?	Express your feelings when you hear good news or bad news.	• *What's Wrong with Joe?* • *Exercise Every Day* • *I Like My Dentist.*
UNIT 9 **Your Work**	• Talking about kinds of work • Understanding everyday life at work • Looking for a job • Applying for a job • Discussing safety at work • Leaving a job	• Could you explain that, please? • I didn't get that. • Could you say that again? • What job would you like to have in the future? • What hours do you work? • I'm looking for a job. • Are any companies hiring now? • You need to fill out an application. • What does that sign mean? • He was fired.	Ask for clarification if you don't understand something.	• *A Bad Interview* • *A Day Job or a Night Job?* • *Out of Work*
UNIT 10 **Your Free Time**	• Going out • Talking about your free time • Watching TV and movies • Going to the park • Talking about sports • Discussing future learning plans	• I love to ski. • So do I. • I don't. • Would you like to go to the movies? • That sounds great. • I'm sorry, I can't. • What do you do in your free time? • What kinds of videos do you like? • How often do you go to the park? • What sports are on TV this weekend? • What's your plan for learning more English?	Express agreement and disagreement about what you like.	• *I Love to Fly* • *Free-time Fun* • *The Beautiful Park*

Listening	CASAS	LAUSD	LCPs
• Answering questions about a health conversation and a medical appointment conversation. • Listening to directions in a hospital.	0.1.1, 0.1.2, 0.1.4, 0.1.5, 0.1.6, 0.2.1, 0.2.2, 0.2.4, 2.2.1, 2.5.3, 2.5.4, 3.1.1, 3.1.2, 3.1.3, 3.2.1, 3.3.1, 3.4.1, 3.5.4, 3.5.5, 4.6.1, 7.4.1, 7.4.7	I.7, II.9 a–d, II.10, II.11.a–c, II.14.a & b, III.C. 22. & 23.b, VI.A.44 & 45 & 46, VIII.58.a – c, VIII.59.a & b	24.02, 24.03, 24.04, 36.04, 39.01, 39.02, 43.02, 49.01, 49.02, 49.03, 49.17
• Answering questions on a phone conversation about a want ad • Answering questions on conversations about people's jobs • Listening to questions about jobs and choosing answers	0.1.1, 0.1.2, 0.1.4, 0.1.5, 0.1.6, 0.2.1, 0.2.2, 0.2.4, 2.2.1, 4.1.2, 4.1.3, 4.1.6, 4.1.7, 4.1.8, 4.3.1, 4.3.2, 4.3.3, 4.4.1, 4.4.2, 4.6.1, 4.6.4, 7.4.1, 7.4.7	I.7, II.9 a–d, II.10, II.11.a–c, II.14.a & b, IV.B. 48 & 49, VII.50 & 52 & 53 & 54 & 55 & 56.a & b, VII.57, VIII.58.a-c, VIII.59.a & b	35.01, 35.02, 35.03, 35.04, 35.05, 35.06, 36.01, 36.02, 36.03, 36.04, 36.05, 38.01, 39.01, 39.02, 43.02, 49.01, 49.02, 49.03, 49.17
• Completing a chart based on a free-time conversation • Answering questions about a going-out conversation. • Answering questions about yourself	0.1.1, 0.1.2, 0.1.4, 0.1.5, 0.1.6, 0.2.1, 0.2.2, 0.2.4, 2.2.1, 2.5.5, 2.5.6, 2.6.1, 2.6.2, 2.6.3, 2.7.2, 2.7.5, 2.7.6, 3.5.9, 4.6.1, 5.6.1, 7.4.1, 7.4.4, 7.4.7, 8.3.2	I.7, II.9 a–d, II.10, II.11.a–c, II.14.a & b, III.C.22, VIII.58.a–c, VIII.59.a & b	36.04, 39.01, 39.02, 43.02, 49.01, 49.02, 49.03, 49.17

TO THE TEACHER

Welcome to the Fourth Edition!

Since the first edition of *A Conversation Book*, we have believed that students learn English through their own "lexical" approach—building their vocabulary by talking with one another about topics relevant to their lives. In each edition, we have updated the pedagogy, art, design, topics, and activities. Structure practice has always been, and still is, drawn from the topics, not vice versa. This has made *A Conversation Book* communicative and student centered from the start.

Look who's talking!

The basic principle of *A Conversation Book* has always been for the students to do most of the talking in the class. The teacher takes the role of facilitator and structures the classes, but students' knowledge, experience, and desire to learn are what drive the conversations and the learning. Through a variety of activities, students learn vocabulary and structures as they strive for fluency of expression. And since the topics are familiar to students, they are able to improve their English conversation skills more quickly.

Cross-cultural approach

Learning a foreign language can be threatening and sometimes even overwhelming. We believe that a classroom atmosphere in which differences in backgrounds and belief systems are recognized and valued helps reduce this stress as it enriches the learning experience. To us, a cross-cultural approach is an essential component of English conversation classes, enabling everyone to relax and enjoy the new experiences and new cultural information as they develop the ability to communicate with other English speakers around the world.

Program overview

Due to the flexible nature of the course, *A Conversation Book* can be used in classes from about 50 to 90 hours/semester. Each of the ten units consists of a unit Preview lesson and six two-page topical lessons, followed by one page each of Listening Practice, Review, and Assessment. This design builds schema at the beginning of the unit, develops vocabulary, practices structure in the context of related topics through the six unit lessons, and wraps up each unit with reinforcement and self-assessment.

* **A student audio CD** is provided in the back of some Student Books. It includes the Conversation Chants and Listening Practice .
* **A class audio program CD** is also available with the picture dictionary vocabulary practice and all the model conversations, in addition to the Conversation Chants and Listening Practice.
* **The Teachers' Guide** provides step-by-step instructions on how to implement each lesson, as well as warm-up and expansion activities.

Activities

Among the many activities in the text, these are the backbone of the pedagogy:

* **Preview Questions** introduce the unit topic with questions about a photograph on the Preview page. They help the

teacher identify in advance what the students already know and what they need to learn.

* **Conversation Tips** are in the Preview as gambits to help students speak "real" English. They are recycled in the unit and beyond.
* **Conversation Chants** give rhythm and intonation practice with real-life bits of conversation and fun. There are three chants in every unit.
* **Picture Dictionary** activities provide boxed words to study; they are matched to the opening picture, and pronunciation is modeled in the audio program. Students are encouraged to add words to the word list.
* **Model conversations** include contextualized formulaic expressions and vocabulary about the topic. The audio program provides the listening component for each of these brief conversations.
* **How about you?** activities give partners opportunities to interview each other, converting the model conversations into conversations about themselves.
* **Cross-cultural exchanges** encourage students to compare and contrast cultures, fostering an appreciation of the richness of the class' experiences and the diversity of the cultures of English speakers.
* **Games** add a light touch—and fun—while learning.
* **Use your English!** activities get students outside the classroom—talking about life, finding out about their community, or doing Internet activities.

Acknowledgments

Our thanks to colleagues and friends who have worked on this project with us: Carolyn Graham, our new co-author; Sarah Lynn, who has joined us in the writing of this new edition; Laura Le Dréan, our editor at Longman; Karen Davy, our development editor; Robert Ruvo, our production editor, and Shana McGuire, editorial assistant. Most of all, our thanks to Gene and Munchi for their endless patience.

Tina Carver and Sandi Fotinos-Riggs

♫ A NOTE FROM CAROLYN GRAHAM

What is a jazz chant?

A jazz chant is a rhythmic expression of natural spoken American English. It is not a distortion of the spoken form. It simply draws attention to the powerful rhythm that is present in the natural speech of a native speaker of American English.

The rhythm is the very simple **one, two, three, four** that is found in early traditional American jazz and flows right into the most modern sounds of hip-hop and rap. Jazz chanting is not rapping, however. There is a very important distinction. Rapping is a poetic distortion of the language but is not meant to sound like a natural conversation. *Jazz chanting is an exact reproduction of the natural speech pattern.* I found all of my best jazz chants simply by carefully listening to the language I heard around me at home and on the streets of New York City.

What is a conversation chant?

A conversation chant is simply a jazz chant written for two or more voices. You will see that many of my chants in this book use a simple question-response pattern to reinforce and expand on the material introduced in each unit.

For example, in Unit 1, Lesson 3 people ask one another how they are and answer with different vocabulary, both positive (*fine, happy, great*) and negative (*not so great, tired,* etc.). In my chant "*How's Brad?*" I use words introduced in the unit under *Feelings* (*sad, mad, confused, excited, worried, happy*) and add rhyming words to help students hear and learn the sounds: *How's Brad? He's very sad. How's Tad? He's very mad.* I want the students to hear the *Brad/sad- Tad/mad* rhyming pattern. This chant also offers practice in the sound of the contractions (*How's, He's, Jack's, I'm, They're, We're*), the negative pattern with "*not*" (*I'm not sad I'm not mad*), and the use of "*so*" (*so is Sue*).

In Unit 7, Lesson 6, I offer a *Yes/No question, short-response chant* moving from present to past and back to present, using the verb *be* and other verbs (*Are you ready to go? Yes, I am. Did you pack your sunhat? Yes, I did. Are your bags all packed? Yes, they are.*) Now I bring in an information question and answer. (*Where's your computer? It's in the car.*) This gives a nice opportunity to practice the contrasting intonation pattern of the rising *Yes/No* question and the falling information question. This chant also includes singular/plural contrasts (it/they). Conversation chants like these constantly reinforce grammar, vocabulary, stress, and intonation.

I was very pleased when my friends Sandi Fotinos-Riggs and Tina Carver invited me to contribute some chants to the new edition of their wonderful book. The chants wrote themselves. This happens when the basic material is really good. When I say "really good," what I mean is *Is this real language? Is it useful and appropriate for the age of the student we are teaching? Will it bring some joy into the language classroom?* I hope and believe that the answers are all **yes**. The conversation chants in this book are meant to offer a fun way to practice the sounds of English, reinforce basic grammar patterns, and build conversational vocabulary. I hope you and your students will enjoy chanting them as much as I enjoyed writing them.

Carolyn Graham

Unit-by-Unit Teaching Suggestions

Preview

Page 1

PREVIEW QUESTIONS

SETUP: (**1**) Have the class look at the photograph. Read each question aloud, and call on individual students to respond. (**2**) For question 4, write students' responses on the board so that the class can see the various possible responses. For example: *I'm fine, thanks. I'm doing well. Not so well. I feel great. I feel tired.*

CONVERSATION TIP

SETUP: (**1**) Write *Is that _____?* on the board. Tell students they can ask this question to confirm their understanding when they hear new information. (**2**) Have students read the conversation silently. (**3**) Role-play the conversation with a volunteer. (**4**) Have students practice the conversation in pairs.

VARIATIONS AND EXPANSIONS: (**1**) Also write on the board the negative response to *Is that _____? No. It's not _____. It's _____.* (**2**) Prompt students with other names. For example: "My name is Guillermo." "My name is Tsewang." Have students ask you the question to confirm their understanding. Model both the affirmative and negative responses as appropriate. (**3**) Have students work in pairs to practice the conversation with their own information.

CONVERSATION CHANT: I'M WORRIED

SETUP: (**1**) The dots over the words indicate where the stress falls. As you play the audio program, make hand motions or clap to reinforce the stress on the dotted syllables. (**2**) Have students listen once through as they read along. (**3**) Play the audio program again, pausing after each line, and have students repeat each line. (**4**) Have the class chant chorally.

VARIATIONS AND EXPANSIONS: (**1**) Once students are familiar with the chant, divide the class into two groups. The indented chant lines represent a second voice. Have one group chant the lines that start at the left margin, and have the other group chant the lines that are indented (**2**) Have students clap or make a hand motion to indicate where the stress falls as

they chant. (**3**) Have groups switch and chant the opposite lines. (**4**) Have students circle all the words that rhyme. Call on volunteers to read the rhyming pairs aloud and then write them on the board.

Lesson 1: Introductions

Pages 2–3

1. INTRODUCTIONS

SETUP: (**1**) Set the context: It's the first day of class, and students are making introductions. (**2**) Have students work individually or in pairs to look at the picture and complete the matching exercise. (**3**) Go over the answers with the class. Then play the audio program, pausing between items, and have students repeat chorally. (**4**) Have the class brainstorm other vocabulary in the picture (for example: *sitting down, standing up, writing his/her name*). Write the words on the board, and have students add the new words to the list in their books.

VARIATIONS: (**1**) Say or write a word or phrase, and have students point to the item in the picture. (**2**) Point to an item in the picture, and have students say the word or phrase. (**3**) Encourage students to keep a vocabulary notebook, where they write down new words and phrases as they learn them.

2. WHAT ARE THEY DOING?

SETUP: Call on a volunteer to read each question aloud. As a class, discuss the answers. For example:
  1. *Paco and Keiko are shaking hands.*
  2. *Maria and Tom are making a name card.*
  3. *Paco is talking.*
  4. *Keiko is smiling.*

VARIATIONS AND EXPANSIONS: (**1**) Write the present forms of the verb *to be* on the board: *I am, You are, He/She/It is, We are, They are.* Have students refer to the forms as they answer the questions. (**2**) For homework, have students write their answers to the questions.

3. WHAT ARE THEY SAYING?

SETUP: (**1**) Point out that these conversations use the Conversation Tip strategy from the Preview page. (**2**) Introduce and practice the first conversation before going on to the second one. (**3**) Have students close their books as they listen to the audio program for the first time. Then have students open their books and read along as they listen to the audio program again. Finally, play the audio a third time, pausing after each line for students to repeat chorally. (**4**) As students practice each of the conversations in pairs, encourage them to act it out by standing as they speak and shaking hands. (**5**) Circulate to give individual feedback on pronunciation and to answer students' questions as necessary.

VARIATIONS AND EXPANSIONS: (**1**) Have students listen to the conversation on the audio program and place dots over the stressed words (as in the conversation chants). Review the stress marks with the class. Practice the conversation chorally, paying special attention to word stress. (**2**) Write this conversation framework on the board with blanks in the places of names:

A: *Hi. I'm* _____.
B: *Nice to meet you,* _____. *My name's* _____.
A: *Sorry. Is that* _____?
B: *Yes, that's right.*
A: *Nice to meet you, too,* _____.

Invite pairs of students to perform the conversations for the class, using their own information.

Language and Culture Note: The standard handshake in the United States is brief (two shakes) and firm. Women often shake hands with other women, as well as with men. Men almost always shake hands when introduced to one another.

4. MEET YOUR GROUP!

SETUP: (**1**) Bring name tags and markers to class. (**2**) Have students write their names on the name tags and then circulate around the room introducing themselves to their new classmates. (**3**) Encourage students to shake hands as they introduce themselves. (**4**) Circulate to give individual feedback on pronunciation.

VARIATIONS AND EXPANSIONS: (**1**) Write the following conversation models on the board for students' reference:

A: *Hello. My name's* _____.
B: *Nice to meet you,* _____. *I'm* _____.

A: *Nice to meet you, too,* _____.
A: *Is that* _____?
B: *Yes, that's right.*

A: *Is that* _____?
B: *No, it's not* _____. *It's* _____.

(**2**) After a few minutes, have students return to their seats and then introduce themselves one by one as the class responds. For example:

Student: Hi. My name is Lydia.
Class: Nice to meet you, Lydia.

5. CONVERSATION CHANT: WHAT'S YOUR FIRST NAME?

SETUP: (**1**) Review the alphabet with the class. Have the class recite it chorally. Then, to assess individual pronunciation, have students recite the alphabet in a round-robin, in which each student says one letter. (**2**) Play the audio program. Tell students to read along as they listen to the chant. As you play the audio program, make hand motions or clap to reinforce the stress on the dotted syllables. (**3**) Play the audio program again, pausing after each line, and have students repeat. (**4**) Have the class chant chorally. (**5**) Replace *Sandy* in the chant with different students' names to practice pronouncing and spelling the names of all the students in the class.

VARIATIONS: (**1**) Once students are familiar with the chant, divide the class into two groups. The indented chant lines represent a second voice. Have one group chant the questions that start at the left margin, and have the other group chant the responses that are indented. (**2**) Have students clap or make a hand motion to indicate where the stress falls as they chant.

6. HOW MANY?

SETUP: (**1**) Tell students to turn to page 169 of their books. Review cardinal numbers 1–100. Have the class recite the numbers chorally. Then, to assess individual pronunciation, have students recite the numbers in a round-robin, with each student saying one or two consecutive numbers. (**2**) Use the pictures embedded in the questions to introduce the vocabulary: *men, women, long hair, short hair,* and *glasses.* (**3**) Model the questions for the class, and have students listen and repeat. (**4**) Have students work in groups to look around the class and answer the questions. (**5**) Have each group report their numbers. As a class, compare answers.

VARIATIONS: (**1**) Write the present forms of the verb *to have* on the board: *I have, You have, He/She/It has, We have, They have.* Have students refer to the forms as they answer the questions. (**2**) To review students' names, ask the class: "Who has long hair?" "Who has short hair?" "Who has glasses?"

7. SEE YOU LATER

SETUP: (1) Set the context for the conversation: Class is over, and students are saying good-bye. **(2)** Have students close their books as they listen to the audio program for the first time. Then play the audio program while students read along. Finally, play the audio a third time, pausing after each line for students to repeat chorally. **(3)** Have students then practice the conversation in groups of three. **(4)** Circulate to give individual feedback on pronunciation.

VARIATIONS AND EXPANSIONS: (1) Have students listen to the conversation on the audio program and place dots over the stressed words (as in the conversation chants). Review the stress marks with the class. Practice the conversation chorally, paying special attention to word stress. **(2)** Invite three students to perform the conversation for the class. Make sure they stand as they speak and also wave good-bye. **(3)** As class ends, have students leave the room individually or in pairs, saying good-bye to the other students, who in turn respond.

Language and Culture Note: It is common to wave good-bye as a person is walking away.

USE YOUR ENGLISH!

SETUP: (1) In EFL settings, have students greet other students in their school in English. **(2)** If your students live in an English-speaking community, they can find their own conversation partner in their community, through connections with neighbors, family, or coworkers. If your students do not live in an English-speaking community, find them a conversation partner through your school. **(3)** Tell students to write down the name of their conversation partner and share it at the beginning of the next class.

Lesson 2: Countries

Pages 4–5

1. MAP OF THE WORLD

SETUP: (1) Have students work individually or in pairs to look at the map and complete the matching

exercise. **(2)** Go over the answers with the class. Then play the audio program, pausing between items, and have students repeat chorally. **(3)** Have the class brainstorm several names of countries on each continent. Write the names of the countries on the board, and have students add the new words to the list in their books; alternatively, tell students to write at least ten new words in their vocabulary notebooks.

VARIATIONS: (1) Say or write a word, and have students point to the item on the map. **(2)** Point to an item on the map, and have students say the word.

2. WHAT'S ON THE MAP?

SETUP: (1) Call on a volunteer to read questions 1 and 2 aloud. As a class, discuss the answers. **(2)** Have students work in pairs to ask and answer questions 3 and 4.

VARIATION: In EFL classes, have the whole class answer questions 3 and 4 together.

Language and Culture Note: In total there are seven continents on Earth: North America, South America, Europe, Africa, Asia, Australia, and Antarctica.

3. WHERE IS SHE FROM?

SETUP: (1) Have students work individually to read the sentences silently and put the lines in order. **(2)** Play the audio program, and have students check their answers. **(3)** Play the audio program again, pausing after each line so students can repeat chorally. **(4)** Have students practice the conversation in pairs. **(5)** Circulate to give individual feedback on pronunciation.

EXPANSION: To help students internalize the language, write the conversation on the board. Phrase by phrase, erase portions of the conversation and have students practice it, filling in the blanks. See to what extent you can erase the conversation with students still able to recall it.

Language and Culture Note: The United States has a very mobile population, so it is common for Americans to ask one another where they are from. It is equally polite and common to ask immigrants where they are from.

4. WHERE ARE YOU FROM?

SETUP: (1) Model the questions for the class. **(2)** Have students work individually to write their answers to the questions before speaking with a partner. (3) Circulate to correct pronunciation and to answer students' questions as necessary. (4) Write the following subject pronouns and possessive adjectives on the board: *she/her, he/his*. Invite students to tell the class about their partners. For example: *This is Kadisha. She is from Somalia. Her country is in Africa. People speak Somali in Somalia.* (5) Write the names of countries, continents, and languages on the board as students mention them. Practice the pronunciation of any new words with the class.

VARIATIONS AND EXPANSIONS: (1) List matching subject pronouns (*he, she*) and possessive pronouns (*his, her*) on the board. Have students refer to these as they tell the class about their partners. (2) Students may also want to ask one another: "What languages do you speak?" (3) In U.S. classes, have students use pushpins to identify their native countries on a world map.

5. WHERE IN THE WORLD IS THAT COUNTRY?

SETUP: (1) Have the class turn to page 161 to look at the map and answer the questions. Have the class continue working together on the questions on pages 162–166. (2) Have students work in groups of three to answer the questions on pages 167 and 168. (3) Lead a class discussion to compare answers.

VARIATIONS AND EXPANSIONS: (1) If you run out of class time, you can assign pages 167 and 168 for homework and then have students compare their answers at the beginning of the next class. (2) Have students conduct a survey on the nationalities of the school's student body. Tell students to briefly interview their schoolmates in the hallways or in their classes and write down the information. Then have them report the results back to the class. Suggest that students tally the results and make a bar graph illustrating the information.

6. WHAT'S THE COUNTRY?

SETUP: (1) Have students think of a country they know something about and write at least two sentences about the country on a slip of paper. The sentences can describe the country's location and its languages. If that information doesn't distinguish the country enough, however, tell students to add a sentence about what the country is famous for (for example: a food, a

celebrity, a sport). Circulate and answer students' questions as necessary. (2) When everyone has finished writing their sentences, have students fold their papers and come to the front of the room and put them in a pile. (3) Have students take turns pulling slips from the pile and reading the sentences aloud. (4) Have the class guess the names of the countries.

VARIATION: After students successfully identify the name of a country, ask: "Who in our class is from _____?"

USE YOUR ENGLISH!

SETUP: Have students do this activity as a homework assignment. (1) To prepare students for these independent conversations, model a conversation about your country with a volunteer, using the questions in the box. (2) Tell students to write down information they learn from their conversation partners. For example: *My conversation partner is from Belgium. His country is in Europe. People speak French, Dutch (Flemish), and German in Belgium.* At the beginning of the next class, students can share this information in small groups or simply hand in their reports to you.

Lesson 3: Feelings

Pages 6–7

1. FEELINGS

SETUP: (1) Have students work individually or in pairs to look at the pictures and complete the matching exercise. (2) Go over the answers with the class. Then play the audio program, pausing between items, and have students repeat chorally. (3) With the class, brainstorm other vocabulary in the pictures (for example: *upset, satisfied, terrified*). Write the words on the board, and have students add the new adjectives to the list in their books; alternatively, tell students to write at least ten new words in their vocabulary notebooks.

VARIATIONS AND EXPANSION: (1) Say or write a word, and have students point to the item in the pictures. (2) Point to an item in the pictures, and have students say the word. (3) Ask: "Which feelings are good? Which are bad?" Have students categorize the feeling words into two groups: *negative* and *positive*.

2. HOW ARE THEY?

SETUP: (**1**) Write this language model on the board: *He/She is feeling* _____. (**2**) For question 1, point to an illustration and ask individual students: "How is he (or she) feeling?" (**3**) For question 2, ask a volunteer to read the question aloud. Tell students to choose at least one adjective. (**4**) Ask: "How are you feeling today?" and have students take turns answering. Encourage students to give complete-sentence answers (for example: *I'm feeling tired today.*).

VARIATIONS AND EXPANSIONS: (**1**) Bring an assortment of magazines to class. Have students work in pairs to look at pictures of people in the magazines and identify their feelings. Have students share their pictures and ideas with the class. (**2**) For homework, have students write their answers to the questions.

3. HOW ARE YOU TODAY?

SETUP: (**1**) Set the context: Two students are greeting each other in school. (**2**) Have students close their books as they listen to the audio program for the first time. Then have students open their books and read along as they listen to the audio program again. Finally, play the audio a third time, pausing after each line for students to repeat chorally. (**3**) Have students practice the conversation in pairs. (**4**) Circulate to give individual feedback on pronunciation.

VARIATIONS AND EXPANSIONS: (**1**) Have students listen to the conversation on the audio program and place dots over the stressed words (as in the conversation chants). Review the stress marks with the class. Practice the conversation chorally, paying special attention to word stress. (**2**) Invite pairs of students to perform the conversation for the class. (**3**) Pass out blank cards to pairs of students. Tell students to write each line from the conversation on a different card. Then have the pairs mix up their cards and put them in order again.

Language and Culture Note: "How are you?" is the most common question asked when greeting someone. "How are you feeling?" usually requires a more complete (and honest) answer and is asked in a longer conversation. Other more informal questions asked in a greeting include "How's it going?" and "How are you doing?"

4. HOW ARE YOUR CLASSMATES TODAY?

SETUP: (**1**) Have the class brainstorm other ways to reply to the questions "How are you?" and "How's your English class?" Write students' ideas on the board. For example: *How are you? Great! / Not so well. How's your English class? My class is excellent. / My class is boring.* (**2**) Practice pronouncing the new expressions on the board. (**3**) Divide the class into groups of four to take turns asking and answering the questions. (**4**) Circulate to give individual feedback on pronunciation and to answer students' questions as necessary. (**5**) Ask each student to report to the class on one of his or her classmates. For example: *Trang is fine today. Her English class is great!*

5. CONVERSATION CHANT: HOW'S BRAD?

SETUP: (**1**) Play the audio program. Tell students to read along as they listen to the chant. As you play the audio program, make hand motions or clap to reinforce the stress on the dotted syllables. (**2**) Play the audio program again, pausing after each line, and have students repeat. (**3**) Have the class chant chorally.

VARIATIONS: (**1**) Once students are familiar with the chant, divide the class into two groups. The indented chant lines represent a second voice. Have one group chant the questions that start at the left margin, and have the other group chant the responses that are indented. (**2**) Have students clap or make a hand motion to indicate where the stress falls as they chant. (**3**) Have students circle all the words that rhyme. Call on volunteers to read the rhyming pairs aloud and then write them on the board.

6. HOW AM I FEELING?

SETUP: (**1**) Model the activity of miming a feeling and ask: "How am I feeling?" (**2**) Divide the class into small groups. Tell students to take turns miming and identifying feelings. Circulate to encourage students to give complete-sentence answers (for example: *You're feeling bored.*) and to answer students' questions as necessary.

VARIATIONS: (**1**) Do this activity as a whole-class exercise, with one student at a time standing up to mime a feeling. (**2**) Have students mime other feeling words from the brainstorming activity in Exercise 1.

USE YOUR ENGLISH!

SETUP: Have students do this activity as a homework assignment. (**1**) To prepare students for these independent conversations, model a conversation with a volunteer. (**2**) Tell students to write down the names of the people they spoke with (for example: *Trang Nguyen, Enrico Sillari, Bertha Baptiste*). At the beginning of the next class, students can hand in their lists to you as evidence of their conversations.

VARIATION: If you have a schoolwide break time, encourage students to mingle with students from other classes to ask: "How are you today?"

Lesson 4: Clothes and Colors
Pages 8–9

1. CLOTHES

SETUP: (**1**) Write the word *clothes* on the board. With the class, brainstorm words for clothes and write them on the board. (**2**) Have students work individually or in pairs to look at the pictures and complete the matching exercise. (**3**) Go over the answers with the class. Then play the audio program, pausing after each item, and have students repeat chorally. (**4**) With the class, brainstorm other vocabulary in the pictures (for example: *short sleeves, long sleeves, jacket*), and have students add the new words to the list in their books; alternatively, tell students to write at least ten new words in their vocabulary notebooks.

VARIATIONS AND EXPANSIONS: (**1**) Say or write a word (for example: *dress, sandals*) and have students point to the item in the pictures. (**2**) Have students work in pairs to take turns identifying the items in the pictures. Write on the board: *This is a _____. These are _____.* Have students use the skeletal sentences to practice the singular and plural nouns. Circulate and make sure students are pronouncing the final *-s* in the plural nouns. (**3**) Write on the board: *That is a _____. Those are _____.* Point to clothes you are wearing and have students identify the clothing items. (**4**) Draw two large intersecting circles on the board (a Venn diagram). Write *men* in one circle and *women* in the other. In the intersection of the two circles, write *both*. Have students

categorize the clothing words from this lesson into clothes for a *woman*, a *man*, or *both*.

2. COLORS

SETUP: (**1**) Have students read the questions and the model answers silently. (**2**) Call on volunteers to read the questions aloud, and have other volunteers give the answers.

VARIATIONS AND EXPANSIONS: (**1**) Have students do this exercise in pairs or small groups. (**2**) Show a magazine picture of a person for ten seconds. Then have students say or write what the person in the picture is wearing. See how many details they can remember! (**3**) Describe what a student is wearing, but don't mention his or her name. Have the class identify the student. (**4**) For homework, have students write a description of what they are wearing.

3. TRUE OR FALSE?

SETUP: (**1**) Model the activity for the class. Write on the board: *Yes, that's true. No, that's false.* Make a statement about the clothes you are wearing. Have students respond with one of the two phrases on the board. Encourage students to follow with an answer to the question *What am I wearing?* in order to make a final, true statement. (**2**) Divide the class into small groups. Give students a few minutes to compose their statements before they start the activity. (**3**) Circulate to offer help with vocabulary and to give individual feedback on pronunciation.

VARIATIONS AND EXPANSIONS: (**1**) Show the class a magazine picture of a person. Say false statements about what the person is wearing. Have students correct you. (**2**) For homework, have students choose a picture from anywhere in their books and write sentences about the clothing and colors they see.

4. CONVERSATION CHANT: LOOK AT TED!

SETUP: (**1**) Play the audio program. Tell students to read along as they listen to the chant. As you play the audio program, make hand motions or clap to reinforce the stress on the dotted syllables. (**2**) Play the audio again, pausing after each line, and have students repeat. (**3**) Have the class chant chorally.

VARIATIONS: (**1**) Once students are familiar with the chant, divide the class into two groups. The indented chant lines represent a second voice. Have one group chant the lines that start at the left margin, and have the other group chant the lines that are indented. (2) Have students clap or make a hand motion to indicate where the stress falls as they chant.

Language and Culture Note: It is not polite to point at someone when noticing what the person is wearing. This chant is a conversation between two people who are looking at and talking about other people, but they are not pointing.

5. YOU LOOK GREAT IN BLACK!

SETUP: (1) Explain to the class that it is common and appropriate to compliment a person on the clothes that he or she is wearing. An appropriate response to a compliment is "Thank you." (2) Have students stand up and walk around the room and compliment four other students on their clothes. Remind students to acknowledge the compliment with a "Thank you."

EXPANSION: If you have some more advanced students, explain that after receiving a compliment, often the person will say something about the piece of clothing. For example: "I got it at Macy's" or "My husband gave it to me." Encourage students who are at that level to add that information in their conversations with their classmates.

USE YOUR ENGLISH!

SETUP: Have students do these activities as homework assignments. (1) To prepare students for these independent conversations, model each conversation with a volunteer. (2) Tell students to write a report of their conversations. For example: *My conversation partner is wearing a dress today. Her clothes are pink, white, and gray. Her favorite color is pink.* At the beginning of the next class, students can hand in their reports to you.

Lesson 5: In Your Classroom
Pages 10–11

1. THE CLASSROOM

SETUP: (1) Write the phrase *things in the classroom* on the board. With the class, brainstorm classroom words and write them on the board. (2) Have students work individually or in pairs to look at the

picture and complete the matching exercise. (3) Go over the answers with the class. Then play the audio program, pausing between items, and have students repeat chorally. (4) Have the class brainstorm other vocabulary in the picture (for example: *globe, student, teacher*), and have students add the new words to the list in their books; alternatively, tell students to write at least twelve new words in their vocabulary notebooks.

VARIATIONS AND EXPANSIONS: (1) Say or write a word, and have students point to the item in the picture. (2) Point to an item in the picture, and have students say the word. (3) Write on the board: *What's this? It's a _____. / It's an _____.* Point to items in your classroom and ask: "What's this?" Have individual students respond. (4) Have students work in pairs and take turns pointing to and identifying items in the classroom.

2. WHAT'S IN THE CLASSROOM?

SETUP: (1) Write on the board: *There's a/an _____. There are _____.* (2) Call on volunteers to read the questions aloud. Have students take turns giving answers.

VARIATIONS AND EXPANSIONS: (1) Make false statements about items in your classroom, and have students correct you. For example:

Teacher: There are three wastebaskets in our
            classroom.
Student: No, that's not right. There's one
            wastebasket in our classroom.

(2) For homework, have students write five questions and answers about the picture. For example:

Q: How many doors are there in the classroom?
A: There's one door in the classroom.

3. WHAT'S THAT IN ENGLISH?

SETUP: (1) Quickly review the English alphabet so that students will feel more confident when spelling words during the activity. (2) Set the context: A student wants to know the English word for something in the classroom. (3) Have students close their books as they listen to the audio program for the first time. Then have students open their books and read along as they listen to the audio program again. Finally, play the audio a third time, pausing after each line for students to repeat chorally. (4) Have students practice the conversation in groups of three. (5) Have students use the conversational model to ask questions about items in your classroom. Circulate to answer students' questions as necessary. (**6**) Ask the class: "What new words did you learn?" Write a list on the board of all the new words students learned in their group conversations.

VARIATIONS AND EXPANSIONS: (**1**) Have students listen to the conversation on the audio program and place dots over the stressed words (as in the conversation chants). Review the stress marks with the class. Practice the conversation chorally, paying special attention to word stress. (**2**) Invite three students to perform the conversation for the class. (**3**) Ask students questions about items in the classroom. Pretend to misunderstand them each time to provide practice in giving corrections. For example:

Teacher: *What's that in English, please?*
Student: *It's a notebook.*
Teacher: *A boat book?*
Student: *No. It's not a boat book. It's a notebook.*
N-o-t-e-b-o-o-k.
Teacher: *Oh, OK. Thanks.*

(**4**) Brainstorm with students other questions they need to ask in the classroom. For example: *What does _____ mean? Excuse me, can you please repeat that?* etc. Write these questions on a large sheet of paper and post it in the room for students' reference.

Language and Culture Note: It is OK to point at things but not at people.

4. WHERE IS IT?

SETUP: (**1**) Have students look again at the picture on page 10. (**2**) Play the audio program, and have students listen once through as they read along on page 11. (**3**) Play the audio again, pausing after each line, and have students listen and repeat. (**4**) Have students work in pairs to look at the picture on page 10 and add two more questions and answers. (**5**) Match pairs up to form groups of four. Have students ask and answer one another's questions. (**6**) Go over some questions and answers together as a class to make sure students understand the location words and phrases.

VARIATION AND EXPANSION: (**1**) You may want to practice the location words and phrases before students do group work. Place a classroom item (such as a book) in different places around the room and make statements about its location. (**2**) Check understanding by asking individual students to say the location of various items in the classroom.

5. YOUR CLASSROOM

SETUP: (**1**) Have students work in small groups to write four questions about the locations of items in the classroom. (**2**) Have students read their questions to the class. Call on individual students to answer the questions.

VARIATIONS AND EXPANSIONS: Make false statements about the locations of items in your classroom. Have students correct your statements. For example:

Teacher: *The blackboard is next to the bookcase.*
Student: *That's false. The blackboard is next to the door!*

6. WHAT IS IT?

SETUP: (**1**) Model the activity. Write on the board: *Is it under/next to/on/in/behind/in front of _____?* Have students guess the item you're thinking about by asking you questions using the model on the board. (**2**) Have students work in small groups to do the activity.

VARIATIONS AND EXPANSIONS: (**1**) Students may want to write some of their questions for you to correct before they ask them in their groups. (**2**) Have students take turns standing up and describing the location of an item for the class; the first classmate to guess the item gets the next turn.

USE YOUR ENGLISH!

SETUP: Have students do this activity as a homework assignment. (**1**) To prepare students for these independent conversations, have students list what they can say about their classroom to their conversation partners. Brainstorm ideas on the board. (**2**) Tell students to take notes on what they said. For example:
In my classroom, there are two boards. There's one door. There are twenty desks and chairs.
At the beginning of the next class, students can hand in their reports to you.

Lesson 6: Taking a Break

Pages 12–13

1. ACTIONS

SETUP: (**1**) Have students work individually or in pairs to look at the picture and complete the matching exercise. (**2**) Go over the answers with the class. Then play the audio program, pausing between items, and have students repeat chorally. (**3**) Have the class brainstorm other vocabulary in the picture (for example: *shaking hands, listening, reading*). Write the words on the board, and have students add the new words to the list in their books; alternatively, tell students to write at least twelve new verbs in their vocabulary notebooks.

VARIATIONS AND EXPANSIONS: (**1**) Say or write a word and have students point to the item in the picture. (**2**) Mime an action and have students identify it.

2. WHAT ARE THEY DOING?

SETUP: (**1**) Write on the board: *He's _____ing. She's _____ing. They're _____ing.* (**2**) Call on a volunteer to read each question aloud. As a class, discuss the answers. (**3**) When students have difficulty composing their answers, point to the board for reference.

VARIATIONS AND EXPANSIONS: (**1**) Have students ask and answer the questions in pairs. (**2**) For homework, have students write their answers to the questions. (**3**) Show the class the illustration on page 12, and point to various students in the picture and introduce their "number." For example: "This is Student 1." "This is Student 2." Then ask questions about the picture. For example: "What's Student 2 doing?" "Who's yawning?" "Is Student 13 waving hello or good-bye?"

3. WHAT AM I DOING?

SETUP: (**1**) Model the activity of miming an action and ask: "What am I doing?" (**2**) Have students work in small groups of three to four, taking turns miming and identifying actions.

VARIATIONS AND EXPANSIONS: (**1**) Have the class do this activity together, with one student at a time standing up to mime an action. (**2**) Have students mime other actions from the brainstorming activity in Exercise 1.

4. FOLLOW INSTRUCTIONS.

SETUP: (**1**) Play the audio program and have students listen while reading along. Mime the actions to illustrate their meaning. (**2**) Have students work in small groups to add two more instructions. Circulate to answer questions as necessary. (**3**) Have students work in their groups to take turns calling out instructions as the other group members listen and perform the action.

VARIATIONS AND EXPANSIONS: (**1**) Have all the groups tell you their additional instructions. Write their ideas on the board. Then call out instructions for the whole class to follow. (**2**) To make the activity more challenging, call out a sequence of actions for students to follow. For example: "Stand up. Wave. Smile. Sit down." (**3**) Add more classroom instructions to the list. Write on the board, for example: *Open your book. Hand in the homework. Raise your hand. Write your name on the board. Erase the board.* Model the pronunciation and then illustrate each action by miming. Then have individual students perform actions as you give instructions. For example: "Julia, write your name on the board." "Chang, open your book."

5. CLASS RULES

SETUP: (**1**) Have students work in small groups to write class rules. Circulate to listen in and to answer students' questions as necessary. (**2**) Have all the groups report their ideas to the class as you write them on the board. (**3**) Have the class agree on the most important class rules. This list can exceed the limit of six on page 13.

EXPANSION: Write the final list of rules on a large sheet of paper, and post the list in the room for students' reference.

USE YOUR ENGLISH!

SETUP: Have students do this activity as a homework assignment. (**1**) Explain that the question "What are you doing right now?" is probably heard most often when two people are on the telephone. Tell students to call two friends and ask the question in that context. (**2**) To prepare students for these independent conversations, model a phone conversation in which you ask a student "What are you doing right now?"

Listening Practice
Page 14

1. WHAT DO YOU HEAR?

SETUP: (**1**) Tell students to read through the sentences silently. (**2**) Play the audio program. (**3**) Review the answers with the class. If there is confusion about any answers, replay the audio program.

VARIATIONS AND EXPANSIONS: (1) Have students first listen with their books closed and then read the sentences. (2) Once finished with the whole exercise, have pairs of students take turns listening to each other read the sentences and then identifying which one their partners say.

2. QUESTIONS AND ANSWERS

SETUP: (1) Have students read the answers and then listen to the audio program. (2) If students are uncertain about their answers, replay the audio program.

VARIATIONS AND EXPANSIONS: (1) Have students first listen and then read the answers. (2) After finishing the whole activity, have students compose questions for the uncircled answers. (3) Have students listen to the audio program again and take dictation on the questions. Write the questions on the board so students can correct their dictations, or have students self-correct by referring to the Audioscript in the back of their books.

3. ABOUT YOU

SETUP: (1) Play the audio program, pausing after each question so students have time to write their responses. (2) When students have answered all three questions, have them share their responses in small groups. (3) Have several volunteers read their answers aloud to the class.

VARIATION: Have students take dictation on the questions and then write their responses after the dictation is corrected. Write the questions on the board so students can correct their dictations, or have students self-correct by referring to the Audioscript in the back of their books.

Review

Page 15

1. GET TO KNOW YOUR PARTNER

SETUP: (1) Divide the class into pairs. (2) Have students ask and answer the questions, writing their partners' information on the lines. Circulate to listen in and to answer students' questions as necessary. (3) Have students take turns telling

the class about their partners. For example: *My partner's name is Celoni. He's from Spain. He speaks Spanish, Catalan, and English. He's happy today. His favorite color is green.*

VARIATION: For homework, have students use the information that they learned in this activity to write a paragraph about their partners.

2. WHAT'S YOUR PARTNER WEARING?

SETUP: (1) Divide the class into pairs. (2) Tell students they have fifteen seconds to study their partner's clothes. (3) Have student pairs sit back-to-back and say what they remember.

VARIATIONS AND EXPANSIONS: (1) Instead of having students do this activity orally, tell them to write a list of what their partners are wearing and then compare their lists to reality. (2) Walk behind the class so no one can see you and ask: "What am I wearing?" Have students describe what you are wearing. If time allows, ask students to take turns standing behind the class while the class tries to remember their clothes.

3. WHO AM I?

SETUP: (1) Write questions on the board to help prompt students' self-descriptions. For example: *Are you a man or a woman? Do you have long/short hair? Do you have glasses? What are you wearing? Where are you from?* (2) Collect the papers, mix them up, and then have each student select one. Make sure no student has received his or her own description. (3) Have students read the descriptions to the class. (4) Have the class guess who the described person is.

4. WHAT'S IN YOUR CLASSROOM?

SETUP: (1) Divide the class into small groups of three to four. (2) Have each group list ten things in the classroom. (3) Have groups take turns reading an item from their lists. Write the item on the board as students check their spelling on their lists. Have everyone check each item off as it is mentioned so there are no repeat mentions.

5. QUESTION PRACTICE

SETUP: (1) Have students work individually to write two questions from each lesson. (2) Put students into pairs to take turns asking and answering their questions. Circulate to listen in and to answer students' questions as necessary.

VARIATION: Have students call out the questions as you write them all on the board. Then put students into pairs to practice asking and answering all the questions.

Assessment

Page 16

PART 1: QUESTIONS

SETUP: Have students work individually to write the questions. Challenge students not to look at the previous lessons but to construct their questions from memory.

VARIATIONS: Have students write their questions on a separate sheet of paper to hand in to you for correction at the end of the assessment.

PART 2: SPEAKING

SETUP: Divide the class into pairs, and have students ask and answer the questions. Circulate to listen in and to answer students' questions as necessary.

VARIATIONS: Have students write their partners' responses to their questions and hand in their work for correction at the end of the assessment.

PART 3: LISTENING

SETUP: (1) Have students first read the answers silently. Then play the audio program. (2) If students are uncertain about any of the answers, replay the audio program. (3) Check answers with the whole class.

VARIATION AND EXPANSION: (1) Have students write the number of the question and the letter of their response on a separate sheet to hand in to you for correction at the end of the assessment. (2) As an added challenge, have students compose questions for the uncircled answers.

PART 4: WRITING

SETUP: (1) Ask the class: "What are the people doing in the picture?" (2) Have students work individually to write their conversations. Circulate to answer questions as necessary. (3) Have students share their conversations in small groups as you circulate to see their work.

VARIATIONS: (1) Have students write their conversations on a separate piece of paper to hand in to you for correction. (2) Have students share their conversations with a partner. Then ask volunteer pairs to perform one of their conversations for the class.

UNIT 2 — EVERYDAY LIFE

Preview

Page 17

PREVIEW QUESTIONS

SETUP: (1) Have the class look at the photograph. Read each question aloud, and call on individual students to respond. (2) For questions 3 and 4, write students' responses on the board so they can see the various possible responses. Be sure to write the responses in the simple present tense since that is the focus of this unit. For example:

> **3.** *Every morning I take a shower. I drink a cup of coffee every morning.*
> **4.** *I do homework every night. Every night, I watch TV.*

CONVERSATION TIP

SETUP: (1) Write *How about you?* on the board. Tell students they can say this—instead of repeating a question—to show interest and get information. (2) Have students read the conversation silently. (3) Act out the conversation with a volunteer. (4) Have students practice the conversation in pairs. (5) Circulate to correct pronunciation.

EXPANSION: (1) Prompt students with other questions. For example: "How are you?" "Where are you from?" Have students answer the questions and then show interest and find out about you by asking "How about you?" (2) Have students work in pairs to practice the conversation with their own information.

CONVERSATION CHANT: WHAT'S YOUR COUSIN'S NAME?

SETUP: (1) The dots over the words indicate where the stress falls. As you play the audio program, make hand motions or clap to reinforce the stress on the dotted syllables. (2) Have students listen once through as they read along. (3) Play the audio program again, pausing after each line, and have students repeat. (4) Have the class chant chorally.

VARIATIONS AND EXPANSIONS: (1) Once students are familiar with the chant, divide the class into two groups. The indented chant lines represent a second voice. Have one group chant the questions that start at the left margin, and have the other group chant the responses that are indented. (2) Have students clap or make a hand motion to indicate where the stress falls as they chant. (3) Have groups switch and chant the opposite lines. (4) Have the whole class chant the questions, as volunteers take turns answering with their own cousins' and uncles' names. (5) Have students circle all the words that rhyme. Call on volunteers to read the rhyming pairs aloud and then write them on the board.

Lesson 1: Your Family

Pages 18–19

1. FAMILY PICTURES

SETUP: (1) Set the context: These are family pictures of a *nuclear* family: a mother and father and their children. (2) Have students work individually or in pairs to look at the pictures and complete the matching exercise. (3) Go over the answers with the class. Then play the audio program, pausing between items, and have students repeat chorally. (4) Have the class brainstorm other vocabulary in the pictures (for example: *bride, groom, siblings, spouse*). Write the words on the board, and have students add the new words to the list in their books; alternatively, tell students to write at least ten new words in their vocabulary notebooks.

VARIATIONS: (1) Say or write a word or phrase, and have students point to the item in the pictures. (2) Point to an item in the pictures, and have students say the word or phrase. (3) Draw two large intersecting circles on the board. Label one circle *female* and the other circle *male*. At the intersection of the two circles, write *both*. Have students categorize the words in the list as they refer to *female*, *male*, or *both*. For example: *female: sister, mother, daughter*; *male: brother, father, son*; *both: children, parents, married couple.*

2. THAT'S ME.

SETUP: (1) Have students close their books as they listen to the audio program for the first time. Then have students open their books and read along as they listen to the audio program again and point to the people in the pictures as they hear them mentioned. Finally, play the audio again, pausing after each line so students can repeat chorally. (2) As students practice the conversation in pairs, encourage them to act it out by pointing to the people in the pictures as they talk about them. (3) Circulate to give individual feedback on pronunciation.

VARIATIONS AND EXPANSIONS: (1) To reinforce students' comprehension of the conversation, have them label the people in the second family picture with the names mentioned in the conversation. (2) Have students listen to the conversation on the audio program and place dots over the stressed syllable (as in the conversation chants). Review the stress marks with the class. Practice the conversation chorally, paying special attention to word stress. (3) Invite pairs of students to perform the conversation for the class.

Language and Culture Notes: It is acceptable to compliment a person on the good looks of his or her relatives (for example: *Your wife is pretty.*). To acknowledge the compliment, the person usually says "Thank you."

3. WHO ARE THEY?

SETUP: Call on a volunteer to read each question aloud. As a class, discuss the answers. For example:
1. *The woman is Donald's wife, Laura.*
2. *The man is Donald.*
3. *The boy is Ben, and the girl is Becky. They are Donald's children.*

VARIATIONS AND EXPANSIONS: (1) Write the possessive adjectives (*my, your, his, her, our, their*) on the board before students answer the questions. Point out that the possessive adjective refers to the owner (the father)—not to the noun that follows it. For example: ***his** son and **his** daughter.* Have students refer to the adjectives on the board as they answer the questions. (2) For homework, have students write their answers to the questions.

4. YOUR FAMILY

SETUP: (1) Model the pronunciation of each question before students break up into pairs. (2) Circulate to listen in and to answer students' questions. (3) Set a time limit for this activity; tell students they have only five minutes to discuss the questions. (4) When the time is up, invite students to tell the class about their own family or about their partner's family.

VARIATIONS AND EXPANSIONS: (1) Write the following skeletal sentence models on the board for students' reference:

I have _____ brothers/sisters/children.
Their names are _____.
My brother/sister/daughter/son is _____ years old.

(2) In addition to *married*, give students the vocabulary of *single* and *divorced*. (3) For homework, have students draw a simple family tree of their nuclear family and label the people in the family tree. They can write an accompanying paragraph about their family using the questions as a guide. (4) Take notes as students tell the class about their families. Then write incomplete sentences on the board, and have students circulate to ask one another questions to find out whose name completes each sentence. For example:

_____ *has seven brothers and sisters.*
_____ *is an only child.*
_____ *has two children.*
_____ *has four sons.*

5. MORE FAMILY PICTURES

SETUP: (1) Set the context: This is a picture of Donald's *extended* family: a family of three or more generations. (2) Have students work individually or in pairs to look at the picture and complete the matching exercise. (3) Go over the answers with the class. Then play the audio program, pausing after each item, and have students repeat chorally. (4) Have the class brainstorm other family relationships in the picture (for example: *sister-in-law, daughter-in-law, mother-in-law, father-in-law*). Write the words on the board, and have students add the new words to the list in their books; alternatively, tell students to write at least ten new words in their vocabulary notebooks.

VARIATIONS: (1) Draw two large intersecting circles on the board. Label one circle *female* and the other circle *male*. At the intersection of the two circles, write *both*. Have students categorize the words in the list as they refer to *female, male,* or *both*. For example: ***female:** aunt, niece, grandmother;* ***male:** uncle, nephew, grandfather;* ***both:** grandparents, cousin, dog, cat.* (2) Ask the class: "How many brothers/sisters/cousins/ nieces/nephews does Donald have?" (3) To further clarify these extended family relationships, draw on the board a family tree of Donald's extended family. Draw a circle around Donald in the family tree and point to different members in the tree and ask: "Who is this?" (Answer: *That's Donald's _____.*) Then circle Donald's son Ben, point to other members of the tree, and ask: "Who is this?" (Answer: *That's Ben's _____.*) Continue asking questions in this manner about different extended family relationships.

6. HOW ABOUT YOU?

SETUP: (**1**) Model the pronunciation of the questions. (**2**) Have students ask and answer the questions in groups of three or four. (**3**) Set a time limit; tell students they have only five minutes to discuss these questions. (**4**) Circulate to listen in and to answer students' questions as necessary. (**5**) When the time is up, invite students to tell the class about their own families, or if the class is more advanced, have them tell about their partner's family.

VARIATIONS AND EXPANSIONS: (**1**) Have students ask one another about the names and ages of extended family members (see Exercise 4). (**2**) Invite students to tell the class about their group members' extended families. (**3**) Take notes as students tell the class about their families. Then write incomplete sentences on the board, and have students circulate to ask one another questions to find out whose name completes each sentence. For example:

_____ *has six aunts.*
_____ *has one cousin.*
_____ *has thirty cousins.*

(**4**) For homework, have students draw a family tree of their extended family, labeling each person with his/her relationship, age, and name. You may also ask them to write an accompanying paragraph about their extended family.

USE YOUR ENGLISH!

SETUP: (**1**) Tell students to do the first activity as a homework assignment. To prepare students for this assignment, have them brainstorm what they will tell their family about their English class. Write their ideas on the board. Tell the class that the purpose of this activity is to encourage home–school communication. You understand that students will speak to their families in their native language. (**2**) For homework, tell students to bring pictures of their families to class. At the beginning of class, show a volunteer a picture of your own family and tell the student about your family, modeling the conversation for the class. Then divide the class into small groups of three or four students,

and have them take turns showing their family pictures to one another. When the conversations wind down, have all the students stand up, form new groups, and sit in their new groups to share their pictures.

EXPANSION: For homework, ask students to write about a family picture, explaining who is in the picture. Have students submit the picture with the writing to you for correction and comment.

Lesson 2: Time

Pages 20–21

1. TIME

SETUP: (**1**) Have students work individually or in pairs to look at the clock times and complete the matching exercise. (**2**) Go over the answers with the class. Then play the audio program, pausing after each item, and have students repeat chorally. (**3**) Have the class brainstorm other ways to say the times. For example: *half past eight (8:30), a quarter to seven (6:45), a quarter past seven (7:15), twelve o'clock (midnight/noon).* Have students add the new expressions to the list in their books; alternatively, tell students to write at least ten different times in their vocabulary notebooks.

VARIATIONS AND EXPANSIONS: (**1**) Say or write a time, and have students point to the clock face on the page. (**2**) Point to a clock face on the page, and have students say the time. (**3**) Draw an analog or a digital clock face on the board with different times on it, and call on students to tell you the time. (**4**) Say several different times, and have students write them in numbers. Check answers by asking volunteers to write the times on the board.

Language and Culture Note: In the United States, people tell the time in twelve-hour cycles rather than in a twenty-four-hour cycle. To distinguish between 9:00 in the morning and 9:00 at night, for example, people use *A.M.* or *P.M.* Any time between 12:00 midnight and 12:00 noon is *A.M.* Any time between 12:00 noon and 12:00 midnight is *P.M.*

2. A STUDENT'S DAY

SETUP: (**1**) Write the simple present forms of the verbs *wake up, sleep, go, have, do* on the board.

Underline the final -s in the third-person singular form. For example:

I wake up
You wake up
He/she/it wakes up
We wake up
They wake up

Model the pronunciation of each of the five verbs, focusing on the -s sound. (**2**) Give students a few minutes to silently read the questions and their partial answers. (**3**) Read a question aloud, and call on a volunteer to respond.

VARIATION: Have students silently read the questions and write their answers before you call on volunteers to answer the questions.

3. HOW ABOUT YOU?

SETUP: (**1**) Model the questions and partial answers for the class. (**2**) Have students work in pairs to take turns asking and answering the questions. (**3**) Set a time limit; tell students they have only seven minutes to discuss these questions. (**4**) Circulate to listen in and to answer students' questions as necessary.

VARIATIONS AND EXPANSIONS: (**1**) Invite students to tell the class about their partner's day. (**2**) For homework, tell students to write a schedule of what they do every weekday and then write an accompanying paragraph. (**3**) Take notes as students tell the class about their daily routines. Then write incomplete sentences on the board, and have students circulate to ask one another questions to find out whose name completes each sentence. For example:

_____ *sleeps ten hours a night.*
_____ *sleeps six hours a night.*
_____ *has dinner at 10:00.*
_____ *does his homework at 7:00 in the morning.*

4. ARE YOU AN EARLY BIRD OR A NIGHT OWL?

SETUP: (**1**) Set the context: Two students are talking about their sleeping habits. (**2**) Have students close their books as they listen to the audio program for the first time. Then have students open their books and read along as they listen to the audio program again. Finally, play the audio a third time, pausing after each line for students to repeat chorally. (**3**) As students practice

the conversation in pairs, circulate to give individual feedback on pronunciation.

VARIATIONS AND EXPANSIONS: (**1**) Have students listen to the conversation on the audio program and place dots over the stressed words (as in the conversation chants). Review the stress marks with the class. Practice the conversation chorally, paying special attention to word stress. (**2**) Invite pairs of students to perform the conversation for the class. (**3**) Pass out blank cards to pairs of students. Have students write each line from the conversation on a different card. Have the pairs mix up their cards and then put them in order again.

5. A SLEEP SURVEY

SETUP: (**1**) Model the questions and the possible responses (*Yes, I do. / No, I don't. / Yes, I am. / No, I'm not.*) for the class. (**2**) Divide the class into small groups of three to four students. Have students work in their groups to ask and answer the questions; tell them to tally their group's responses. (**3**) Ask a spokesperson from each group to report their numbers to the class.

VARIATIONS AND EXPANSIONS: (**1**) Have each group add one more yes/no question to their survey. (**2**) Have students survey other students in the school and report their findings to the class.

6. CONVERSATION CHANT: MY DOG'S A NIGHT OWL!

SETUP: (**1**) Play the audio program. Tell students to read along as they listen to the chant. As you play the audio program, make hand motions or clap to reinforce the stress on the dotted syllables. (**2**) Play the audio program again, pausing after each line, and have students repeat. (**3**) Have the class chant chorally.

VARIATIONS: (**1**) Have students clap or make a hand motion to indicate where the stress falls as they chant. (**2**) Have students circle all the words that rhyme. Call on volunteers to read the rhyming pairs aloud and then write them on the board.

USE YOUR ENGLISH!

SETUP: Have students do this activity as a homework assignment. (**1**) To prepare students for this independent conversation, brainstorm with the class all the questions from this lesson. Write students' ideas on the board. (2) Tell students to write down the information they learn from their conversation partners. For example: *My conversation partner sleeps six hours every night. He gets up at 5:00 in the morning. He usually goes to bed at 11:00.* (3) At the beginning of the next class, students can share this information in small groups or simply hand in their reports to you.

Lesson 3: Morning Routines

Pages 22–23

1. A MORNING ROUTINE

SETUP: (1) Have students work individually or in pairs to look at the pictures and complete the matching exercise. Point out that some numbers will be used more than once. (2) Go over the answers with the class. Then play the audio program, pausing between items, and have students repeat chorally. (3) With the class, brainstorm other vocabulary in the pictures (for example: *upset, satisfied, terrified*). Write the words on the board, and have students add the new words to the list in their books; alternatively, tell students to write at least ten new words in their vocabulary notebooks.

VARIATIONS AND EXPANSIONS: (1) Say or write a word or phrase, and have students point to the picture. (2) Point to a picture, and have students say the word or phrase. (3) Have students work in pairs to take turns pointing and identifying items in the pictures. (4) Say a clock time, and have students identify the corresponding picture.

2. FIRST, NEXT, LAST

SETUP: Call on a volunteer to read each question aloud. As a class, discuss the answers.

VARIATIONS AND EXPANSIONS: (1) Before students ask and answer the questions, write the simple present forms of the verb *brush* in the phrase *brush his hair* on the board. Underline the final *-es*. For example:

I brush my hair.
You brush your hair.
He brush<u>es</u> his hair.
She brush<u>es</u> her hair.

We brush our hair.
They brush their hair.

Point out that you added an *-e* to the third-person singular *-s* and that this adds a syllable, too. Contrast the pronunciation of *brush* and *brushes*. Circle the possessive adjectives, and explain that in English, parts of the body are always preceded by a possessive adjective or a possessive noun form (for example: *Ed's hair*). Assess students' understanding of these rules; invite volunteers up to the board to conjugate *watch* and *comb* in the phrase *comb his hair.* Did they remember the possessive adjectives? Did they remember to add *-es* to *he/she watches*? Write the other verbs in this exercise on the board (*get, have, leave, make his bed, read, shave,* and *take*), and invite volunteers up to the board to write out the conjugations. Review the pronunciation of all the verbs with special emphasis on the *-s* of the third-person singular. (2) Have students work in pairs to take turns pointing to the pictures and retelling the whole story. (3) For homework, have students write their answers to the questions.

3. HOW ABOUT YOU?

SETUP: (1) Have the class brainstorm other phrases to describe their morning routines. Write the verbs on the board. (2) Have students work in pairs to take turns describing their morning routines. (3) Circulate to give individual feedback on pronunciation and to answer students' questions as necessary.

VARIATIONS AND EXPANSIONS: (1) Invite students to describe their partner's morning routine to the class. (2) For homework, have students write a paragraph describing their morning routine.

4. FIND SOMEONE WHO . . .

SETUP: (1) Model (or ask volunteers to model) the questions that students will need to ask. For example: *Do you sing in the shower? Do you watch TV in the morning? Do you have coffee in the morning?* (2) Have students walk around the classroom asking and answering the questions. Set a time limit for this activity; tell the class they have five minutes to complete their charts. (3) Have students report their information to the class.

VARIATIONS AND EXPANSIONS: (1) Encourage students to add one more sentence to the list. (2) For homework, have students write affirmative and negative sentences about themselves using the ideas in this activity. For example: *I sing in the* *shower. I don't watch TV in the morning.* (**3**) Have students choose one question, survey twenty other students in the school, and then report their findings to the class. For example: *Eleven students have coffee in the morning, and nine don't.*

5. WHAT AM I DOING?

SETUP: (**1**) Model the activity of miming an activity and ask: "What am I doing?" (**2**) Have students work in groups to take turns miming and identifying the activity.

VARIATION: Have the class do this together, with one student at a time standing up to mime an activity.

USE YOUR ENGLISH!

SETUP: (**1**) To prepare students for this independent conversation, model a conversation with a volunteer, using the question in the box. Tell students to write down information they learn from their conversation partners. For example: *My conversation partner gets up at 8:00. She eats breakfast and watches the news.* At the beginning of the next class, students can hand in their reports to you. (**2**) Bring a song you like to class or encourage students to bring an English-language song they want to learn. If possible, make multiple copies of the lyrics from the CD insert and distribute them to the class. Play the song and encourage students to sing along as they read the lyrics. Answer questions about unfamiliar vocabulary as necessary.

Lesson 4: Housework

Pages 24–25

1. DOING HOUSEWORK

SETUP: (**1**) Have students work individually or in pairs to look at the pictures and complete the matching exercise. (**2**) Go over the answers with the class. Then play the audio program, pausing between items, and have students repeat chorally. (**3**) With the class, brainstorm other vocabulary in the pictures (for example: *polish the furniture, do the laundry*). Write the phrases on the board, and have students add them to the list in their books; alternatively, tell students to

write at least ten new words and phrases in their vocabulary notebooks.

VARIATIONS AND EXPANSIONS: (**1**) Say or write a word or phrase, and have students point to the picture. (**2**) Point to a picture, and have students say the word or phrase. (**3**) Have students work in pairs to take turns pointing to and identifying actions in the pictures.

2. WHO DOES WHAT?

SETUP: Call on volunteers to read each question aloud. Discuss the answers with the class. For example:
   1. *She cooks, dusts, and folds the laundry.*
   2. *He washes and dries the dishes, cleans the refrigerator, and changes the light bulbs.*

VARIATIONS AND EXPANSIONS: (**1**) Before the class discusses the questions, conjugate the verbs *wash* and *dry* on the board. Underline the final *-s* endings. For example:

I wash the dishes.	*I dry the dishes.*
You wash the dishes.	*You dry the dishes.*
He/She wash<u>es</u> the dishes.	*He/She dri<u>es</u> the dishes.*
We wash the dishes.	*We dry the dishes.*
They wash the dishes.	*They dry the dishes.*

Point out you added an *-e* to the third-person singular *-s* form of *wash* and that this adds a syllable, too. Contrast the pronunciation of *wash* and *washes*. Point out that the *-y* changes to *-i* in *dries*. Write the other verbs in this exercise on the board (*change, clean, cook, dust, fold, iron,* and *vacuum*), and invite volunteers up to the board to write out the conjugations. Review the pronunciation of all the verbs, with special emphasis on the *-s* of the third-person singular. (**2**) For homework, have students write their answers to the questions.

3. HOW ABOUT YOU?

SETUP: (**1**) Model the questions for the class, and have students listen and repeat. (**2**) Have students work in pairs to take turns asking and answering the questions. (**3**) Circulate to give individual feedback on pronunciation and to answer students' questions as necessary.

VARIATIONS AND EXPANSIONS: (**1**) Lead a brief brainstorming session with the class to think of more questions that students can ask and answer about who does what housework at their homes. (**2**) For homework, have students write a paragraph describing who does what housework at their homes. Write a sample paragraph on the board about housework at your home. Have students copy the paragraph to use as a model for their own.

4. DO YOU DO HOUSEWORK?

SETUP: (**1**) Set the context: Two students are talking in class. (**2**) Have students close their books as they listen to the audio program for the first time. Then have students open their books and read along as they listen to the audio program again. Finally, play the audio a third time, pausing after each line for students to repeat chorally. (**3**) As students practice the conversation in pairs, circulate to give individual feedback on pronunciation.

VARIATIONS: (**1**) Have students listen to the conversation on the audio program and place dots over the stressed words (as in the conversation chants). Review the stress marks with the class. Practice the conversation chorally, paying special attention to word stress. (**2**) Invite two students to perform the conversation for the class.

5. A HOUSEHOLD SURVEY

SETUP: (**1**) Have the class brainstorm other housework activities, and write them on the board. (**2**) Have students work alone to write their answers before getting into groups. (**3**) Call on volunteers to report what they learned in their groups. They can talk about themselves or about their classmates. For example: *Javier cooks every day, and he vacuums every week. He never cleans the refrigerator.*

EXPANSION: Have students survey other students in the school and report their findings to the class.

6. CROSS-CULTURAL EXCHANGE

SETUP: (**1**) Model the questions for the class. (**2**) Have students work in small groups of three to four students to ask and answer the questions. (**3**) Invite students to report what they learned in their groups.

VARIATION AND EXPANSION: (**1**) Group the students according to gender (men only and women only). If you have a multicultural ESOL setting, group the students according to cultural background. When students report their group discussions, draw contrasts in their differing answers. (**2**) Dictate the following statements: (a) *Women are better at housework than men.* (b) *Children don't do enough housework.* Have students discuss their reactions in groups or as a class.

7. CONVERSATION CHANT: LAZY SUSAN

SETUP: (**1**) Play the audio program. Tell students to read along as they listen to the chant. As you play the audio program, make hand motions or clap to reinforce the stress on the dotted syllables. (**2**) Play the audio again, pausing after each line, and have students repeat. (**3**) Have the class chant chorally.

VARIATIONS: (**1**) Once students are familiar with the chant, divide the class into two groups. Have one group chant the lines that start at the left margin, and have the other group chant the lines that are indented. (**2**) Have students clap or make a hand motion to indicate where the stress falls as they chant. (**3**) Have students circle all the words that rhyme. Call on volunteers to read the rhyming pairs aloud and then write them on the board.

USE YOUR ENGLISH!

SETUP: Have students do this activity as a homework assignment. (**1**) To prepare students for this independent conversation, have them take a few minutes to brainstorm a list of all the housework they do. Then model the conversation with a volunteer, using the questions in the box. (**2**) Tell students to write down information they learn from their conversation partners. For example: *My conversation partner cooks and washes the dishes every day. She vacuums and dusts every week. She never irons.* At the beginning of the next class, students can share this information in small groups or simply hand in their reports to you.

Lesson 5: Everyday Life
Pages 26–27

1. BARBARA'S DAY

SETUP: (**1**) Set the context: This is a description of a typical day in a woman's life. (**2**) Have students work individually or in pairs to look at the pictures and complete the matching exercise. (**3**) Go over the answers with the class. Then play the audio program, pausing between items, and have students repeat chorally. (**4**) Have the class brainstorm other vocabulary in the pictures (for example: *walk to school, get groceries*). Write the words on the board, and have students add the new words to the list in their books; alternatively, tell students to write at least ten new words and phrases in their vocabulary notebooks.

VARIATIONS AND EXPANSIONS: (**1**) Say or write a word or phrase, and have students point to the picture. (**2**) Point to a picture, and have students say the word or phrase. (**3**) Have students work in pairs to take turns pointing to and identifying actions in the pictures.

2. BEFORE OR AFTER?

SETUP: (**1**) For question 1, point to the first picture and ask the class: "What do you think? What time does Barbara feed the baby?" Write a student's response on the board (for example: *At 7:30*), and have all the students write that time into the corresponding clock face. Circulate around the room to check students' work. Continue to point and ask until all the clock faces are filled in and checked. (**2**) Read the questions aloud, and call on student volunteers to answer each question. For example: *She does the dishes after she goes to class. She reads to the children before she studies.*

VARIATIONS AND EXPANSIONS: (**1**) Before the class discusses the questions, write the simple present forms of the verb *study* on the board. Underline the final *-s* ending:

> *I study*
> *You study*
> *He/She stud<u>ies</u>*
> *We study*
> *They study*

Point out that the *-y* changes to *-i* in *studies*. Write other verbs in this exercise on the board (*feed, read, sweep*), and invite volunteers up to the board to write out the simple present forms. Review the pronunciation of these verbs, with special emphasis on the *-s* of the third-person singular. (**2**) Make true/false statements about what Barbara does; have students say whether they are true or false and correct the false statements. For example:

Teacher: Barbara goes to class before she feeds the baby. True or false?
Student: False. Barbara goes to class after she feeds the baby.

(**3**) For homework, have students write a paragraph describing Barbara's day.

3. HOW ABOUT YOU?

SETUP: (**1**) Model the questions for the class. (**2**) Have students work in pairs to take turns asking and answering the questions. Circulate to give individual feedback on pronunciation and to answer students' questions as necessary.

VARIATIONS AND EXPANSIONS: (**1**) Have students tell the class about their partner's day. For example: *Jenny studies before class. She goes to work after class. She does the dishes every day.* (**2**) For homework, have students write about what they do on a normal weekday and the times they do each activity. Have students submit their writing to you for correction and comment.

4. YESTERDAY, TODAY, TOMORROW

SETUP: (**1**) Explain to students that in English the days of the week always begin with a capital letter. (**2**) Play the audio program once through, and have students listen along. Then play the audio program a second time, pausing after each line for students to repeat chorally. (**3**) Have a volunteer read each question aloud to the class. Call on another volunteer to respond, and write the full answer on the board (for example: *Today is Tuesday*).

VARIATION: Students can do this activity in pairs.

Language and Culture Note: In the United States, the first day of the week is Sunday.

5. DAYS OF THE WEEK

SETUP: (**1**) Have students fill in the calendar individually and then talk about their calendar with a partner. Circulate to listen in and to answer students' questions as necessary. (**2**) To assure that students use the correct preposition in their statements, write the phrases *on Sunday morning, on Tuesday afternoon*, and *on Friday evening* on the board.

VARIATION AND EXPANSION: (**1**) Ask different students about their partners' week. For example: "What does Jimmy do on Thursday afternoon?" (**2**) Make multiple copies of the calendar, and distribute two to each student. Have students write in the calendar five activities they do during the week. Have them tell their partners about the five activities without showing their calendars. The partners must listen and complete their blank calendars correctly. Then have the partners switch roles.

USE YOUR ENGLISH!

SETUP: Have students do this activity as a homework assignment. (**1**) To prepare students for this assignment, have them take a few minutes in class to list what they plan to do tomorrow. Then have students share their lists in pairs. (**2**) Tell students to check off each item after they finish it tomorrow. At the beginning of the next class, students can hand in their checked-off lists to you.

EXPANSION: In the next class, have students compare their lists. What things on their lists did they do? What things didn't they do?

Lesson 6: Telephone Calls

Pages 28–29

1. TELEPHONE CALLS

SETUP: (**1**) Have students work individually or in pairs to look at the pictures and complete the matching exercise. (**2**) Go over the answers with the class. Then play the audio program, pausing between items, and have students repeat chorally. (**3**) Have the class brainstorm other vocabulary related to phone calls (for example: *land line, voicemail*), Write the words on the board, and have students add the new words to the list in their books; alternatively, tell students to write at least ten new words or phrases in their vocabulary notebooks.

VARIATIONS AND EXPANSIONS: (**1**) Say or write a word or phrase, and have students point to the item in the pictures. (**2**) Point to an item in the pictures, and have students say the word or phrase.

2. WHAT'S HAPPENING?

SETUP: (**1**) Have students silently read the phone conversations. (**2**) Call on volunteers to read the phone conversations aloud. (**3**) Answer any questions about vocabulary. (**4**) Read each question in this section aloud, and call on volunteers to respond.

VARIATIONS AND EXPANSIONS: (**1**) Have students ask and answer the questions in pairs. (**2**) For homework, have students write their answers to the questions.

3. HOW ABOUT YOU?

SETUP: Have students work in pairs to take turns asking and answering the questions. While students are working, circulate to answer questions as necessary.

VARIATIONS AND EXPANSIONS: (**1**) Invite students to report on what they learned about their partners. For example: *Kim has a cell phone, and she loves to talk to her friends on the phone.* (**2**) Ask the class: "How many students have a cell phone?" "How many students have a cordless phone?" and "How many students have an answering machine?" Count the raised hands and write the number on the board each time. (**3**) With the class, brainstorm the advantages and disadvantages of different kinds of phone service (for example: land line vs. cell phone, answering machine vs. voicemail). Ask the class: "What's good about cell phones?" Write their ideas on the board (for example: *You can take them everywhere. They're good for emergencies.*). Then ask: "What's good about land line phones?" and write students' ideas on the board (for example: *They don't cost a lot. You can make international calls.*). Finally, ask the class: "Which is better: a land line or a cell phone? Why?" You can repeat this procedure asking questions about answering machines and voicemail.

4. ROLE PLAY

SETUP: (**1**) Have students work in pairs to read the phone conversations on page 28 again. Answer any questions students may have about the language. (**2**) Have students write their own phone conversations. (**3**) Circulate around the class, answering questions and correcting students' writing where necessary. (**4**) Have each pair present one of their role plays to the class. As students perform, encourage them to mime dialing and holding a phone. (**5**) Have the rest of the class listen and identify the type of phone situation (making a call, leaving a message, getting a wrong number).

VARIATIONS AND EXPANSIONS: (**1**) To further familiarize students with phone language, photocopy the three conversations on page 28 and cut each line of each conversation into a slip of paper. Mix the slips from the three conversations together. Have pairs of students read the slips of paper, sort them into the three separate conversations, and then put each conversation in order. (**2**) Have students submit their written conversations to you for correction before they perform the conversations in the following class.

5. PREPAID PHONE CARDS

SETUP: (1) Play the audio program one time through, and have students listen along. Then play the audio program a second time, pausing after each line for students to repeat chorally. (2) Have students work in pairs to ask and answer the questions. Circulate to listen in and to answer students' questions as necessary.

VARIATIONS AND EXPANSION: (1) Have students draw phone keypads. Explain that the * is the "star" key and the # is the "pound" key. Then have students practice following the phone card directions using their keypads. (2) Bring in other samples of phone cards so students can practice reading them and following their directions.

Language and Culture Note: In the United States, the number of minutes advertised on a phone card is for calls inside the country. International calls are more expensive and therefore use up the "minutes" more quickly.

6. CROSS-CULTURAL EXCHANGE

SETUP: (1) Model the questions for the class. (2) Have students ask and answer the questions in small groups. Circulate to listen in and to answer questions as necessary. (3) Invite students to report on what they learned in their groups.

EXPANSION: For homework, have students write their own answers to the questions.

7. FIND SOMEONE WHO . . .

SETUP: (1) Model (or have volunteers model) the questions students will need to ask. For example: *Do you have a cell phone? Do you talk on the phone every day? Do you like to use English on the phone?* (2) Have students walk around the room asking and answering the questions. Set a time limit; tell the class they have five minutes to complete their charts. (3) Have students report their information to the class.

VARIATIONS AND EXPANSIONS: (1) Encourage students to add one more sentence to the list. (2) For homework, have students write affirmative and negative sentences about themselves using the ideas in this activity. For example: *I have a cell phone. I don't have a cordless phone.* (3) Have students choose one question, survey twenty other students in the school, and then report their findings to the class. For example: *Nineteen students have a cell phone, and one doesn't.*

USE YOUR ENGLISH!

SETUP: Have students do this activity as a homework assignment. (1) To prepare students for this assignment, brainstorm the names of phone companies in your area. Write the names on the board, and have each student choose one company to investigate. (2) Tell students to write down the numbers they find. At the beginning of the next class, students can share this information in small groups or simply hand in their information to you.

EXPANSION: Identify other numbers students might need to find (for example: their children's schools, their local supermarket, their local pharmacy). Brainstorm the names of these places, and then tell students to find those numbers in the phone book, too.

Listening Practice
Page 30

1. WHAT DO YOU HEAR?

SETUP: (1) Tell students to read through the sentences silently. (2) Play the audio program. (3) Review the answers with the class. If there is confusion about any answers, have students listen to the audio program again.

VARIATIONS AND EXPANSIONS: (1) Have students first listen and then read the sentences. (2) Once finished with the whole exercise, have pairs of students take turns listening to each other read the sentences and identifying which sentence their partners say.

2. QUESTIONS AND ANSWERS

SETUP: (1) Have students read the answers silently. (2) Play the audio program. (3) Check answers with the whole class. If students are uncertain about any of their answers, replay the audio program.

VARIATIONS AND EXPANSIONS: (1) Have students first listen and then read the answers. (2) After finishing the whole activity, have students compose questions for the uncircled answers. (3) Have students listen to the audio program again and take dictation on the questions. Write the questions on the board so students can correct their work, or have students self-correct by referring them to the Audioscript in the back of the book.

3. HOW ABOUT YOU?

SETUP: (1) Pause the audio program after each question so that students have time to write their responses. (2) When students have answered all four questions, have them share their responses in small groups. (3) Call on volunteers to read their answers to the class.

VARIATION: Have students take dictation on the questions and then write their responses after the dictation is corrected. Write the questions on the board so students can correct their work, or have students self-correct by referring them to the Audioscript in the back of the book.

Review

Page 31

1. GET TO KNOW YOUR PARTNER.

SETUP: (1) Divide the class into pairs. (2) Have students ask and answer questions about their families, taking notes as they listen. If students have trouble getting started, refer them to Lesson 1. Circulate to listen in and to answer questions as necessary. (3) Have students tell the class about their partners. For example: *Lizette has a big family. She has three brothers and four sisters.*

EXPANSION: For homework, have students write a paragraph about their partners using information they learned from this activity.

2. WHAT TIME . . . ?

SETUP: (1) To model the questions, write question stems 1 and 2 on the board and ask volunteers to complete each question. Write their ideas on the board. Then ask other volunteers to answer each question. For example:
    1. What time is *English class? It's at 9:00.*
    2. What time do *you get up? I get up at 6:00.*
(2) Point out the verb in each question (*is, do*) to underscore the different structures of these two types of questions. (3) Have students work individually to complete the questions and compose a third one. Circulate to correct students' questions as necessary. (4) Have students walk around the room, asking and answering their questions.

3. HOUSEWORK: WHO AM I?

SETUP: (1) Have students brainstorm different kinds of housework. Write their ideas on the board. (2) Have students work individually to write a kind of housework and the frequency with which they do it. (3) Collect the papers, mix them up, and then have each student select one. Make sure no student has received his or her own paper. (4) Have students read the information to the class. (5) Have the class guess who the person is.

4. WHAT DO YOU DO?

SET UP: (1) Model the questions for the class. (2) For question 2, write a response stem on the board for student reference (for example: *On Mondays, I usually . . .*). (3) Have students work in pairs to ask and answer the questions. Circulate to listen in and to answer students' questions as necessary.

5. FAVORITE DAY

SETUP: (1) Model a response to the question by describing your favorite day of the week and saying why it's your favorite. For example: *Saturday is my favorite day of the week because on Saturday I go shopping and spend time with my children.* (2) Have students answer the questions in small groups. Circulate to listen in and to answer students' questions as necessary.

EXPANSION: For homework, have students write a paragraph about their favorite day of the week.

Assessment

Page 32

PART 1: QUESTIONS

SETUP: Have students work individually to write the questions. Challenge students not to look at the previous lessons but to construct their questions from memory.

VARIATION: Have students write their questions on a separate sheet of paper and hand them in for correction at the end of the assessment.

PART 2: SPEAKING

SETUP: (**1**) Divide the class into pairs, and have students ask and answer the questions. (**2**) Circulate to listen in and to answer students' questions as necessary.

VARIATION: Have students write their partners' responses to their questions and hand them in for correction at the end of the assessment.

PART 3: LISTENING

SETUP: (**1**) Have students first read the answers silently. Then play the audio program. (**2**) Check answers with the whole class by asking volunteers to read the correct sentence aloud. If there is confusion about any of the answers, replay the audio program.

VARIATIONS AND EXPANSION: (**1**) Have students write the number of the question and the letter of their response on a separate sheet to hand in to you for correction at the end of the assessment. (**2**) As an added challenge, have students compose questions for the uncircled answers.

PART 4: WRITING

SETUP: (**1**) Ask the class: "What are the people doing in the pictures?" Lead a brief brainstorming session about what the people could be saying. (**2**) Have students work individually to write their conversations. Circulate as students are writing, and answer questions as necessary.

VARIATIONS: (**1**) Have students write their conversations on a separate piece of paper to hand in to you for correction. (**2**) Have students share their conversations with a partner. Then ask volunteer pairs to perform one of their conversations for the class.

Preview

Page 33

PREVIEW QUESTIONS

SETUP: (1) Have the class look at the photographs. Read each question aloud, and call on individual students to respond. (2) For questions 3–5, write students' responses on the board so everyone can see the various possible responses. For example:

3. *I cook. I clean. I watch TV.*
4. *I have to do laundry. I have to help my children with homework.*
5. *I want to watch TV. I want to call my sister.*

CONVERSATION TIP

SETUP: (1) Write on the board: *How do you say this in English? How do you spell that?* Tell students they can ask these questions to learn new words. (2) Have students look at the picture and read the conversation silently. (3) Act out the conversation with a volunteer. (4) Have students practice the conversation in pairs. (5) Circulate to correct pronunciation.

EXPANSION: Point to objects in the room to prompt students to ask you the questions about the objects. For example:

(Teacher points to a binder.)
Student: How do you say this in English?
Teacher: Binder.
Student: How do you spell that?
Teacher: B-i-n-d-e-r.

When you spell a word, have students write the word on a paper and then spell it back to you so you can assess how well they recognize the names of the letters in English.

CONVERSATION CHANT: KATHY'S DOG MOVED TO PARIS

SETUP: (1) The dots over the words indicate where the stress falls. As you play the audio program, make hand motions or clap to reinforce the stress on the dotted syllables. (2) Have students listen once through as they read along. (3) Play the audio again, pausing after each line, and have students repeat. (4) Have the class chant chorally.

VARIATIONS AND EXPANSION: (1) Have students clap or make a hand motion to indicate where the stress falls as they chant. (2) Have students circle all the words that rhyme. Call on volunteers to read the rhyming pairs aloud and then write them on the board.

Lesson 1: Your Home

Pages 34–35

1. HOMES

SETUP: (1) Have students work individually or in pairs to look at the pictures and complete the matching exercise. (2) Go over the answers with the class. Then play the audio program, pausing between items, and have students repeat chorally. (3) Write on the board the two Conversation Tip questions from the Preview section of the unit: *How do you say this in English? How do you spell that?* As you brainstorm more vocabulary items, encourage students to point to items in the pictures and ask the questions. New vocabulary may include: *driveway, door, window.* Write the words on the board, and have students add the new words to the list in their books; alternatively, tell students to write at least ten new words in their vocabulary notebooks.

VARIATIONS: (1) Say or write a word or phrase, and have students point to the item in the pictures. (2) Point to an item in the pictures and have students say the word or phrase. (3) Have students label each picture with one of the following words: *apartment building, house, mobile home,* or *condo.*

2. DIFFERENT HOMES

SETUP: Call on a volunteer to read each question aloud. As a class, discuss the answers. For example:

1. *All these homes have windows, doors, and roofs.*
2. *The apartment building has three floors. The mobile home has one floor. The house has a balcony.*

VARIATION AND EXPANSION: (1) Write students' responses on the board using the following rubric.

For similarities, write: *All the homes have* . . . . For differences, write: *The condo has* . . . *, The apartment has* . . . *, The mobile home has* . . . *, The house has* . . . . (**2**) For homework, have students write their answers to the questions.

3. YOUR HOME

SETUP: (**1**) Model the pronunciation of the questions. (**2**) Have students work in pairs to take turns asking and answering the questions. (**3**) Circulate to listen in and to answer students' questions as necessary.

VARIATION AND EXPANSION: (**1**) Have students draw a picture of their home (from the outside) and then explain the picture to a partner. (**2**) For homework, have students write their answers to the questions and then submit their work to you for correction.

4. LEI'S NEW PHONE NUMBER AND ADDRESS

SETUP: (**1**) Set the context: A young woman is calling her parents from her new apartment. (**2**) Have students close their books as they listen to the audio program for the first time. Then have students open their books and read along as they listen to the audio program again. Finally, play the audio a third time, pausing after each line for students to repeat chorally. (**3**) Have students then practice the conversation in pairs. (**4**) Circulate to give individual feedback on pronunciation.

VARIATIONS AND EXPANSION: (**1**) Have students listen to the conversation on the audio program and place dots over the stressed words (as in the conversation chants). Review the stress marks with the class. Practice the conversation chorally, paying special attention to word stress. (**2**) Invite pairs of students to perform the conversation for the class. (**3**) Pass out blank cards to pairs of students. Have students write each line from the conversation on a different card, mix up their cards, and then put them in order again.

Language and Culture Notes: When giving telephone and address numbers, *zero* is referred to as "oh." For example: The ZIP code 10471 is pronounced "one-oh-four-seven-one." Usually address numbers are read as single- or two-digit numbers, not as composite numbers: For example: 219 East 57th Street is read as "two-nineteen," not "two hundred

and nineteen." 1079 Broadway is read as "ten-seventy-nine," not as "one thousand seventy-nine."

5. HOW ABOUT YOU?

SETUP: (**1**) Review the pronunciation of phone numbers and ZIP codes. Write the telephone number (212) 662-3538 on the board, and model the two possible ways to read the number: "two-one-two six-six-two three-five-three-eight" or "two-one-two six-six-two thirty-five, thirty-eight." Write other phone numbers on the board, for example: (781) 349-9874 or (219) 885-6475, and call on students to read them aloud in the two possible styles. (**2**) Review the pronunciation of ordinal numbers. The *-th* in 4th, 6th, 7th, 8th, and 9th is difficult for non-native speakers to hear. Write *57* and *57th* on the board, and put a letter under each item (*a* and *b*). Ask students: "What do you hear?" Say one of the numbers and have the class call out what they hear. For example:

Teacher: 57th
  Class: b
Teacher: 57
  Class: a

Change the numbers but keep the contrast between cardinal and ordinal numbers. For example: 24 and 24th; 36 and 36th; 48 and 48th; 59 and 59th. Once students begin to hear the difference between the cardinal and ordinal numbers, have individual students call out a number on the board (*24* or *24th*) and have the rest of the class identify it. For example:

Student 1: 24
  Class: a
Student 1: 24th
  Class: b

(**3**) Model the pronunciation of the questions. (**4**) Have students work in pairs to ask and answer the questions. If students prefer not to share this information, they can give made-up answers to questions 1 and 2. (**5**) Circulate to listen in and to answer students' questions as necessary.

VARIATIONS AND EXPANSIONS: (**1**) Set a time limit; tell students they have only five minutes to discuss these questions. (**2**) For homework, have students write complete-sentence answers to the questions. (**3**) Dictate questions that students have learned so far: *What's your name? How do you spell that? Where are you from? What street do* you live on? Do you have an apartment number? If yes, what is it? What city and state do you live in? What's your ZIP code? Write the questions on the board so students can correct their dictations. (**4**) Get a simple personal information form (name and address), and have pairs of students interview one another to complete the form using the above questions. If students want, they can make up the information.

6. CONVERSATION CHANT: A HOUSE IS NOT A HOME

SETUP: (**1**) Have students listen once through as they read along. As you play the audio program, make hand motions or clap to reinforce the stress on the dotted syllables. (**2**) Play the audio program again, pausing after each line, and have students repeat. (**3**) Have the class chant chorally.

VARIATIONS AND EXPANSION: (**1**) Have students clap or make a hand motion to indicate where the stress falls as they chant. (**2**) Have students circle all the words (or syllables) that rhyme. Call on volunteers to read the rhyming pairs aloud and then write them on the board. (**3**) Write these questions on the board, and have students discuss their answers in small groups: *Where do you want to live? What kind of home do you want? What do you want your home to have?* (**4**) For more advanced students, discuss the following questions: *The title of the chant is "A House Is Not a Home." What does that mean? What is the difference between a "house" and a "home"?*

USE YOUR ENGLISH!

SETUP: Have students do this activity as a homework assignment. (**1**) To prepare students for this independent conversation, use the question in the box to model the conversation with a student. (**2**) Tell students to write down the name and address of their conversation partners. At the beginning of the next class, students can share this information in small groups or simply hand in their reports to you.

EXPANSION: Brainstorm with the class about when it's OK for a person to ask for your address and telephone number (for example: registering for school, in a doctor's office). Then brainstorm when it

is not OK (for example: meeting someone for the first time, telling a stranger who calls you on the phone).

Lesson 2: The Kitchen
Pages 36–37

1. THE KITCHEN

SETUP: (**1**) Write *kitchen* on the board. Brainstorm with the class items that are usually found in a kitchen. Write their ideas on the board (for example: *table, sink, refrigerator*). (**2**) Have students work individually or in pairs to look at the picture and complete the matching exercise. (**3**) Go over the answers with the class. Then play the audio program, pausing between items, and have students repeat chorally. (**4**) Write on the board the two Conversation Tip questions from the Preview on page 33: *How do you say this in English? How do you spell that?* As you brainstorm other vocabulary items in the picture, encourage students to point to items in the picture and ask the questions. New vocabulary may include: *table, counter, drinking coffee, looking in the refrigerator.* Write the words and phrases on the board and have students add them to the list in their books; alternatively, tell students to write at least twelve new words and phrases in their vocabulary notebooks.

VARIATIONS: (**1**) Say or write a word or phrase, and have students point to the item in the picture. (**2**) Point to an item in the picture and have students say the word or phrase. (**3**) Have students work in pairs to take turns pointing to items in the picture and asking the two Conversation Tip questions. For example:

A: (*Pointing to an item in the picture*) *How do you say this in English?*
B: *It's a washing machine.*
A: *How do you spell that?*
B: *W-a-s-h-i-n-g m-a-c-h-i-n-e.*

Circulate to listen in and to answer students' questions as necessary.

2. IN THE KITCHEN

SETUP: Call on volunteers to read the questions aloud. As a class, discuss the answers.

VARIATION AND EXPANSION: (**1**) Write students' responses on the board in the correct present progressive forms. For example: *The mother is doing laundry. The dog is eating.* (2) Have students work in small groups to look at the picture and write a list of all the things they see. Set a two-minute time limit. After two minutes, find out which group has the longest list. (3) For homework, have students write their answers to the questions and submit them to you for correction.

3. HOW ABOUT YOU?

SETUP: (1) Model the pronunciation of the questions. (2) Have students work in pairs to take turns asking and answering the questions. Circulate to listen in and to answer students' questions as necessary.

VARIATIONS AND EXPANSIONS: (1) Have the partners report back to the class. For example: *Tito has a stove, a refrigerator, a table, and two chairs in his kitchen. He cooks, washes dishes, and eats meals in his kitchen.* (2) Have students draw a picture of their kitchen and then explain the picture to a partner. (3) For homework, have students write their answers to the questions and submit them to you for correction.

4. THE SAME OR DIFFERENT?

SETUP: (1) Write on the board: *There's _____* and *There are _____.* Say a singular noun (for example: *a dishwasher*) and point to the first model. Say a plural noun (for example: *chairs*) and point to the second model. Continue calling out singular and plural nouns, and call on students to make sentences with *There's* and *There are.* For example:

   Teacher: a refrigerator
Student 1: There's a refrigerator.
   Teacher: pans
Student 2: There are pans.

(2) Write on the board: *There's no a dishwasher.* Cross out the indefinite article *a.* Explain that no article follows the word *no.* (3) Divide the class into groups. Have each group choose one person to write the lists. (4) Set a time limit of ten minutes for groups to find the similarities and differences between the two pictures. (5) Have all the groups report their ideas to the class as you write them on the board. Be sure to write the similarities on the left side of the board and the differences on the right, as the exercise is presented on page 37.

EXPANSION: For homework, have students write a comparison of their own kitchen with the kitchen in the picture on page 36, following the language in this exercise as a model.

5. FIND SOMEONE WHO . . .

SETUP: (1) Model (or have volunteers model) the questions students will need to ask. For example: *Do you do laundry in the kitchen? Do you use an electric mixer? Do you have a toaster?* Have a volunteer write the model questions on the board. The rest of the class can help with spelling and copy the questions in their notebooks. (2) Have students circulate around the classroom asking and answering the questions. Set a six-minute time limit for this information-gathering part. (3) Have students report their information to the class. For example: *Juan does laundry in the kitchen. Lee uses an electric mixer.*

VARIATIONS AND EXPANSIONS: (1) Encourage students to add one more sentence to the list. For example: *_____ does homework in the kitchen.* (2) For homework, have students make sentences about themselves using the ideas in this activity. For example: *I don't do laundry in the kitchen. I use an electric mixer.* (3) Have students choose one question from this activity and survey other students in the school. Have students report their findings to the class. For example: *Twelve students have a dishwasher, and eighteen don't.*

USE YOUR ENGLISH!

SETUP: Have students do these activities as homework assignments. (1) To prepare students for this independent conversation, model the conversation with a student volunteer, using the questions in the box. Tell students to write down information they learn from their conversation partners. For example: *My conversation partner has a sink, stove, and refrigerator in her kitchen. My conversation partner cooks, eats, washes dishes, and talks on the phone in her kitchen.* At the beginning of the next class, students can hand in their reports to you. (2) Encourage students to write labels on various items in their kitchens.In class, you can answer vocabulary questions and model the correct pronunciation of any new words. After several classes, ask students: "Did you put the labels in your kitchen? Did you learn the new words?"

Lesson 3: The Dining Area and Living Room

Pages 38–39

1. THE DINING ROOM

SETUP: (1) Write the words *dining room* on the board. Brainstorm with the class items that are usually found in a dining room. Write their ideas on the board. (2) Have students work individually or in pairs to look at the picture and complete the matching exercise. (3) Go over the answers with the class. Then play the audio program, pausing between items, and have students repeat chorally. (4) Write on the board the two Conversation Tip questions from the Preview on page 33: *How do you say this in English? How do you spell that?* As you brainstorm more vocabulary items, encourage students to point to items in the picture and ask these questions. New vocabulary may include: *candles, table, chairs, cabinet.* Write the words on the board, and have students add the new words to the list in their books; alternatively, tell students to write at least ten new words and phrases in their vocabulary notebooks.

VARIATIONS AND EXPANSION: (1) Say or write a word or phrase, and have students point to the item in the picture. (2) Point to an item in the picture, and have students say the word or phrase. (3) Have students work in pairs to take turns pointing and identifying items in the picture. (4) Point to the words *dining area* in the lesson title and *dining room* in the exercise title. Ask: "What's a dining room? What's a dining area?" Explain the difference: A *dining room* is a room with walls and a door that is used only for eating meals. A *dining area* is part of a room—perhaps a living room or a kitchen—where people eat meals.

2. WHAT ARE THEY DOING?

SETUP: Call on a volunteer to read each question aloud. As a class, discuss the answers. For example:

1. *The sister is setting the table.*
2. *She is putting a plate on the table.*
3. *One brother is pouring the milk. The other brother is doing his homework.*
4. *The mother is bringing the food.*

VARIATIONS AND EXPANSIONS: (1) On the board, write the framework for statements with present progressive verbs: *He's _____ing. She's _____ing. They're _____ing.* Have students refer to the forms as they answer the questions.

(2) For homework, have students write their answers to the questions and submit them for correction.

3. HOW ABOUT YOU?

SETUP: (1) Model the pronunciation of the questions. (2) Have students work in pairs to take turns asking and answering the questions. (3) Circulate to listen in and to answer students' questions as necessary.

VARIATIONS AND EXPANSIONS: (1) Have students draw a typical table setting for dinner. Have them explain where they place their eating utensils and the food. In an EFL classroom, do this activity together as a class by drawing the place setting on the board. In an ESOL classroom, pair students from different cultural backgrounds to compare their place settings. Have them draw their place settings on a piece of paper. (2) For homework have students write their answers to the questions and submit them for correction.

4. THE LIVING ROOM

SETUP: (1) Write the words *living room* on the board. Brainstorm with the class items that are usually found in a living room. Write students' ideas on the board. (2) Have students work individually or in pairs to look at the picture and complete the matching exercise. (3) Go over the answers with the class. Then play the audio program, pausing between items, and have students repeat chorally. (4) Write on the board the two Conversation Tip questions from the Preview on page 33: *How do you say this in English? How do you spell that?* As you brainstorm more vocabulary items, encourage students to point to items in the picture and ask these questions. New vocabulary may include: *picture, clock, armchair.* Write the words on the board, and have students add the new words to the list in their books; alternatively, tell students to write at least ten new words in their vocabulary notebooks.

VARIATIONS AND EXPANSIONS: (1) Say or write a word or phrase, and have students point to the item in the picture. (2) Point to an item in the picture, and have students say the word or phrase. (3) To review the vocabulary in this lesson, play a drawing game. Write the vocabulary items from this lesson on slips of paper. Have student take turns coming up to the front of the classroom, taking a slip of paper, and drawing the item on the board. The rest of the class guesses the item. To keep the pace moving, set a time limit of one minute for each turn.

5. WHAT ARE THEY SAYING?

SETUP: (**1**) Set the context: This conversation takes place among the people in the picture in Exercise 4. (**2**) Have students close their books as they listen to the audio program for the first time. Then have students open their books and read along as they listen to the audio program again. Finally, play the audio a third time, pausing after each line for students to repeat chorally. (**3**) As students practice the conversation in groups of four, circulate to give individual feedback on pronunciation.

VARIATIONS AND EXPANSIONS: (**1**) Have students listen to the conversation on the audio program and place dots over the stressed words (as in the conversation chants). Review the stress marks with the class. Practice the conversation chorally, paying special attention to word stress. (**2**) Invite groups of students to perform the conversation for the class. (**3**) Pass out blank cards to the groups. Have students write each line from the conversation on a different card, mix up their cards, and then put them in order again.

Language and Culture Note: When a person declines an invitation, it is considered polite to explain why. In this conversation, each family member declines the invitation to play a video game and then gives a reason why he or she can't.

6. IN THE LIVING ROOM

SETUP: Call on a volunteer to read each question aloud. As a class, discuss the answers. For example:
1. *There's a sofa. There's a headset.*
2. *One brother is playing a video game. Another brother is listening to music and doing homework.*

VARIATIONS AND EXPANSIONS: (**1**) To provide students with guidance for the first question, write these sentence stems on the board: *There's a(n)* _____. *There are* _____. (**2**) For question 2, write students' responses on the board in the correct present progressive forms to model the grammar. (**3**) For homework, have students answer the questions and submit their answers to you for correction.

7. HOW ABOUT YOU?

SETUP: (**1**) Model the pronunciation of the questions. (**2**) Have students work in pairs to take turns asking and answering the questions.

(**3**) Circulate to listen in on students' conversations and to answer questions as necessary.

EXPANSIONS: (**1**) Have students draw a picture of their own living room and dining area. Then put students into pairs to share their pictures and tell each other what's in each room and what they do in each room. For example: *This is my living room. In my living room, there is a big TV and a big sofa. I watch TV in the living room.* (**2**) For homework, have students write a paragraph about their living room, answering the questions in this activity.

USE YOUR ENGLISH!

SETUP: Have students do this activity as a homework assignment. (**1**) To prepare students for this independent conversation, model a conversation about your living room with a volunteer, using the questions in the box. (**2**) Tell students to write down information they learn from their conversation partners. For example: *My conversation partner has a couch, a bed, a TV, and a table in his living room. He watches TV in the living room. His cousin sleeps on the bed at night.* At the beginning of the next class, students can share this information in small groups or simply hand in their reports to you.

EXPANSION: Brainstorm with the class other questions from this lesson that they can ask their conversation partners, such as: *Is there a dining room or dining area in your home? What's in it? Where do you eat dinner at home?*

Lesson 4: Neat and Messy Bedrooms
Pages 40–41

1. TWO BEDROOMS

SETUP: (**1**) Write the word *bedroom* on the board. Brainstorm with the class items that are usually found in a bedroom. Write their ideas on the board. (**2**) Read the two picture titles aloud to the class. (**3**) Have students work individually or in pairs to complete the matching exercise. (**4**) Go over the answers with the class. Then play the audio component, pausing between items, and have students repeat chorally. (**5**) Write on the board the two Conversation Tip questions from the Preview on page 33: *How do you say this in English?*

How do you spell that? As you brainstorm more vocabulary items, encourage students to point to items in the pictures and ask these questions. New vocabulary may include: *drawer, dirty clothes, clock radio.* Write the words on the board, and have students add the new words to the list in their books; alternatively, tell students to write at least ten new words in their vocabulary notebooks.

VARIATIONS AND EXPANSIONS: (1) Say or write a word, and have students point to the item in the pictures. (2) Point to an item in one of the pictures, and have students say the word. (3) Have students work in pairs to take turns pointing and identifying items in the pictures. (4) Make false statements about items in the pictures, and have students correct you. For example:

Teacher: There are dirty dishes on the dresser in the neat bedroom.
Student: No, that's not right. There are dirty dishes on the dresser in the messy bedroom.

2. A NEAT AND A MESSY BEDROOM

SETUP: (1) Write on the board: *Both bedrooms have _____. In the messy room, the _____. In the neat room, the _____.* (2) Call on a volunteer to read each question aloud. As a class, discuss the answers.

VARIATION: For homework, have students write their responses to the questions and submit their work to you for correction.

3. WHAT ARE THEY SAYING?

SETUP: (1) Set the context: The two girls in the picture are speaking to each other on the phone. (2) Have students close their books as they listen to the audio program for the first time. Then have students open their books and read along as they listen to the audio program again. Finally, play the audio a third time, pausing after each line for students to repeat chorally. (3) As students practice the conversation in groups of three, encourage them to act it out by pretending to hold a phone as they speak. (4) Circulate to give individual feedback on pronunciation.

VARIATION: Invite one or two groups to perform the conversation for the class.

Language and Culture Note: When a person declines an invitation, it is considered polite to explain why. In this conversation, Briana declines

the invitation to see a movie and then explains why she can't go.

4. WHO'S WHO?

SETUP: (1) Have students look again at the pictures on page 40. (2) Read each question aloud, and call on volunteers to respond. For example:

    1. *The girl on the left is Briana. The girl on the right is Nicole.*
    2. *Briana is wearing pajamas. Nicole is wearing a shirt and shorts. They are talking on the phone.*
    3. *Briana wants to go to a movie. She has to clean her room because it is messy.*

EXPANSION: Write the sentence stems *I want to _____.* and *I have to _____.* on the board. Have students work in pairs to write other possible endings. (For example: *I want to watch a movie, but I can't. I have to work.*) Invite the pairs to share their ideas with the class.

5. ROLE PLAY

SETUP: (1) Brainstorm with the class possible invitations. For example: *Do you want to go for a walk? Do you want to go to a play?* Write their ideas on the board. (2) Have students work in groups of three to complete the phone conversation. (3) Circulate around the class answering questions and correcting the writing where necessary. (4) Have the groups present their role plays. Encourage students to move about freely and mime the actions of speaking on the phone. (5) Have the rest of the class listen and answer these questions: *What is the invitation? Why can't she/he go?*

VARIATION: Have students submit their written work to you for correction before they perform the conversations in the following class.

6. HOW ABOUT YOU?

SETUP: (1) Model the pronunciation of the questions. (2) Have students work in pairs to take turns asking and answering the questions. (3) Circulate to listen in and to answer students' questions as necessary.

VARIATIONS AND EXPANSIONS: (1) Have students draw a picture of their own bedrooms and then share their pictures in pairs, telling one another what's in the room. (2) For homework, have students write their answers to the questions and submit their work for correction.

7. NEAT OR MESSY?

SETUP: (**1**) Write the following questions on the board: *What's your name? How do you spell it?* (**2**) Have students circulate around the classroom asking one another the questions. Set a time limit of four minutes for this activity. (**3**) When students are finished, ask the class: "How many students have a neat bedroom? How many students have a messy bedroom?"

EXPANSION: Have students survey students outside of the classroom. Tell them to briefly interview their schoolmates in the hallways or in their classes and write down their answers. Then have them report the results back to the class. For example: *Twelve students say their bedroom is neat. Nine students say their bedroom is messy.*

USE YOUR ENGLISH!

SETUP: Have students do these activities as homework assignments. (**1**) To prepare students for this independent conversation, model a conversation with a volunteer, using the questions in the box. Tell students to write down information they learn from their conversation partners. For example: *My conversation partner has a nice bedroom. It is usually neat.* At the beginning of the next class, students can hand in their reports to you. (**2**) Encourage students to write labels on various items in their bedrooms. In class, you can answer vocabulary questions and model the correct pronunciation of any new words. After several classes, ask students: "Did you put the labels in your bedroom? Did you learn the new words?"

EXPANSIONS: Brainstorm with the class other questions they can ask their conversation partners. For example: *How many bedrooms are in your home? How many windows are there in your bedroom? What's in your bedroom?*

Lesson 5: The Bathroom

Pages 42–43

1. THE BATHROOM

SETUP: (**1**) Write the word *bathroom* on the board. Brainstorm with the class items that are usually found in a bathroom. Write their ideas on the board.

(**2**) Have students work individually or in pairs to look at the picture and complete the matching exercise. (**3**) Go over the answers with the class. Then play the audio program, pausing between items, and have students repeat chorally. (**4**) Write on the board the two Conversation Tip questions from the Preview on page 33: *How do you say this in English? How do you spell that?* As you brainstorm more vocabulary items, encourage students to point to items in the picture and ask these questions. New vocabulary may include: *shower, medicine cabinet, faucet.* Write the words on the board, and have students add the new vocabulary to the list in their books; alternatively, tell students to write at least ten new words in their vocabulary notebooks.

VARIATIONS AND EXPANSIONS: (**1**) Say or write a word, and have students point to the item in the picture. (**2**) Point to an item in the picture, and have students say the word. (**3**) Have students work in pairs to take turns pointing and identifying items in the picture.

Language and Culture Note: Point out that parts of the body are often preceded by possessive adjectives (for example: *brushing **her** teeth, washing **his** hair*).

2. WHAT ARE THEY DOING?

SETUP: (**1**) With the class, identify the *mother, father, daughter,* and *son* in the picture. (**2**) Have students work in pairs to ask and answer the questions.

VARIATION AND EXPANSION: (**1**) Write on the board: *The mother is _____. The son is _____. The daughter is _____.* Have students refer to these forms as they answer the questions. (**2**) Ask the class: "What is the father doing?" For example: *He's giving his son a bath. He's washing his son's hair.*

3. YOUR BATHROOM

SETUP: (**1**) Model the pronunciation of the questions. (**2**) Have students work in pairs to take turns asking and answering the questions. (**3**) Circulate to listen in and to answer students' questions as necessary.

VARIATIONS AND EXPANSIONS: (**1**) Have students draw a picture of their own bathroom and share their pictures in pairs, telling each other what's in the room. (2) For homework, have students answer the questions and submit their writing to you for correction.

4. A BRAND SURVEY

SETUP: (1) Model the conversation. (2) Write on the board the Conversation Tip question *How do you spell that?* for student reference during the survey activity. (3) Have students ask and answer the questions in groups of three. Circulate to listen in and to answer students' questions as necessary. (4) When students are finished, have them report their findings to the class. (5) Ask the class: "Which toothpaste brands are the most popular? Soap brands? Shampoo brands?" For higher-level classes, you can also ask: "Why do you like these brands?"

EXPANSION: Have students survey other students in the school about the brands of toothpaste, soap, and shampoo that they prefer. Tell students to briefly interview their schoolmates in the hallways or in their classes and write down the information. Then have them tally the results and report the numbers to the class. For example: *Twelve students use Colgate. Ten students use Aqua Fresh.* Students can even make a bar graph illustrating the information.

5. FIND SOMEONE WHO . . .

SETUP: (1) Model (or ask volunteers to model) the questions that students will need to ask. For example: *Do you like to take baths? Do you usually take showers? Do you sometimes use bubble bath?* (2) Have students circulate around the classroom asking and answering the questions. Set a five-minute time limit for this part. (3) Have students report their information to the class. For example: *Alice likes to take baths. Pierre usually takes showers.*

VARIATIONS AND EXPANSIONS: (1) Encourage students to add one more sentence to the list. For example: _____ *brushes his/her teeth three times a day.* (2) For homework, have students make sentences about themselves using the ideas in this activity. For example: *I don't like to take baths. I usually take showers. I never use bubble bath.* (3) Have students choose one question and survey other students in the school. Tell students to briefly interview their schoolmates in the hallways or in their classes and write down the information. Have students report their findings to the class.

For example: *Ten students like to take baths, and twenty-three don't.*

6. CONVERSATION CHANT: WHERE'S MY TOOTHBRUSH?

SETUP: (1) Play the audio program. Tell students to read along as they listen to the chant. As you play the audio program, make hand motions or clap to reinforce the stress on the dotted syllables. (2) Play the audio again, pausing after each line, and have students repeat. (3) Have the class chant chorally.

VARIATIONS AND EXPANSION: (1) Once students are familiar with the chant, divide the class into two groups. The indented chant lines represent a second voice. Have one group chant the questions that start at the left margin, and have the other group chant the responses that are indented. (2) Have students clap or make a hand motion to indicate where the stress falls as they chant. (3) Have groups switch and chant the opposite lines. (4) Have students circle all the words that rhyme. Call on volunteers to read the rhyming pairs aloud and then write them on the board. (5) Have students work in pairs to ask and answer questions about the location of items in the bathroom illustrated on page 42. For example:

A: *Where are the towels?*
B: *They're above the toilet. Where's the toothpaste?*
A: *It's next to the sink.*

USE YOUR ENGLISH!

SETUP: Have students do these activities as homework assignments. (1) To prepare students for this independent conversation, model a conversation with a volunteer, using the questions in the box. Tell students to write down information they learn from their conversation partners. For example: *My conversation partner uses Crest toothpaste. Her favorite brand of shampoo is Pert. She likes Lever2000 soap.* At the beginning of the next class, students can hand in their reports to you. (2) Encourage students to write labels on various items in their bathrooms. In class, you can answer vocabulary questions and model the correct pronunciation of any new words. After several classes, ask students: "Did you put the labels in your bathroom? Did you learn the new words?"

VARIATIONS AND EXPANSIONS: Brainstorm with the class other questions from this lesson that they can ask their conversation partners, such as: *Do you like to take baths? Do you use bubble bath?*

Lesson 6: Problems at Home

Pages 44–45

1. PROBLEMS

SETUP: (**1**) Write *house problems* on the board. Brainstorm with the class problems they have with their homes. Write their ideas on the board. (**2**) Have students work individually or in pairs to look at the pictures and complete the matching exercise. (**3**) Go over the answers with the class. Then play the audio program, pausing between items, and have students repeat chorally. (**4**) Write on the board the two Conversation Tip questions from the Preview on page 33: *How do you say this in English? How do you spell that?* As you brainstorm more vocabulary items, encourage students to point to items in the pictures and ask these questions. New vocabulary may include: *doll, icicles.* Write the words on the board, and have students add the new words to the list in their books; alternatively, tell students to write at least eight new words in their vocabulary notebooks.

VARIATIONS AND EXPANSIONS: (**1**) Say or write a word or phrase, and have students point to the item in the pictures. (**2**) Point to an item in the pictures, and have students say the word or phrase. (**3**) Have students work in pairs to take turns pointing and identifying items in the pictures.

Language and Culture Note: Point out that *mice* is the irregular plural form of *mouse.*

2. WHAT ARE THE PROBLEMS?

SETUP: (**1**) Have students work in pairs to match the problems on the left with the sentences on the right. Circulate to listen in and to answer students' questions as necessary. (**2**) Review the answers with the class. Note that for item 1 the order of the sentences is important; *c* precedes *e*.

3. WHAT'S WRONG?

SETUP: Call on a volunteer to read each question aloud. As a class, discuss the answers. For example:

There are mice and cockroaches in her kitchen. The toilet is completely clogged. The radiator doesn't work.

EXPANSION: For homework, have students write their responses to the questions.

4. CALLING FOR HELP

SETUP: (**1**) Have students close their books as they listen to the audio program for the first time. Then have students open their books and read along as they listen to the audio program again. Finally, play the audio again, pausing after each line for students to repeat chorally. (**2**) As students practice the conversation in pairs, encourage them to act it out by pretending to hold a phone as they speak. (**3**) Circulate to give individual feedback on pronunciation.

VARIATION: Invite one or two pairs of students to perform the conversation for the class.

5. WHO CAN THEY CALL?

SETUP: (**1**) Have students work in small groups to reread the phone conversation in Exercise 4. Have them underline the questions to highlight the structure of the conversation. For example: *May I help you? What's the problem? Can you help? What's your address?* Also tell students that they can use the sentences from Exercise 2 in their phone conversations. For example: *The plunger and drain opener aren't working. The toilet's completely clogged!* (**2**) Have the groups write their own phone conversations. Circulate around the class answering questions and correcting the writing where necessary. (**3**) Have two students in each group present one of their phone conversations. (**4**) Have the rest of the class watch their classmates' role plays and then identify the type of problem (toilet problem or heat problem).

VARIATIONS AND EXPANSIONS: (**1**) Have students submit their written conversations to you for correction before they perform the conversations in the following class. (**2**) Have students write their own ads for an exterminator. Have them share their ads in small groups. (**3**) For homework, have students look up plumbers or exterminators in the yellow pages (print or Internet) and read one ad. Have them either photocopy the ad or write down its information to bring to class. Have students share their advertisements. Answer any vocabulary

and pronunciation questions that students
may have.

Language and Culture Note: Some heating
systems in the United States use oil; others
use natural gas. A plumber can fix the heating
system, but does not provide the heat energy
(oil or natural gas). Natural gas or oil companies
supply the fuel.

6. PROBLEMS AT HOME

SETUP: (**1**) Have students brainstorm their
list of home problems in small groups. (**2**) Have
each group choose one person to write their
list on the board. (**3**) Go over all the lists with
the class.

EXPANSIONS: (**1**) As you discuss each problem,
ask the class: "Who can you call for this problem?"
(for example: *a plumber, a carpenter, the landlord*).
(**2**) Have pairs of students choose one home
problem, write a phone conversation about the
problem, and present their conversation to the
class. For example:

Carpenter: *Woodworks. May I help you?*
    Caller: *Yes! My front door doesn't close.*
                Can you help?
Carpenter: *I can come tomorrow at 6:00. What's*
                your address?
    Caller: *1324 Broadway. Thank you so much!*

USE YOUR ENGLISH!

SETUP: Have students do these activities as homework
assignments. (**1**) To prepare students for this
independent conversation, model a conversation with
a volunteer, using the questions in the box. Tell
students to write down information they learn from
their conversation partners. For example: *My
conversation partner has problems with her front door.
It doesn't open well.* At the beginning of the next class,
students can hand in their report to you or share their
information in small groups. (**2**) Show students how to
find the information in the yellow pages (look under
plumbing service and repair and *exterminators*).
If you live in an English-speaking community,
encourage students to look in the yellow pages.
For EFL classes, have students look in the yellow
pages on the Internet. At the beginning of the
next class, have students share the information
they found.

EXPANSION: Ask the class: "What plumbers
do you recommend?" "What exterminators do you
recommend?"

Listening Practice
Page 46

1. WHAT DO YOU HEAR?

SETUP: (**1**) Tell students to read through the
sentences silently. (**2**) Play the audio program.
(**3**) Review the answers with the class. If there is
confusion about any answers, replay the audio.

VARIATIONS AND EXPANSIONS: (**1**) Have
students first listen with their books closed and
then open their books to read the sentences.
(**2**) Once students have completed the exercise,
have them work in pairs to take turns listening to
each other read the sentences and identifying
which one they hear.

2. QUESTIONS AND ANSWERS

SETUP: (**1**) Have students read the answers and then
listen to the audio program. (**2**) Review the answers
with the class. If there is confusion about any
answers, replay the audio.

VARIATIONS AND EXPANSIONS: (**1**) Have students
first listen and then read the answers. (**2**) After
students finish the activity, have them compose
questions for the uncircled answers. (**3**) Have
students listen to the audio program again and take
dictation on the questions. Write the questions on the
board so students can correct their dictations, or have
students self-correct by referring to the Audioscript
in the back of the book.

3. ABOUT YOU

SETUP: (**1**) Play the audio program, pausing after
each question so students have time to write their
responses. (**2**) When students have answered all
three questions, have them share their responses in
small groups. (**3**) Then have students read their
answers to the class.

VARIATION: Have students take dictation on the
questions and then write their responses after the
dictation is corrected. Write the questions on the

board so students can correct their dictations, or have students self-correct by referring to the Audioscript in the back of the book.

Review

Page 47

1. MAKE A LIST!

SETUP: (**1**) Divide the class into groups. (**2**) Have students choose one person to write the words down as the group brainstorms vocabulary. Set a ten-minute time limit for this part of activity. (**3**) Call out the name of a room, and have groups take turns reading an item from their lists that belongs in that room. Write the item on the board as students check their spelling. Have everyone check off each item as it is mentioned so there are no duplications.

EXPANSION: For homework, have students write a list of things they have in the rooms of their own homes.

2. HOW DO YOU SAY THIS?

SETUP: (**1**) Write the questions on the board: *How do you say this? How do you spell that?* (**2**) Divide the class into groups and give each group a section of the room to label. Supply each group with paper slips, markers, and transparent tape. (**3**) Circulate around the room helping students with vocabulary and spelling questions as necessary. Set a fifteen-minute time limit for this activity. (**4**) When time is up, have each group present the objects they labeled. For example: *(Student holds up a ruler) This is a ruler. (Student points to the label.) R-u-l-e-r.*

3. HOW ABOUT YOU?

SETUP: (**1**) Model the pronunciation of the questions. (**2**) Tell students if they don't want to give their own street address or e-mail address, they can reply with a fake address or they can say "I'd rather not say." (**3**) Have students circulate around the classroom asking and answering the questions.

VARIATION: Have students ask and answer the questions in small groups.

Language and Culture Note: Explain the conventions of saying an e-mail address: . is *dot.* _ is *underscore.* - is *hyphen. com, net,* and *org* are pronounced as words. For example: The e-mail address **Marcy_Jim@comcast.net** is said as: "Marcy underscore Jim at Comcast dot net"; the e-mail address **Sylvia.Jackson-Edouard@juno.com** is said as: "Sylvia dot Jackson hyphen Edouard at juno dot com."

4. WHAT AM I DOING?

SETUP: (**1**) Model the activity of miming an action and ask: "What am I doing? What room am I in?" (**2**) Divide the class into groups. (**3**) Have students in each group take turns miming and identifying the action and its location. Circulate to answer students' questions as necessary.

VARIATION AND EXPANSION: (**1**) Have the class do this activity together, with one student at a time standing up to mime an action. (**2**) Write phrases from this unit on the board for students to act out. For example: *doing laundry, making a sandwich, drinking coffee, looking in the refrigerator for something to eat, bringing food to the table, setting the table, pouring milk or water, playing a video game, using a laptop computer, listening to a CD player with a headset, talking on the phone, brushing your teeth, putting on lipstick, taking a bath.*

Assessment

Page 48

PART 1: QUESTIONS

SETUP: Have students work individually to write their questions. Challenge students not to look at the previous lessons but to construct their questions from memory.

VARIATION: Have students write their questions on a separate sheet of paper to hand in to you for correction at the end of the assessment.

PART 2: SPEAKING

SETUP: (**1**) Divide the class into pairs, and have students ask and answer the questions. (**2**) Circulate to listen in and to answer students' questions as necessary.

VARIATION: Have students write their partners' responses to their questions and hand in their work for correction.

PART 3: LISTENING

SETUP: (**1**) Have students first read the answers silently. Then play the audio program. (**2**) If there is confusion about any of the answers, replay the audio. (**3**) Check answers with the whole class.

VARIATION AND EXPANSION: (**1**) Have students write the number of the question and the letter of their response on a separate sheet to hand in to you for correction at the end of the assessment. (**2**) As an added challenge, have students compose questions for the uncircled answers.

PART 4: WRITING

SETUP: (**1**) Set the context: This man has a problem in his home. (**2**) Have students work individually to write their conversations. Circulate to answer questions as necessary.

VARIATIONS: (**1**) Have students write their conversations on a separate piece of paper to hand in to you for correction. (**2**) Have students share their conversations with a partner. Then ask volunteer pairs to perform one of their conversations for the class.

FOOD

Preview

Page 49

PREVIEW QUESTIONS

SETUP: Have the class look at the photograph. Read each question aloud, and call on individual students to respond. Encourage students to use the present progressive in their answers to questions 2 and 3. For example:

2. *They're eating lunch.*
3. *They're eating hamburgers and corn.*

The present progressive is not necessary for the answers to question 4 (for example: *I'm hungry! This is delicious! Please pass the iced tea.*).

EXPANSION: Ask additional questions about the photograph, such as: "How many people are eating together?" (*Nine.*) "Is this a family meal?" (*Yes.*) "Why are they eating outside the house?" (*It's a summer barbecue.*)

CONVERSATION TIP

SETUP: (1) Write *please, thank you*, and *thanks* on the board. Tell students these are common words in English. (2) Have students read the conversations silently. (3) Role-play the conversations with various volunteers. After each conversation, ask the class: "Where are these people? What is the context?" Encourage students to use their imaginations. For example:

Conversation 1: *In a home. People are talking at a family meal.*
Conversation 2: *In a home. People are talking at a family meal.*
Conversation 3: *In a store. A customer is buying fruit.*
Conversation 4: *In a restaurant. Two people are on a date.*

(4) Have students practice the conversations in pairs. (5) Circulate to correct pronunciation.

CONVERSATION CHANT: IT'S TIME TO EAT!

SETUP: (1) The dots over the words indicate where the stress falls. As you play the audio program, make

hand motions or clap to reinforce the stress on the dotted syllables. (2) Have students listen once through as they read along. (3) Play the audio program again, pausing after each line, and have students repeat. (4) Have the class chant chorally.

VARIATIONS AND EXPANSIONS: (1) Once students are familiar with the chant, divide the class into two groups. The indented chant lines represent a second voice. Have one group chant the lines that start at the left margin, and have the other group chant the lines that are indented. (2) Have students clap or make a hand motion to indicate where the stress falls as they chant. (3) Have groups switch and chant the opposite lines. (4) Have students circle all the words that rhyme. Call on volunteers to read the rhyming pairs aloud and then write them on the board.

Language and Culture Note: When the cook is calling the family to the table, he or she usually says: "It's time to eat!"

Lesson 1: Vegetables

Pages 50–51

1. VEGETABLES

SETUP: (1) Write the word *vegetables* on the board. Have the class brainstorm familiar names of vegetables, and write them on the board. (2) Have students work individually or in pairs to look at the picture and complete the matching exercise. (3) Go over the answers with the class. Then play the audio program and have students repeat chorally. (4) Have the class brainstorm other vocabulary in the picture (for example: *cabbage, artichokes, beets*). Write the words on the board, and have students add the new words to the list in their books; alternatively, tell students to write at least ten new words in their vocabulary notebooks.

VARIATIONS: (1) Say or write a word, and have students point to the item in the picture. (2) Point to an item in the picture, and have students say the word. (3) Have students work in pairs to take turns pointing and identifying items in the picture. (4) To practice this new vocabulary, play a drawing game. Write the names of the vegetables on slips of paper. Have student take turns coming up to the front of the classroom, taking a slip of paper, and drawing the vegetable on the board. The rest of the class guesses the vegetable. To keep the pace moving, set a time limit of one minute for each turn.

Language and Culture Note: Broccoli, corn, celery, and lettuce are listed in the singular form because they are non-count nouns. To count them, use the following nouns: a *bunch of broccoli, an ear of corn, a bunch of celery*, and *a head of lettuce*. This is also true with the following vegetables: *a head of cauliflower, a head of cabbage, a head of garlic (with its many cloves), a bunch of spinach*, and *a bunch of parsley*.

2. HOW ABOUT YOU?

SETUP: (**1**) Model the pronunciation of the questions. (**2**) Have students first work individually to write their answers to the question. (**3**) Have students work in pairs to take turns asking and answering the questions. (**4**) Invite students to report what they learned about each other. (**5**) Tally the results on the board. Find out: *What is the most popular vegetable in the class? What's a vegetable no one likes?*

VARIATION AND EXPANSION: (**1**) Before doing this activity, you may want the class first to learn the Conversation Chant on page 51. (**2**) In a multicultural ESL class setting, pair students from different cultural backgrounds to talk about their food tastes. (**3**) Draw two large intersecting circles on the board. Label one circle *raw* and the other circle *cooked*. At the intersection of the two circles, write *raw and cooked*. Ask the class: "How do you eat cucumbers? Do you eat cucumbers raw? Or do you eat them cooked?" Write the class response into the diagram. If students have differing opinions, write the item into both places. Continue asking questions until students have categorized all the vegetables according to whether they eat them raw, cooked, or both. For example: *raw:* cucumbers; *cooked:* potatoes, corn, broccoli; *raw and cooked:* carrots, green beans, lettuce, mushrooms, onions, peppers. In a multicultural setting, students can make their own charts and then compare them in small groups of mixed cultural backgrounds. (**4**) For homework, have students write their answers to the questions.

3. LET'S MAKE A SALAD.

SETUP: (**1**) Set the context: Two friends are talking about making a salad. (**2**) Have students close their books as they listen to the audio program. Then have students open their books and read along as they listen to the audio program. Finally, play the audio a third time, pausing after each line for students to repeat chorally. (**3**) As students practice the conversation in pairs, circulate to give individual feedback on pronunciation.

VARIATIONS AND EXPANSIONS: (**1**) Have students listen to the conversation on the audio program and place dots over the stressed words (as in the conversation chants). Review the stress marks with the class. Practice the conversation chorally, paying special attention to word stress. (**2**) Invite pairs of students to perform the conversation for the class. (**3**) Ask the class: "What do you put in your salads?" Call on volunteers for their responses.

4. WHAT DO YOU NEED?

SETUP: (**1**) Have students work in pairs to make a list of the vegetables they put in each dish. (**2**) Invite several volunteer pairs to share their lists with the class. Write students' ideas on the board so they can check their spelling.

VARIATIONS AND EXPANSION: (**1**) Have students first work individually to make their lists of ingredients. Then put students into pairs or small groups to compare lists. (**2**) Have the class brainstorm other vegetable dishes (for example: chili, potato soup, vegetable stew), and ask: "What do you need to make _____?"

5. CONVERSATION CHANT: HE LIKES CUCUMBERS.

SETUP: (**1**) Play the audio program. Tell students to read along as they listen to the chant. As you play the audio program, make hand motions or clap to reinforce the stress on the dotted syllables. (**2**) Play the audio again, pausing after each line, and have students repeat. (**3**) Have the class chant chorally.

VARIATIONS AND EXPANSION: You may want to do this chant before Exercise 2 so that students can practice how to talk about what vegetables they like and dislike. (**1**) Once students are familiar with the chant, divide the class into two groups. The indented chant lines represent a second voice. Have one group chant the lines that start at the left margin, and have the other group chant the lines that are indented. (**2**) Have students clap or make a hand motion to indicate where the stress falls as they chant. (**3**) Have groups switch and chant the opposite lines. (**4**) Have students circle all the words that rhyme. Call on volunteers to read the rhyming pairs aloud and then write them on the board. (5) Write on the board: *So do I. So does she. So does he. So do they.* Have students work in groups of three or four to talk about the vegetables they like and then compose true statements following this pattern:

> *Maria likes mushrooms. So does Chen.*
> *Nguyen likes tomatoes. So do Phong and Tomas.*

Have the groups read some of their statements to the class.

USE YOUR ENGLISH!

SETUP: Have students do this activity as a homework assignment. (1) To prepare students for this independent assignment, have them brainstorm the names of vegetable stands and supermarkets in the area. Have each student choose one to visit with their conversation partners. Remind them to take paper and pen to list all the vegetables they see. For example: *At Manny's Grocery, there are carrots, lettuce, eggplant, onions, scallions, potatoes, and sweet potatoes.* (2) At the beginning of the next class, students can share this information in small groups or simply hand in their reports to you.

EXPANSION: Bring a supermarket flyer to class. Show the flyer to the class, covering the names of the vegetable, and ask students: "What's this?" "What are these?"

Lesson 2: Fruit

Pages 52–53

1. FRUIT MARKET

SETUP: (1) Write the word *fruit* on the board. Have the class brainstorm the names of fruits. Write their ideas on the board. (2) Have students work individually or in pairs to look at the picture and complete the matching exercise. (3) Go over the answers with the class. Then play the audio program, pausing between items, and have students repeat chorally. (4) Have the class brainstorm the names of other fruits in the picture (for example: *blueberries, raspberries, blackberries, kiwi, watermelon, cantaloupe*). Write the words on the board, and have students add the new words to the list in their books; alternatively, tell them to write at least ten new words in their vocabulary notebooks.

VARIATIONS: (1) Say or write a word, and have students point to the item in the picture. (2) Point to an item in the picture, and have students say the word. (3) Have students work in pairs to take turns pointing and identifying items in the picture.

Language and Culture Note: Even though *grapefruit* is a count noun, in American English it does not usually change form from the singular and plural. For example, it is acceptable to say: "I'd like three grapefruit." This is also true with the following fruits: kiwi, cantaloupe, watermelon, and pineapple.

2. WHAT ARE THEY SAYING?

SETUP: (1) Point out that these conversations use the Conversation Tip strategy from the Preview page. (2) Set the context: A customer is buying fruit from a grocer. (3) Have students close their books as they listen to the audio program for the first time. Then have students open their books and read along as they listen to the audio program again. Finally, play the audio a third time, pausing after each line for students to repeat chorally. (4) Circulate to give individual feedback on pronunciation.

VARIATIONS AND EXPANSIONS: (1) Have students listen to the conversation on the audio program and place dots over the stressed words (as in the conversation chants). Review the stress marks with the class. Practice the conversation chorally, paying special attention to word stress. (2) Invite pairs of students to perform the conversation for the class. (3) To help students internalize the language, write the conversation on the board. Phrase by phrase, erase portions of the conversation and have students practice it, filling in the blanks. See to what extent you can erase the conversation with students still able to recall it.

Language and Culture Note: The phrase *I'm all set* is very common and, in this context, means "I don't need anything else." It is rather informal.

3. ROLE PLAY

SETUP: (1) Have students work in pairs to write their own conversations. (2) Circulate around the class answering questions and correcting the writing where necessary. (3) Have the pairs present their role plays. Encourage students to move about freely and mime the actions. (4) Write the question *What does the customer buy?* on the board. Have students watch their classmates' role plays and write down their answer to the question. After each role play, call on a student to answer the question. If the response is not correct, have the pair perform the role play again.

VARIATIONS AND EXPANSIONS: (1) Students can expand the premise of the role play to include buying fruits and vegetables. (2) Have students submit their written conversations to you for correction before they perform the conversations in the following class.

4. WHAT'S YOUR FAVORITE FRUIT?

SETUP: (1) Model the activity by asking a student: "What's your favorite fruit?" and writing the student's response on the board (for example: *Rafik—strawberries*). (2) Set a time limit of five minutes for this activity. (3) Call on individual students and ask them for their results. (4) Ask the class: "What is the most popular fruit in this class?"

EXPANSIONS: (1) Have students survey other students in the school and report their findings. Students can present their findings in a bar graph. (2) In a multicultural ESL setting, have students bring to class a fruit that is common in their native culture and present it to the class, answering the following questions: "What's this fruit called? Where is it from? How do people eat it? What time of year do people usually eat it?" (3) In an EFL class, have the class pretend to be English-speaking visitors. Have students present local kinds of fruit to the "visitors" and answer questions about the fruit.

5. LET'S MAKE A FRUIT SALAD!

SETUP: (1) Divide the class into groups of four. Have students decide what to bring, fill in the chart, and answer the questions. Each student should be responsible for at least one item. Circulate to listen in and to answer students' questions as necessary. (2) In the next class, have the groups meet and prepare their salads. Set a time limit of ten minutes for preparing the salads. (3) Have students line up all the salads on a table. Put a number card in front of each salad, and have the class vote on the best salad. (4) Have students serve the salad and enjoy!

VARIATIONS AND EXPANSIONS: (1) Bring to class backup supplies of knives, forks, plates, serving spoons, and napkins. (2) As students eat the salads, introduce vocabulary for describing taste (for example: *sweet, crunchy, juicy, delicious, tart*). Encourage students to describe the salads as they eat them.

USE YOUR ENGLISH!

SETUP: Have students do these activities as homework assignments. (1) To prepare students for talking with their conversation partners, model a conversation about the fruits you like with a volunteer, using the question in the box. Tell students to write down information they learn about their conversation partners. For example: *My conversation partner likes plums, oranges, and strawberries.* At the beginning of the next class, students can hand in their report to you. (2) To prepare students for the second assignment, have them brainstorm the names of fruit markets and supermarkets in the area. Have each student choose one to visit with their conversation partners. Remind them to take paper and pen to list all the fruits they see. For example: *At Alice's Fruit Stand, I see strawberries, blueberries, cantaloupe, kiwi, watermelon, and pears.* At the beginning of the next class, students can share this information in small groups or simply hand in their reports to you.

EXPANSION: Bring a supermarket flyer to class. Show the flyer to the class, covering the names of the fruit on sale, and ask students: "What's this?" "What are these?"

Lesson 3: The Supermarket
Pages 54–55

1. AT THE SUPERMARKET

SETUP: (1) Write the word *supermarket* on the board. Have the class brainstorm foods you can buy in a supermarket. Write their ideas on the board. (2) Have students work individually or in pairs to look at the picture and complete the matching exercise. (3) Go over the answers with the class. Then play the audio program, pausing between items, and have students repeat chorally. (4) Have the class brainstorm the other foods in the picture (for example: *canned tomatoes, canned tuna, yogurt, cheese, frozen pizza*). Have students add the new words and phrases to the list in their books; alternatively, tell students to write at least ten new words and phrases in their vocabulary notebooks.

VARIATIONS AND EXPANSIONS: (1) Say or write a word or phrase in the picture, and have students point to the item. (2) Point to an item in the picture, and have students say the word or phrase. (**3**) Have students write a shopping list of what they usually buy at the supermarket. Have students compare their lists in pairs. (**4**) For homework, tell students to look in their refrigerators and write a list of all the food they see. In the next class, have volunteers read their lists aloud.

2. WHERE CAN I FIND THE MILK?

SETUP: (**1**) Point out that this conversation uses the Conversation Tip strategy from the Preview page. (**2**) Set the context: The woman in the picture is asking where to find something in the supermarket. (**3**) Have students close their books as they listen to the audio program for the first time. Then have students open their books and read along as they listen to the audio program again and point to the dairy section when they hear it mentioned. Finally, play the audio again, pausing after each line so students can repeat chorally. (**4**) As students practice the conversation in pairs, encourage them to act it out by standing and pointing as they speak. (**5**) Circulate to give individual feedback on pronunciation.

VARIATIONS AND EXPANSIONS: (**1**) Have students listen to the conversation on the audio program and place dots over the stressed words (as in the conversation chants). Review the stress marks with the class. Practice the conversation chorally, paying special attention to word stress. (**2**) Invite pairs of students to perform the conversation for the class.

3. EXCUSE ME.

SETUP: (**1**) Tell the class that beef, chicken, and pork are in the Meat and Poultry Section. Have them write the words *Meat and Poultry* above the images of chicken, beef, and pork in the picture on page 54. (**2**) Write on the board the skeletal conversation model for this role play:

A: *Excuse me. Where can I find the* _____ ?
B: *In the* _____ *section.*
A: *Thanks.*

(**3**) As students write their role plays in pairs, circulate around the class answering questions and correcting the writing where necessary. (**4**) Have the pairs present their role plays. (**5**) Write the question *What is the customer looking for?* on the board. Have students watch their classmates' role plays and write down their answer to the question. After each role play, call on students to answer the question. If their response is not correct, have the pair perform the role play again.

VARIATIONS AND EXPANSIONS: (**1**) Name a section of a supermarket and have the class brainstorm foods that belong in that section. For example: *Dairy Section: milk, butter, cheese.* Write students' ideas on the board. Students can refer to these lists as they compose their role plays. (**2**) Tell the class that there are also other sections in a supermarket, such as *Health and Beauty* and *Produce*. Have the class brainstorm the items in these sections. For example: **Health and Beauty**: *soap, shampoo.* **Produce**: *lettuce, apples, bananas.* Students can also use this vocabulary in their role plays. (**3**) For homework, tell students to visit a supermarket and write down all the sections they see in the supermarket. In class, have students compare their lists in groups of three or four. Invite the groups to report their information as you write a class list on the board.

4. SPECIALS OF THE WEEK

SETUP: (**1**) Model how to read items in the ads. For example: *Dell's Ice Cream. Four ninety-nine for 56 ounces.* (**2**) Call on volunteers to read items in the ads aloud. (**3**) Write the following questions on the board: *Which market has a good price for chicken? For orange juice? For bread? For ice cream?* (**4**) Have students work in pairs to complete the price chart and answer the questions. Ask individual students questions about the information in their charts. For example: "How much is chicken at Johnnie's Grocery?" "How much is chicken at Super Mart?"

VARIATIONS AND EXPANSIONS: (**1**) Bring in (or have students bring in) flyers from local supermarkets and have students compare the prices of several items. (**2**) Explain liquid measurements: *A pint has 16 fluid ounces; a quart has 32 fluid ounces; a half-gallon has 64 fluid ounces; a gallon has 128 fluid ounces.* Have students determine the size of the orange juice on special at Johnnie's Grocery and Super Mart (*a quart*).

5. WHAT SUPERMARKETS DO YOU RECOMMEND?

SETUP: (**1**) Model the pronunciation of the questions for the class. (**2**) Divide the class into groups of three or four to discuss the questions. Circulate to listen in and to answer students' questions as necessary.

VARIATION AND EXPANSION: (**1**) Write these additional questions on the board for the groups to discuss: *Why do you recommend that supermarket? Does it have good prices? Good service? Good locations?* (**2**) Ask a spokesperson from each group to report to the class on their group's supermarket recommendations.

USE YOUR ENGLISH!

SETUP: Have students do this activity as a homework assignment. (**1**) To prepare students for this assignment, have them brainstorm the names of supermarkets. Write their ideas on the board. Have each student choose one supermarket to investigate. (**2**) Tell students to write down information they learn about their supermarket visit. For example: *Oranges: $3.99 for 10 pounds.* At the beginning of the next class, students can either share this information in small groups or report to the whole class.

VARIATIONS AND EXPANSION: (**1**) Assign specific supermarket sections to students to investigate (for example: *Dairy, Frozen Foods, Meat and Poultry, Snacks*) or even specific products (for example: *a gallon of milk, a pound of bananas*). This way, students' information is more comparative in class. (**2**) Encourage students to pick up a flyer at the supermarket they visit so they can compare even more prices in class.

Lesson 4: Breakfast

Pages 56–57

1. BREAKFAST

SET UP: (**1**) Write the word *breakfast* on the board. With the class, brainstorm the names of breakfast foods. Write their ideas on the board. (**2**) Have students work individually or in pairs to look at the picture and complete the matching exercise. (**3**) Go over the answers with the class. Then play the audio program, pausing between items, and have students repeat chorally. (**4**) Brainstorm the other foods in the picture (for example: *butter, cantaloupe, maple syrup*). Have students add the new words to the lists in their books; alternatively, tell students to write at least twelve new words in their vocabulary notebooks.

VARIATIONS AND EXPANSIONS: (**1**) Say or write a word or phrase, and have students point to the item in the picture. (**2**) Point to an item in the picture, and have students say the word or phrase. (**3**) Have students work in pairs to take turns pointing and identifying items in the picture. (**4**) Have students work in pairs to sort the breakfast foods into two categories: *healthy foods* and *unhealthy foods.* Have the pairs share their ideas with the class. As students

talk, write a master list of healthy and unhealthy foods on the board.

Language and Culture Note: The foods featured in this picture are common breakfast foods in the United States. A weekday breakfast in the United States is typically light (toast or cereal), but on a weekend morning Americans often eat large leisurely breakfasts that may include eggs, bacon, potatoes, and pancakes.

2. WHAT ARE THEY EATING FOR BREAKFAST?

SET UP: (**1**) Point to the family in the picture and ask: "What are their names?" Call on student volunteers to name each member of the family in the picture. This will make it easier to answer the questions. For example:
    1. *Ben is eating cold cereal. Donald is eating toast.*
(**2**) Ask a volunteer to read each question aloud. Then call on individual students for the answers.

VARIATION: For homework, have students write their responses to the questions and submit their work to you for correction and comment.

3. WHAT ARE THEY SAYING?

SETUP: (**1**) Set the context: These exchanges are from the family eating breakfast together on page 56. (**2**) Play the audio program and have students look at the picture as they listen. Tell them to point to each person as he or she speaks. (**3**) Play the audio program again and tell students to read along. Then play the audio a third time, pausing after each line, and have students repeat chorally. (**4**) As students practice the conversations in pairs, encourage them to act it out by pretending to pass things while they speak.

VARIATION: Invite pairs of students to perform the conversations for the class.

Language and Culture Note: In the United States, the food is usually brought to the table in serving bowls and served there, rather than serving it at the stove. As people sit at the table, they either pass their plates around and serve one another or they pass the serving bowls to one another and serve themselves. It is appropriate and common to say *please* in requests and *thanks* in responses.

4. ROLE PLAY

SETUP: (**1**) Have students work in small groups of three or four to decide on foods they are eating for their pretend breakfast. Then have them write out their role play. Encourage students to use the exchanges in Exercise 3 as a model for their conversation. (**2**) Circulate to answer questions as necessary and to correct students' writing. (**3**) Have the groups take turns presenting their role plays. Encourage students to use props (table, chairs, and containers for food) and to mime the action of passing food around. (**4**) Write the question *What are they eating for breakfast?* on the board. Have students watch their classmates' role plays and write their answer to the question. After each role play, call on students to answer the question. If their responses are not correct, have the pair perform the role play again.

EXPANSION: Bring some breakfast foods to class (for example: fruit, muffins, coffee, orange juice) and have the whole class sit down together around a table (or tables clustered together) and eat. Encourage students to use the language they practiced earlier in the lesson to ask for and offer the various things on the table.

5. HOW ABOUT YOU?

SETUP: (**1**) Model the pronunciation of the questions. Explain the meaning of question 4 (*Do you ever NOT eat breakfast?*). (**2**) Have students work in pairs to take turns asking and answering the questions. (**3**) Circulate to listen in and to answer students' questions as necessary.

EXPANSIONS: (**1**) On the board, write the question *What time do you have breakfast?* and tell students to add it to the questions in the exercise. (**2**) For homework, have students write a paragraph about their favorite breakfast, answering the questions in this activity.

6. YOUR CLASSMATES' BREAKFAST

SETUP: (**1**) Have students circulate around the classroom asking one another the question and filling in the chart. (**2**) Set a time limit of ten minutes for this activity. (**3**) When students are finished asking and answering the questions, ask the class: "Who drinks coffee for breakfast? Who drinks tea? Orange juice? Who eats eggs for breakfast? Who eats toast for breakfast? Cereal? Pancakes?" Count the raised hands and write the number on the board each time.

EXPANSIONS: (**1**) Have students survey other students in the school. Tell them to briefly interview

their schoolmates in the hallways or in their classes and write down the information. Then have students report the results back to the class. Suggest that groups of students tally the results and make a bar graph illustrating the information. For example: *Four students eat toast. Ten students eat cereal.*

USE YOUR ENGLISH!

SETUP: Have students do this activity as a homework assignment. (**1**) To prepare students for this independent assignment, have the class brainstorm the names and locations of restaurants that serve breakfast. Have students choose one to visit. (**2**) Tell students to write down the name of the restaurant and what they ate. For example: *Frenchie's Diner. Eggs and toast.* At the beginning of the next class, students can share this information in small groups or simply hand in their reports to you.

EXPANSION: In class, ask students: "Do you recommend the restaurant? Why or why not?" Write on the board the names of the restaurants that students recommend.

Lesson 5: Lunch
Pages 58–59

1. LUNCH

SETUP: (**1**) Write the word *lunch* on the board. Have the class brainstorm the names of lunch foods. Write their ideas on the board. (**2**) Have students work individually or in pairs to look at the picture and complete the matching exercise. (**3**) Go over the answers with the class. Then play the audio program, pausing between items, and have students repeat chorally. (**4**) Have the class brainstorm the other items in the picture (for example: *napkins, salad dressing, take-out window*). Write the new vocabulary on the board, and have students add the new words and phrases to the list in their books; alternatively, tell students to write at least ten new vocabulary items in their vocabulary notebooks.

VARIATIONS AND EXPANSIONS: (**1**) Say or write a word or phrase, and have students point to the item in the picture. (**2**) Point to an item in the picture, and have students say the word or phrase. (**3**) Have students work in pairs to take turns pointing and identifying items in the picture.

2. WHAT'S HAPPENING?

SETUP: Call on a volunteer to read each question aloud. Ask other volunteers for their answers. For example:

1. *You can buy hamburgers, cheeseburgers, and salad at this fast-food restaurant.*
2. *She's buying a hamburger, french fries, and a soft drink.*
3. *It costs $3.75.*
4. *Maybe he wants another hamburger.*
5. *Maybe the man wants chicken nuggets.*

EXPANSIONS: For homework, have students write their responses to the questions and submit their writing to you for correction and comment.

3. HOW ABOUT YOU?

SETUP: (**1**) Model the pronunciation of the questions. (**2**) Have students work in pairs to take turns asking and answering the questions. Circulate to listen in and to answer students' questions as necessary.

VARIATION AND EXPANSION: (**1**) Before students get into pairs, tell the class: "Hamburgers and chicken nuggets are fast foods. What are other kinds of fast foods?" Write students' ideas on the board. Students can use this list as a reference when they ask and answer the questions in this activity. (**2**) Invite students to share what they learned in their pairs. (**3**) As a follow-up, ask: "What fast-food restaurants do you recommend? Why?" Call on individual students for their responses.

Language and Culture Note: In the United States, lunch is usually a light meal of a sandwich and soup or salad. It's a quick meal; many workers get only a thirty-minute break to eat lunch. Most people eat lunch between 11:30 A.M. and 2:00 P.M.

4. WHAT'S THE SPECIAL TODAY?

SETUP: (**1**) Point out that this conversation uses the Conversation Tip strategy from the Preview page. (**2**) Set the context: Some people are getting lunch in a cafeteria. (**3**) Have students close their books as they listen to the audio program for the first time. Then have students open their books and read along as they listen to the audio program again. Finally, play the audio a third time, pausing after each line for students to repeat chorally. (**4**) As students practice the conversation in pairs, circulate to give individual feedback on pronunciation.

VARIATIONS AND EXPANSIONS: (**1**) Have students listen to the conversation on the audio program and place dots over the stressed words (as in the conversation chants). Review the stress marks with the class. Practice the conversation chorally, paying special attention to word stress. (**2**) Invite pairs of students to perform the conversation for the class. (**3**) To help students internalize the language, write the conversation on the board. Phrase by phrase, erase portions of the conversation and have students practice it, filling in the blanks. See to what extent you can erase the conversation with students still able to recall it.

Language and Culture Note: *Coming right up!* refers to the food that is about to be served.

5. ROLE PLAY

SETUP: (**1**) Write on the board the skeletal conversation model for this role play:

A: *What's your special today?*
B: _____.
A: *What's the soup today?*
B: _____.
A: *I'd like _____, please.*
B: *Coming right up!*

(**2**) Have students write their role plays in pairs. (**3**) Circulate around the class answering questions and correcting the writing where necessary. (**4**) Have the pairs present their role plays. (**5**) Write the question *What is he/she eating for lunch today?* on the board. Have students watch their classmates' role plays and write down their answer to the question. After each role play, call on students to answer the question. If their responses are not correct, have the pair perform the role play again.

VARIATIONS AND EXPANSIONS: (**1**) Before students work in pairs, have the class brainstorm a lunch menu for a cafeteria. Write their ideas on the board. Have students refer to the menu when they write their role plays. (**2**) Have students submit their written role plays to you for correction before they perform the conversations in the following class.

6. CROSS-CULTURAL EXCHANGE

SETUP: Call on a student volunteer to read each question. Ask other volunteers for their responses.

EXPANSION: For homework, have students write their responses to the questions and submit their work to you for correction and comment.

7. FIND SOMEONE WHO . . .

SETUP: (1) Model (or ask volunteers to model) the questions that students will need to ask. For example: *Do you like fast food? Do you eat fast food often? Do you eat lunch at home?* (2) Have students walk around the classroom asking and answering the questions. Tell the class they have ten minutes to complete their charts. (3) Have students report their information to the class.

VARIATIONS AND EXPANSIONS: (1) Encourage students to add one more sentence to the list. (2) For homework, have students write affirmative and negative sentences about themselves using the ideas in this activity. For example: *I don't like fast food. I never eat fast food.* (3) Have students choose one question and survey other students in the school. Set up group visits in other classes. Have students report their findings to the class. For example: *In Mrs. Johnson's Level 2A class, twenty-seven students like fast food and nine don't.*

USE YOUR ENGLISH!

SETUP: Have students do this activity as a homework assignment. (1) To prepare students for this independent conversation, model a conversation about lunch with a volunteer, using the questions in the box. (2) Tell students to write down information they learn about their conversation partners. For example: *My conversation partner likes to eat pizza and tacos for fast food. My conversation partner's favorite lunch is a cheese sandwich and a bowl of soup.* At the beginning of the next class, students can share this information in small groups or simply hand in their reports to you.

VARIATIONS AND EXPANSIONS: Have the class brainstorm other questions from this lesson that they can ask their conversation partners, such as: *Where do you usually eat lunch? Do you like soup? Do you bring lunch from home?*

1. DINNER

SETUP: (1) Write *dinner* on the board. Have the class brainstorm words associated with dinner. Write their ideas on the board. (2) Have students work individually or in pairs to look at the pictures and complete the matching exercise. (3) Go over the answers with the class. Then play the audio program, pausing between items, and have students repeat chorally. (4) Have the class brainstorm words for other items in the pictures (for example: *plates, fork, salt*). Have students add the new words to the list in their books; alternatively, tell students to write at least ten new words in their vocabulary notebooks.

VARIATIONS AND EXPANSIONS: (1) Say or write a word or phrase, and have students point to the item in the pictures. (2) Point to an item in the pictures, and have students say the word or phrase. (3) Have students work in pairs to take turns pointing and identifying items in the pictures.

Language and Culture Note: In the United States, dinner is usually the largest meal of the day. Families usually eat dinner between 6:00 and 7:30 P.M.

2. WHAT'S DIFFERENT?

SETUP: (1) Point to the families in the pictures and ask: "What are their names?" Call on volunteers to name each member of the family in the picture. This will make it easier to answer the questions. For example: *The Smiths are eating garden salad and roast beef. The Fukimayas are eating rice and fish.* (2) Call on a volunteer to read each question aloud. Ask other volunteers to give their responses.

EXPANSION: For homework, have students write their responses to the questions and submit their writing to you for correction and comment.

3. HOW ABOUT YOU?

SETUP: (1) Model the pronunciation of each question before students break up into pairs. (2) Circulate to give individual feedback on pronunciation. (3) Set a time limit; tell students they have only five minutes to discuss these questions.

VARIATIONS AND EXPANSIONS: (1) Have students choose one of the questions in this activity and survey the whole class or other students in the school. Have students report their findings to the class. For example: *Twenty-five students sometimes eat dinner out, and thirteen never eat dinner out.* (2) Write these questions on the board: *Do you agree or disagree. Why?* Then dictate the following statements:

    a. *It's important for a family to eat dinner together.*

    b. *It's healthy to watch TV and eat dinner at the same time.*

Have students discuss their reactions to these statements in groups or as a class. (3) For homework, have students write complete-sentence answers to the questions and submit them to you for correction and comment.

4. CROSS-CULTURAL EXCHANGE

SETUP: (1) Read each question aloud for the class. (2) Call on student volunteers for their responses.

VARIATIONS AND EXPANSION: (1) If you have a multicultural ESOL setting, mix students by cultural background. (2) Suggest that students go out to dinner together to a traditional "ethnic" restaurant or that students bring traditional dinner dishes to class. (3) For homework, have students write a paragraph response to question 1 and submit their writing to you for correction and comment.

5. CONVERSATION CHANT: LET'S EAT IN.

SETUP: (1) Have students listen once through as they read along. As you play the audio program, make hand motions or clap to reinforce the stress on the dotted syllables. (2) Play the audio program, pausing after each line, and have students repeat. (3) Have the class chant chorally.

VARIATIONS: (1) Once students are familiar with the chant, divide the class into two groups. The indented lines represent a second voice. Have one group chant the lines that start at the left margin, and have the other group chant the lines that are indented. (2) Have students clap or make a hand motion to indicate where the stress falls as they chant. (3) Have groups switch and chant the opposite lines. (4) Have students circle all the words that rhyme. Call on volunteers to read the rhyming pairs aloud and then write them on the board. (5) Write these questions on the board: *Do you prefer to eat in or to eat out? Why? Is it hard to be on a diet and eat out? Why?* Have students

discuss these questions in small groups of three to four students. Have one student from each group report their ideas to the class.

USE YOUR ENGLISH!

SETUP: Have students do these activities as homework assignments. (1) To prepare students for this independent conversation, model the conversation with a volunteer, using the questions in the box. Tell students to write down information that they learn from their conversation partners. For example: *My conversation partner usually eats dinner at home. He only goes out to dinner once a month.* At the beginning of the next class, students can hand in their reports to you. (2) Model the survey question to the class. Tell students to survey at least four friends and write down their responses. At the beginning of the next class, have students report their findings to the class.

EXPANSION: Have the class brainstorm other questions from this lesson that students can also ask their conversation partners. For example: *What do you like to eat and drink for dinner? Do you ever eat food from other countries in restaurants? What kinds of food? Who eats dinner with you?*

Listening Practice
Page 62

1. WHAT DO YOU HEAR?

SETUP: (1) Have students first read the list of items and then listen to the audio program. (2) Review the answers with the class. If there is confusion about any answers, replay the audio program.

EXPANSION: Have pairs of students create their own conversations about making a shopping list. Have students present their conversations to the class.

2. AT THE SUPERMARKET

SETUP: (1) Introduce the new vocabulary word *aisle*. Show students the aisles in the picture on page 54. (2) Have students listen to the conversations and complete each sign. (3) Review the answers with the class. If there is confusion about any answers, replay the audio program.

EXPANSION: Have students take dictation on one of the conversations. Write the conversation on the board so students can correct their dictations, or have students self-correct by referring to the Audioscript in the back of the book.

3. MEALS

SETUP: (**1**) Have students first read the questions and answers before listening to the audio program. (**2**) Review the answers with the class. If there is confusion about any answers, replay the audio program.

VARIATION: Have students listen for and write down the key words in each conversation that signal the answer to the question (for example: Conversation 1: *toast, morning*).

other students in the school. Have students report their findings to the class. For example: *Fourteen students like to cook, and thirteen don't.*

3. ROLE PLAY

SETUP: (**1**) Have students work in pairs to write their conversations. (**2**) Circulate around the class answering questions and correcting the writing where necessary. (**3**) Match pairs with other pairs. Have each pair present one of their role plays to the other pair. Circulate around the class listening in on the role plays and giving feedback on pronunciation.

VARIATION: Have students submit their written conversations to you for correction before they perform the conversations in small groups the following class.

Review

Page 63

1. WHO IS IT?

SETUP: (**1**) Give students several minutes to compose their responses. (**2**) Collect the papers, mix them up, and then have each student select one. Make sure no student has received his or her own statements. (**3**) Have students read the statements to the class. (**4**) Have the class guess who the person is.

2. FIND SOMEONE WHO . . .

SETUP: (**1**) Model (or have volunteers model) the questions students will need to ask. For example: *Do you eat dinner after 8:00 P.M.? Do you usually eat breakfast? Do you like to cook?* (**2**) Have students walk around the classroom asking and answering the questions. Tell the class they have five minutes to complete their charts. (**3**) Have students report their information to the class.

VARIATIONS AND EXPANSIONS: (**1**) Encourage students to add one more sentence to the list. (**2**) For homework, have students write affirmative and negative sentences about themselves using the ideas in this activity. For example: *I eat dinner before 8:00 P.M. I usually eat breakfast. I don't like to cook.* (**3**) Have students choose one question and survey

Assessment

Page 64

PART 1: QUESTIONS

SETUP: Have students work individually to write the questions. Challenge students not to look at the previous lessons but to construct their questions from memory.

VARIATION: Have students write their questions on a separate sheet of paper to hand in to you for correction at the end of the assessment.

PART 2: SPEAKING

SETUP: (**1**) Divide the class into pairs, and have students take turns asking and answering their questions. (**2**) Circulate to listen in and to answer students' questions as necessary.

VARIATION: Have students write their partners' responses to their questions and hand them in to you for correction at the end of the assessment.

PART 3: LISTENING

SETUP: (**1**) Have students first read the answers and then listen to the audio program. (**2**) Check answers with the whole class by asking volunteers to read the correct sentence aloud. If there is any confusion about any of the answers, replay the audio component.

VARIATIONS AND EXPANSION: (**1**) Have students write the number of the question and the letter of their response on a separate sheet to hand in to you for correction at the end of the assessment. (**2**) As an added challenge, have students compose questions for the uncircled answers.

PART 4: WRITING

SETUP: (**1**) Set the context: Someone is buying fruit and vegetables from a grocer. (**2**) Have students work individually to write their conversations. (**3**) Have students share their conversations in small groups as you circulate to see their work.

VARIATIONS: (**1**) Have students write their conversations on a separate piece of paper to hand in to you for correction. (**2**) Have students share their conversations with a partner. Then ask volunteer pairs to perform one of their conversations for the class.

YOUR COMMUNITY

Preview

Page 65

PREVIEW QUESTIONS

SETUP: Have the class look at the photograph. Read each question aloud, and call on individual students to respond. For question 3, write students' responses on the board so they can see the various possible responses (for example: *Where are we?*).

CONVERSATION TIP

SETUP: (**1**) Set the context: Someone is asking for directions. (**2**) Have students read the conversation silently. (**3**) Ask the class: "Why does Speaker A repeat what Speaker B said?" (**4**) Point out the question mark at the end of A's repetition. Tell students they can turn a statement into a question by using rising intonation. Explain that we often do this when we think we're right but we're not sure. (**5**) Act out the conversation with various volunteers. (**6**) Have students practice the conversation in pairs. (**7**) Circulate to give individual feedback on pronunciation.

CONVERSATION CHANT: NICE NEIGHBORHOOD

SETUP: (**1**) The dots over the words indicate where the stress falls. As you play the audio program, make hand motions or clap to reinforce the stress on the dotted syllables. (**2**) Have students listen once through as they read along. (**3**) Play the audio program again, pausing after each line, and have students repeat. (**4**) Have the class chant chorally.

VARIATIONS AND EXPANSIONS: (**1**) Once students are familiar with the chant, divide the class into two groups. The indented chant lines represent a second voice. Have one group chant the questions that start at the left margin, and have the other group chant the responses that are indented (**2**) Have students clap or make a hand motion to indicate where the stress falls as they chant. (**3**) Have groups switch and chant the opposite lines. (**4**) Have students circle all the words

that rhyme. Call on volunteers to read the rhyming pairs aloud and then write them on the board. (**5**) Write these questions on the board: *Do you like your neighborhood? Do you have good restaurants in your neighborhood? How about movie theaters? Do you have a park?* Have students discuss these questions in pairs. After a few minutes, call on volunteers to report to the class what they learned about their partner.

Lesson 1: Neighborhood and Neighbors

Pages 66–67

1. THE NEIGHBORHOOD

SETUP: (**1**) Have students work individually or in pairs to look at the picture and complete the matching exercise. (**2**) Go over the answers with the class. Then play the audio program, pausing between items, and have students repeat chorally. (**3**) Have the class brainstorm other words and actions in the picture (for example: *parking meter, streetlight, running, mailing a letter*). Have students add the new words to the list in their books; alternatively, tell students to write at least ten new words and phrases in their vocabulary notebooks.

VARIATIONS: (**1**) Say or write a word or phrase, and have students point to the item in the picture. (**2**) Point to an item in the picture, and have students say the word or phrase. (**3**) Have students work in pairs to take turns pointing to and identifying items in the picture.

2. WHAT'S HAPPENING?

SETUP: (**1**) Read each question aloud to the class. (**2**) Call on volunteers to respond. For question 2, encourage students to give complete sentences and write the responses on the board in the correct present progressive forms (for example: *She is walking the dog. He is riding a bike.*).

VARIATION AND EXPANSION: (**1**) Have students work in groups of three or four to write a list of all the things they see in the neighborhood. Which group has the longest list? (**2**) For homework, have students write their answers to the questions and turn in their writing for correction.

3. HOW DO YOU LIKE YOUR NEIGHBORHOOD?

SETUP: (1) Set the context: Two people are talking about where they live. (2) Have students close their books as they listen to the audio program for the first time. Then have students open their books and read along as they listen to the audio program again. Finally, play the audio a third time, pausing after each line for students to repeat chorally. (3) As students practice each of the conversations in pairs, circulate to give individual feedback on pronunciation.

VARIATIONS AND EXPANSIONS: (1) Have students listen to the conversations on the audio program and place dots over the stressed words (same as in the conversation chants). Review the stress marks with the class. Practice the conversation chorally, paying special attention to word stress. (2) Invite pairs of students to perform the conversations for the class. (3) Ask the class: "Are these people in the two conversations talking about the same neighborhood?" (*Yes. They're talking about the neighborhood in the picture on page 66.*)

4. HOW ABOUT YOU?

SETUP: (1) Model the pronunciation of the questions. (2) Have students work in pairs to take turns asking and answering the questions. (3) Tell students they have only eight minutes to discuss these questions. (4) Circulate to listen in and answer students' questions as necessary.

VARIATIONS AND EXPANSIONS: (1) Point to the pictures, and ask the class: "What are these neighbors doing? Are they friendly? Helpful? Angry?" Call on volunteers for their responses. (2) With a more advanced class, ask: "What are they saying?" Have pairs of students choose one picture and write a conversation between the neighbors. The pairs can present their conversation to the class or submit it to you for correction. (3) For homework, have students write complete-sentence answers to the questions and turn them in for correction.

USE YOUR ENGLISH!

SETUP: Have students do this activity as a homework assignment. (1) To prepare the class for this independent conversation, model a conversation about your neighborhood with a volunteer, using the questions in the box. (2) Tell students to write down the information they learn from their conversation partners. For example: *My conversation partner doesn't like his neighborhood. It is noisy and dirty.*

At the beginning of the next class, students can share this information in small groups or simply hand in their reports to you.

EXPANSION: Have the class brainstorm other questions from this lesson that they can ask their conversation partners. For example: *Do you like your neighbors? Are they friendly? Helpful? Angry? Noisy? Do your neighbors help you? If yes, how? What problems do you have with your neighbors?*

Lesson 2: Around Town
Pages 68–69

1. COMMUNITY MAP

SETUP: (1) Have students work individually or in pairs to look at the picture and complete the matching exercise. (2) Go over the answers with the class. Then play the audio program, pausing between items, and have students repeat chorally. (3) Have the class brainstorm other vocabulary in the picture (for example: *bakery, cleaners, library, school*). Have students add the new words to the list in their books; alternatively, tell students to write at least ten new words or phrases in their vocabulary notebooks.

VARIATIONS: (1) Say or write a word or phrase, and have students point to the item in the picture. (2) Point to an item in the picture, and have students say the word or phrase. (3) Have students work in pairs to take turns pointing to and identifying items in the picture.

Language and Culture Note: A grocery store is a small, independently owned store that sells fruit, vegetables, and a few staple food items. The person who owns and runs the store is called a *grocer*. A supermarket is a large food store owned by a corporation. It sells fruits, vegetables, and all sorts of food and non-food items.

2. WHAT'S IN THIS COMMUNITY?

SETUP: (1) Model the pronunciation of each question before students break up into groups of three or four. (2) Write the following skeletal sentence models on the board for student reference:

> *There is a* _____.
> *There are* _____s.

Say *a laundromat* and then write the word into the first model. Say *traffic lights* and write it into the second model. (**3**) Set a time limit; tell students they have only seven minutes to discuss these questions. Circulate to listen in and answer students' questions as necessary. (**4**) After the groups complete the exercise, have a spokesperson from each group report to the class on their communities.

VARIATION AND EXPANSIONS: (**1**) Write the following question on the board: *What is in your school's neighborhood?* Have students work in groups of three to write a list of all the places in the school neighborhood. Which group has the longest list? As students report back to class, write a master list on the board. (**2**) Have students draw a map of their neighborhood, identifying important places and things on the map. Have students share their maps in pairs. (**3**) For homework, have students write complete-sentence answers to the questions.

3. WHERE IS IT?

SETUP: (**1**) Have students listen to the audio program as they look at the community map on page 68. (**2**) Play the audio program again as students read along. (**3**) Finally, play the audio again, pausing after each line for students to repeat chorally. (**4**) Circulate while students practice to give individual feedback on pronunciation. (**5**) Have the pairs write an additional conversation about the places on page 68 and perform their conversation for the class.

VARIATIONS AND EXPANSIONS: (**1**) Have students listen to the conversations on the audio program and place dots over the stressed words (as in the conversation chants). Review the stress marks with the class. Practice the conversations chorally, paying special attention to word stress. (**2**) Ask individual students about the locations of places on the map to check understanding. For example:

Teacher: *Where is the florist?*
Student: *It's on the corner of Maple Lane and Central Avenue.*

(**3**) Have each student write two sentences describing the location of one place on the map. Invite students to read their descriptions to the class without naming the place. Can the class identify the place? For example:

Student 1: *It's on the corner of Main Street and Lake Boulevard. It's next to the public library.*
Student 2: *It's the Main Elementary School!*

(**4**) Point out the different names for streets on the map: *boulevard, avenue, street, lane*, and *terrace*. Mention other common names (*road* and *parkway*). Ask students to name examples of boulevards, avenues, and streets in the school neighborhood.

4. WHAT ARE THEY SAYING?

SETUP: (**1**) Point out that these conversations use the Conversation Tip strategy from the Preview page. (**2**) Set the context: A driver is asking for directions. Point to the car in the lower left-hand corner of the map on page 68. (**3**) Have students listen to the audio program and look at the map on page 68, following the directions with their finger. Then play the audio program again while the students read along on page 69. Finally, play the audio a third time, pausing after each line for students to repeat chorally. (**4**) As students practice the conversation in pairs, encourage them to act it out by standing and gesturing as they give the directions. (**5**) Circulate to give individual feedback on pronunciation.

VARIATIONS AND EXPANSIONS: (**1**) Have students listen to the conversation on the audio program and place dots over the stressed words (as in the conversation chants). Review the stress marks with the class. Practice the conversation chorally, paying special attention to word stress. (**2**) Invite pairs of students to perform the conversation for the class.

5. ROLE PLAY

SETUP: (**1**) For student reference, write the following skeletal directions model on the board:

> *Turn left on _____.*
> *Turn right on _____.*
> *Go past _____.*
> *It's on the left.*
> *It's on the right.*

Demonstrate the meaning of *turn left* and *turn right* by actually turning left and right with your back to the students so you have the same left and right directions. (**2**) Have students work in pairs to write their own conversations using the map on page 68. (**3**) Circulate around the class answering questions and correcting students' writing where necessary. (**4**) Have the pairs present their role plays. Encourage them to use gestures as they give directions. (**5**) Have the rest of the class listen and follow the directions with their finger on the map on page 68.

VARIATIONS AND EXPANSIONS: (1) Have students submit their written conversations to you for correction before they perform the conversations in the following class. (2) Have students write a conversation asking for directions to a place in the school neighborhood and perform it for the class.

USE YOUR ENGLISH!

SETUP: Have students do this activity as a homework assignment. (1) To prepare students for this independent conversation, model a conversation asking a stranger for directions with a volunteer. Have the student ask the first question. For example:

Student: *Excuse me. How do I get to the public library?*
Teacher: *The public library? Go straight on Main Street, past Tenth Street. It's on the left. It's next to the movie theater.*
Student: *I go straight on Main Street. I go past Tenth Street, and it's on the left?*
Teacher: *That's right.*
Student: *Thank you.*

(2) Tell students to write down the place they chose with their conversation partners and the directions they received. For example: *Angelina's Pizzeria. Take a left on Central Street. Go past the park. It's on the right.* At the beginning of the next class, have students hand in their reports to you.

EXPANSION: For additional homework, tell students to ask their conversation partners: *What's in your community?* Students can write down what their conversation partners say and submit the reports to you at the beginning of the next class.

Lesson 3: The Post Office

Pages 70–71

1. THE POST OFFICE

SETUP: (1) Write the word *post office* on the board. Ask the class: *What is in a post office?* Write their ideas on the board. (2) Have students work individually or in pairs to look at the picture and complete the matching exercise. (3) Go over the answers with the class. Then play the audio program,

pausing between items, and have students repeat chorally. (4) Have the class brainstorm other vocabulary in the picture (for example: *mail truck, scale*). Write the words on the board, and have students add the new words to the list in their books; alternatively, tell students to write at least eight new words in their vocabulary notebooks.

VARIATIONS AND EXPANSIONS: (1) Say or write a word, and have students point to the item in the picture. (2) Point to an item in the picture, and have students say the word. (3) Have students work in pairs to take turns pointing to and identifying items in the picture.

2. WHAT CAN YOU DO AT THE POST OFFICE?

SETUP: Call on volunteers to read each question aloud. Then have other volunteers answer the questions. For example:

1. *You can mail letters, packages, postcards, and money orders.*
2. *You can buy stamps, boxes, and money orders.*

EXPANSION: For homework, have students visit a local post office and write down all the things a person can buy there. Have students share their lists in class.

3. POST OFFICE CONVERSATIONS

SETUP: (1) Set the context by pointing to the clerks and the customers in the picture on page 70. (2) For each conversation, have students close their books as they listen to the audio program for the first time. Then have students open their books and read along as they listen to the audio program again. Finally, play the audio a third time, pausing after each line for students to repeat chorally. (3) As students practice each of the conversations in pairs, circulate to give individual feedback on pronunciation.

VARIATIONS AND EXPANSION: (1) Help tune students' ears to hear the /d/ in *I'd like*. Write *I like* and *I'd like* on the board and number each item (*1* and *2*). Ask students: "What do you hear?" Say a sentence with one of the phrases, and have students identify what they hear. For example:

Teacher: *I like to write letters.*
Students: *1*
Teacher: *I'd like to mail this letter.*
Students: *2*

(2) Invite pairs of students to perform the conversations for the class. (3) To help students internalize the

language, write one of the conversations on the board. Phrase by phrase, erase portions of the conversation and have students practice it, filling in the blanks. See to what extent you can erase the conversation with students still able to recall it.

Language and Culture Note: *I'd like* is a contraction of the phrase *I would like*. It's a formulaic expression: *would like* + noun / *would like* + infinitive (*to* + base form of verb) and is used to make requests.

4. ROLE PLAY

SETUP: (**1**) Introduce more post office vocabulary. Explain the four most common ways to send mail within North America: *Express Mail (next-day delivery); Priority Mail (2–3 days delivery); First-Class Mail (2–4 days delivery); and for packages, Parcel Post (3–9 days delivery).* (**2**) Have students work in pairs to write their own post office conversations. (**3**) Circulate around the class answering questions and correcting the writing where necessary. (**4**) Have the pairs present their role plays to the class. After each presentation, ask: "What would the customer like?" and call on volunteers to answer.

VARIATIONS: (**1**) Bring props to class for students to use in their role plays (for example: envelopes, stamps, a book of stamps, a cardboard box for a package). (**2**) Have students submit their written conversations to you for correction before they perform the conversations in the following class.

5. CONVERSATION CHANT: LOTS OF MAIL

SETUP: (**1**) Play the audio program. Tell students to read along as they listen to the chant. As you play the audio program, make hand motions or clap to reinforce the stress on the dotted syllables. (**2**) Play the audio program again, pausing after each line, and have students repeat. (**3**) Have the class chant chorally.

VARIATIONS AND EXPANSIONS: (**1**) Once students are familiar with the chant, divide the class into two groups. The indented lines represent a second voice. Have one group chant the lines that start at the left margin, and have the other group chant the lines that are indented. (**2**) Have students clap or make a hand motion to indicate where the stress falls as they chant. (**3**) Have groups switch and chant the opposite lines. (**4**) Have students circle all the words that rhyme. Call on volunteers to read the rhyming pairs aloud and then write them on

the board. (**5**) Write these questions on the board: *Do you get lots of mail? Do you get letters from friends? What kind of mail do you get?* Have students discuss these questions in pairs. After a few minutes, ask for volunteers to report to the class what they learned about their partner.

6. HOW OFTEN . . . ?

SETUP: (**1**) Model the questions. (**2**) Have students work in groups of three or four to take turns asking and answering the questions. (**3**) Circulate to listen in and answer students' questions as necessary. Set a time limit; tell students they have five minutes to complete the chart. (**4**) Invite students to report their findings to the class. For example: *In our group, three people go to the post office once a month. One person never goes.*

VARIATIONS AND EXPANSIONS: (**1**) The complete-sentence responses to these questions use two different sets of word order. To illustrate this, write on the board:

> *I go to the post office <u>once a week</u>.*
> *I <u>never</u> go to the post office.*

Underline the time words in each sentence. Point out that the frequency adverb *never* (as well as other adverbs of frequency—*sometimes, always, often, rarely, seldom*) goes before the verb and the time expressions *once a week/month/year* go at the end of the sentence. Leave the sentences on the board for students' reference as they ask and answer their questions in groups. (**2**) Have students choose one question and survey ten other students in the school and then report their findings to the class. For example: *Seven students write and receive letters once a year. Three students write and receive letters once a month.*

USE YOUR ENGLISH!

SETUP: Have students do this activity as a homework assignment. (**1**) To prepare students for this independent conversations, model the conversation with a volunteer, using the questions in the box. (**2**) Tell students to write down the information they learn from their conversation partners. For example: *My conversation partner never writes letters. He goes to the post office once a month to buy a money order and a book of stamps.* At the beginning of the next class, students can share this information in small groups or simply hand in their reports to you.

EXPANSION: Have the class brainstorm other questions they can ask their conversation partners. For example: *How often do you go to the post office? Which post office do you go to? Do you get a lot of mail? What kind of mail do you get?*

Lesson 4: The bank

Pages 72–73

1. BANKING ITEMS

SETUP: (1) Write the word *bank* on the board. Ask the class: "What items do you use at the bank"? Write their ideas on the board. (2) Have students work individually or in pairs to look at the pictures and complete the matching exercise. (3) Go over the answers with the class. Then play the audio program, pausing between items, and have students repeat chorally. (4) Point out that a withdrawal slip is different from a deposit slip. It usually has spaces for the amount of money to be withdrawn and a line for the customer's signature and date.

VARIATIONS AND EXPANSIONS: (1) Say or write a word or phrase, and have students point to the item in the pictures. (2) Point to an item in the pictures, and have students say the word or phrase. (3) Have students work in pairs to take turns pointing and identifying items in the pictures.

Language and Culture Notes: (1) The short form of the word *identification* is *ID*. (2) In the United States, a driver's license is the most common form of identification. There is no U.S. national identity card. People who do not drive use other forms of identification, such as student, employee, or state ID cards.

2. BANKING

SETUP: (1) Introduce the new vocabulary: *savings account* and *checking account*. (2) Model the first question and answer: *What do you need to make a deposit to your savings account? You need a deposit slip and a check or cash.* (3) Read each question aloud. Call on volunteers to answer the questions.

Remind students to use the words in Exercise 1 to answer the questions.

VARIATION: For homework, have students write their responses to the questions and turn in their work for correction.

3. MAY I HELP YOU?

SETUP: (1) Set the context: A customer is at the bank. (2) Have students close their books as they listen to the audio program for the first time. Then have students open their books and read along as they listen to the audio program again. Finally, play the audio a third time, pausing after each line for students to repeat chorally. (3) As students practice the conversation in pairs, circulate to give individual feedback on pronunciation. (4) Have students work with their partners to write their own bank conversations, using vocabulary from page 72. (5) Circulate around the class answering questions and correcting the writing where necessary. (6) Have the pairs present their role plays to the class.

VARIATIONS: (1) To help students internalize the bank conversation, write it on the board. Phrase by phrase, erase portions of the conversation and have students practice it, filling in the blanks. See to what extent you can erase the conversation with students still able to recall it. (2) To guide students as they write their new conversations, write on the board the following skeletal model conversation:

> Teller: *May I help you?*
> Customer: *Yes, I'd like to _____. Here's my _____.*
> Teller: *May I see some identification?*
> Customer: *Of course.*

(3) Bring props to class for students to use in their role plays (deposit slips, fake checks, withdrawal slips, play money, etc.).

4. HOW ABOUT YOU?

SETUP: (1) Model the pronunciation of the questions. (2) Have students work in pairs to take turns asking and answering the questions. (3) Tell students they have only five minutes to discuss these questions. (4) Circulate to listen in and answer students' questions as necessary.

EXPANSION: For homework, have students write complete-sentence answers to the questions.

5. WHAT DO YOU DO?

SETUP: (1) Read the situations, questions, and choices aloud to the class, and ask students if they have any questions before they work together in groups. (2) Have students work in small groups of three or four to look at the pictures, read the situations, and answer the questions. (3) Circulate around the class to listen in and answer students' questions as necessary. (4) Invite students to report their ideas to the class.

EXPANSION: Have pairs of students write a role play for one of the two situations and perform it for the class.

USE YOUR ENGLISH!

SETUP: Have students do this activity as a homework assignment. (1) To prepare students for this assignment, have them brainstorm ways they can find banks in their community (for example: in the phone book, on the Internet, by asking friends, by looking around). (2) Tell students to write down the information they learn. For example: *In my community, there are four banks: Key Bank, Chase Manhattan Bank, Citizens Bank, and Winter Hill Bank.* At the beginning of the next class, students can submit their reports to you.

EXPANSIONS: (1) Have the class brainstorm additional questions they can ask their conversation partners. For example: *Do you use a bank? Which bank do you use? Is it a good bank? Do you recommend it? Why? Why not?* (2) Have students visit a bank in their community or on the Internet. Have them find the answers to these questions: *Does the bank have savings accounts? Does the bank have checking accounts? Does the bank have ATMs?*

Lesson 5: Help! Fire!

Pages 74–75

1. A FIRE

SETUP: (1) Have students work individually or in pairs to look at the picture and complete the matching exercise. (2) Go over the answers with the class. Then play the audio program, pausing

between items, and have students repeat chorally. Point out that the abbreviation for *Emergency Medical Technician* is pronounced "E-M-T." (3) Have the class brainstorm other vocabulary in the picture (for example: *hose, water, carrying someone, spraying the fire*). Write the words on the board, and have students add the new words and phrases to the list in their books; alternatively, tell students to write at least ten new words and phrases in their vocabulary notebooks.

VARIATIONS AND EXPANSION: (1) Say or write a word or phrase, and have students point to the item in the picture. (2) Point to an item in the picture, and have students say the word or phrase. (3) Have students work in pairs to take turns pointing to and identifying items in the picture.

2. WHAT'S HAPPENING?

SETUP: Call on a student volunteer to read each question aloud. Ask other volunteers to respond.

EXPANSION: For homework, have students write their responses to the questions and turn in their work for correction.

3. REPORTING A FIRE

SETUP: (1) Set the context: Someone is calling 911 on his cell phone to report a fire. (2) Read the lines aloud to the class. Answer any questions about unfamiliar vocabulary. (3) Divide the class into pairs. Have students complete the conversation and present their role plays to the class.

VARIATION: In random order, write on the board possible answers to the operator's questions in the conversation. For example: *155 Main Street. Sandra Banner. (807) 343-6666. It's across the street, on the corner of Main Street and Cherry Avenue. People are running out of the building. Yes. Many people are coughing.* Have students select the correct answer for each question and write it into the conversation in their books. Review the answers with the class.

Language and Culture Note: If a person calls from a land line, the emergency operator can immediately identify the location and phone number of the caller, but if the call comes from a cell phone, the operator must ask about the caller's phone number and address.

4. HOW ABOUT YOU?

SETUP: Read each question aloud to the class. Call on volunteers to respond. Following are possible answers to question 1:

1. *You should leave the house immediately.*
   If there is a lot of smoke, you should crawl on the floor.
   You should call 911 as soon as you can.

VARIATION AND EXPANSION: (1) Bring fire-safety brochures to class (available from the local fire department or from the Internet). Have students read the brochures. Ask questions such as "Do you have an escape route?" (Everyone should have an escape route from each room in their home. There should be two alternative routes for every room—for example, a window and a door.) "Do you have smoke detectors?" (All homes should have several smoke detectors. In the United States, landlords are responsible for supplying and maintaining the smoke detectors in rental properties.) "What is the emergency number?" (In the United States, it is 911.) "What does *stop, drop, and roll* mean?" (If a person is on fire, he or she should stop, drop [fall to the ground], and roll around to put out the fire.) (2) For homework, have students write their responses to the questions.

5. CONVERSATION CHANT: FIREFIGHTERS CLIMBING

SETUP: (1) Play the audio program. Tell students to read along as they listen to the chant. As you play the audio program, make hand motions or clap to reinforce the stress on the dotted syllables. (2) Play the audio program again, pausing after each line, and have students repeat. (3) Have the class chant chorally.

VARIATIONS: (1) Have students clap or make a hand motion to indicate where the stress falls as they chant. (2) Have students circle all the words that rhyme. Call on volunteers to read the rhyming pairs aloud and then write them on the board.

USE YOUR ENGLISH!

SETUP: Have students do this activity as a homework assignment. (1) To prepare students for this independent conversation, model the conversation with a volunteer, using the questions in the box. (2) Tell students to write down the information they learn from their conversation partners. For example: *There is a fire station in my conversation partner's neighborhood. It is across the street from his house!* At the beginning of the next class, students can hand in their reports to you.

Lesson 6: Help! Police!

Pages 76–77

1. A ROBBERY

SETUP: (1) Have students work individually or in pairs to look at the pictures and complete the matching exercise. (2) Go over the answers with the class. Then play the audio program, pausing between items, and have students repeat chorally.

Language and Culture Notes: (1) *Freeze!* means "Stop! Don't move!" Police often use this phrase in an emergency to command someone to stop running. (2) *Steal* means "to take something." A person and a place are *robbed*, but the property is *stolen*.

2. WHAT'S THE STORY?

SETUP: Call on a volunteer to read each question a loud. Ask other volunteers to respond. For example:

1. *Ernesto is in his home.*
2. *He sees a robbery through his window.*
3. *He calls 911.*
4. *They try to take his CD player and his hubcaps.*
5. *Yes, they do.*
6. *The police put handcuffs on the two robbers. Then they take them to the police station.*

EXPANSION: For homework, have students write their responses to the questions.

Language and Culture Note: The simple present tense is often used to tell a story even though the actions took place in the past.

3. TELL THE STORY AGAIN.

SETUP: (1) Have students work in pairs to look at the pictures and retell the story. Remind them to use the simple present tense. (2) Circulate to listen in, correct students' pronunciation, and answer questions as necessary. Pay close attention to whether students produce the third-person singular -*s* (for example: *he sees, he calls,* etc.). (3) Set a time limit; tell students they have only five minutes to complete this task.

VARIATION AND EXPANSION: (1) Have students tell the story in a round-robin. For example:

Student 1: Ernesto looks out the window.
Student 2: He sees two robbers.
Student 3: They are stealing his CD player and his hubcaps.
Student 4: Ernesto calls 911.

(2) Write the story from the book on the board with a lot of space between lines and words. Ask students to give more details, asking questions such as: "What time of day is it?" "What color is Ernesto's car?" Insert those details into the story lines. For example: (insert) *It's 6:00 in the evening. Two young men break into Ernesto's* (insert) *yellow car.*

4. ROLE PLAY

SETUP: (1) Call on two volunteers to read aloud the phone conversation on page 75. **(2)** Have students work in pairs to write a phone conversation between Ernesto and a 911 operator. Encourage them to model their conversation on the 911 call on page 75. **(3)** Circulate around the class answering questions and correcting students' writing as necessary. **(4)** Have the pairs present their role plays to the class.

VARIATION: Have students submit their written conversations to you for correction before they perform the conversations in the following class.

5. WHAT DO YOU DO?

SETUP: (1) Read the questions and answers aloud to the class. Answer any questions students may have about unfamiliar vocabulary. **(2)** Have students work in pairs to look at the pictures, read the situations, check the answers they like best, and add another idea. **(3)** Circulate around the class to listen in and to answer questions as necessary. **(4)** Invite students to report their ideas to the class.

EXPANSIONS: (1) For each possible answer, ask the class: "Is this a good idea? Why or why not?" Write students' ideas on the board so the whole class can see and remember different ideas. **(2)** For homework, have students write their response to each situation and explain why they chose it.

6. WHEN DO YOU CALL 911?

SETUP: (1) Write the following questions on the board: *What is a real emergency? When do you call 911?* **(2)** Have students work in small groups of three or four to decide what kinds of emergencies require a 911 response (for example: *a fire, a robbery, and an accident*). Have each group write down three emergencies in their books. Circulate to listen in and to answer students' questions as necessary. **(3)** Invite students to share their ideas with the class.

Language and Culture Note: The number 911 is called only in real emergencies (fire, robbery, medical emergency, domestic violence, car accidents). Situations such as losing your car keys, getting lost at night, or seeing a car drive through a red light are not real emergencies. In situations like those, you can call the non-emergency number for the local police.

USE YOUR ENGLISH!

SETUP: Have students do this activity as a homework assignment. **(1)** To prepare students for this assignment, explain that there are two numbers for the police: One is the emergency number (911 in the United States); the other is a non-emergency number to report smaller problems. Tell students to find both numbers and write them down. **(2)** At the beginning of the next class, have students share this information with the class.

Listening Practice
Page 78

1. MAY I HELP YOU?

SETUP: (1) Tell students to read through the sentences silently. **(2)** Play the audio program. **(3)** Review the answers with the class. If there is confusion about any answers, replay the audio program.

VARIATION: Have students first listen with their books closed and then open their books to read the questions and answers.

2. 911

SETUP: (1) Have students first read the questions and answers and then listen to the audio program. **(2)** Review the answers with the class. If there is confusion about any answers, play the audio program again.

VARIATION: Have students first listen with their books closed and then open their books to read the questions and answers.

3. WHERE IS IT?

SETUP: (1) Have students first look at the map and read the questions; then play the audio program. **(2)** Review the answers with the class. If there is confusion about the locations of the places, replay the audio program.

EXPANSION: Have students use the map for an information-gap activity. Make multiple copies of the map and distribute two copies to each student. Have students put the *movie theater, drugstore,* and *school* on one map in any place they wish. Then have students work in pairs to take turns describing the locations of these places on their map. Their partner listens and completes the map. The students then compare their maps to make sure they understood each other.

Review

Page 79

1. YOUR NEIGHBORHOOD

SETUP: (**1**) Give students unlined paper to draw their maps. (**2**) Set a time limit; tell students they have ten minutes to draw their maps. (**3**) As students complete their maps, put them into pairs. Have students compare maps and take turns talking about their neighborhoods. Circulate to listen in and to answer questions as necessary.

EXPANSION: Write the following questions on the board for students to discuss in pairs as they share their maps: *What's in your neighborhood? How do you like your neighborhood? Is it safe? Is it noisy?*

2. WHAT'S HAPPENING?

SETUP: (**1**) Ask the class: "What do you think? What's happening outside right now?" Have the class brainstorm ideas and write them on the board. For example: *Cars are going by. People are walking. Children are running.* Use the present progressive tense and remind the class that we use this tense when we talk about what is happening right now. (**2**) Tell students to look out their classroom window or go outside to see what's happening on the street. Give students a ten-minute time limit to look outside and write their observations. (**3**) When students return to class, call on individual students to say what they saw happening in the street.

VARIATION: Students can do this activity for homework and submit their writing to you for correction and comment.

3. WHAT'S THE PLACE?

SETUP: (**1**) Have the class brainstorm different places in the school neighborhood (for example: *U.S. Trust Bank, Vinny's Restaurant, the laundromat*). (**2**) Have students choose one place and write a description of its location and directions to get there. (For example: *It's next to the bank on Summit Drive. You go straight down Summit Drive, past the post office and the pizzeria. It's on the left.*) Circulate to answer questions as necessary. (**3**) Collect the papers, mix them up, and then have each student select one. Make sure no student has received his or her own paper. (**4**) Have students read the papers to the class. (**5**) Have the class guess what the place is.

4. EMERGENCIES

SETUP: (**1**) Divide the class into small groups. Tell each group to choose a secretary who will take notes. (**2**) As the groups brainstorm emergency situations, circulate around the classroom listening in on students' ideas and answering questions as necessary. (**3**) Set a time limit; tell students they have five minutes to write down their ideas. (**4**) Have the groups take turns reading their lists to the class.

EXPANSION: Have pairs of students choose one of the situations and write a conversation between a caller in that situation and the 911 operator. Have the students perform their role plays for the class or submit their conversations to you for correction and comment.

5. MAKE A LIST!

SETUP: (**1**) Call on a volunteer to read each question aloud. Call on student volunteers to respond. For example:

Student 1: *When I go to the bank, I make a deposit or a withdrawal.*
Student 2: *When I go to the bank, I cash my paycheck.*
Student 3: *When I go to the bank, I send money to my family.*

(**2**) Write students' ideas for questions 1, 2, and 4 on the board, and have students copy the lists. Because answers to question 3 will vary, have students share their feelings without writing them down.

VARIATION: (**1**) Have volunteers come up to the board to write the lists for questions 1, 2, and 4.

(2) Have students do this activity in small groups of three and then share their lists with the class.

Assessment

Page 80

PART 1: QUESTIONS

SETUP: Have students work individually to write the questions. Challenge students not to look at the previous lessons but to construct their questions from memory.

VARIATION: Have students write their questions on a separate sheet of paper to hand in to you at the end of the assessment for correction.

PART 2: SPEAKING

SETUP: (1) Divide the class into pairs, and have students take turns asking and answering their questions. (2) Circulate to listen in and to answer students' questions as necessary.

VARIATION: Have students write their partners' responses to their questions and hand in their work at the end of the assessment.

PART 3: LISTENING

SETUP: (1) Have students first read the answers silently. Then play the audio program. (2) Check answers with the whole class by asking volunteers to read the correct sentences aloud. If there is any confusion about any of the answers, replay the audio program.

VARIATION AND EXPANSION: (1) Have students write the number of the question and the letter of their response on a separate sheet to hand in to you for correction at the end of the assessment. (2) As an added challenge, have students compose questions for the uncircled answers.

PART 4: WRITING

SETUP: (1) Set the context: This person is calling 911. Lead a brief brainstorming session about what the person could be saying. (2) Have students work individually to write their conversations. Circulate as students are writing, and answer questions as necessary.

VARIATIONS: (1) Have students write their conversations on a separate piece of paper to hand in to you for correction. (2) Have students share their conversations with a partner. Then ask volunteer pairs to perform one of their conversations for the class.

Preview

Page 81

PREVIEW QUESTIONS

SETUP: (**1**) Have the class look at the photograph. Read each question aloud, and call on individual students to respond. (**2**) For questions 3 and 4, write students' responses on the board so they can see the various possible responses. For example:

> **3.** *They're shopping. They're looking at clothes.*
> **4.** *They're saying, "This is nice." "I like this." "It fits."*

CONVERSATION TIP

SETUP: (**1**) Set the context: These people are asking for and giving information. (**2**) Have students read the conversations silently. (**3**) Ask the class: "Which words does each Speaker A repeat?" (**4**) Act out the conversations with various volunteers. (**5**) Have students practice the conversations in pairs. Circulate to give individual feedback on pronunciation.

CONVERSATION CHANT: AT THE SHOPPING MALL

SETUP: (**1**) Introduce the new vocabulary: *stationery store, hardware store, electronics store, sporting goods store.* Explain (or ask volunteers to explain) what each kind of store sells. For example: *A stationery store sells pens, pencils, paper, notebooks; a hardware store sells paint, tools, light bulbs; an electronics store sells cell phones, radios, TVs, and computers; and a sporting goods store sells balls, sports clothes, sports equipment.* (**2**) The dots over the words indicate where the stress falls. As you play the audio program, make hand motions or clap to reinforce the stress on the dotted syllables. (**3**) Have students listen once through as they read along. (**4**) Play the audio program again, pausing after each line, and have students repeat. (**5**) Have the class chant chorally.

VARIATIONS AND EXPANSIONS: (**1**) Once students are familiar with the chant, divide the class into two groups. The indented chant lines represent a second

voice. Have one group chant the lines that start at the left margin, and have the other group chant the responses that are indented. (**2**) Have students clap or make a hand motion to indicate where the stress falls as they chant. (**3**) Have groups switch and chant the opposite lines. (**4**) Have students circle all the words that rhyme. Call on volunteers to read the rhyming pairs aloud and then write them on the board. (**5**) Write these questions on the board: *What do you need to buy? What do you want to buy?* Then ask: "What is the difference?" For example: *I need to buy milk and bread. I want to buy ice cream. I need to buy a car to drive to work. I want to buy a Lexus.* Have students discuss these questions in pairs and then share their ideas with the class.

Lesson 1: Shopping at the Mall

Pages 82–83

1. AT THE MALL

SETUP: (**1**) Write *shopping mall* on the board. Have the class brainstorm types of stores in a shopping mall, and write the words on the board. (**2**) Have students work individually or in pairs to look at the pictures and complete the matching exercise. (**3**) Go over the answers with the class. Then play the audio program, pausing between items, and have students repeat chorally. (**4**) Brainstorm other vocabulary in the pictures (for example: *flower stand, shoppers, pharmacist*). Write the words on the board, and have students add the new words to the list in their books; alternatively, tell students to write at least twelve new words and phrases in their vocabulary notebooks.

VARIATIONS AND EXPANSIONS: (**1**) Say or write a word or phrase, and have students point to the item in the pictures. (**2**) Point to an item in the pictures, and have students say the word or phrase. (**3**) Have students work in pairs to take turns pointing to and identifying items in the pictures.

2. WHAT CAN YOU GET THERE?

SETUP: (**1**) Call on a volunteer to read each question aloud. Call on other volunteers to respond. For example: *There's a drugstore. There's a toy store. There's a shoe store.* (**2**) Write students' ideas on the board as they speak.

VARIATIONS AND EXPANSION: (1) Have students work in small groups to answer question 2. Call out a kind of store and give students two minutes to list all the items one can buy there. Which group has the longest list? Repeat this activity with different kinds of stores. (2) Point to the pictures and ask the class: "Are there malls like this in your native town/city? How are they similar? How are they different? What can you buy at stores in your native country that you can't buy at this mall?" Call on volunteers to respond to your questions. (3) For homework, have students write their answers to the questions.

3. WHAT'S THE NAME OF THE STORE?

SETUP: (1) Point out that only two of the stores in the pictures on page 82 have names (Moocy's and Carol's Café). (2) Have students work in pairs to list their naming ideas on a separate paper—not in the book. (3) Set a time limit; tell students that they have ten minutes to create store names. (4) Call out a type of store, and ask volunteers for ideas. Write students' ideas on the board, and have the class vote with a show of hands on which is best. (5) Once all the names have been selected, have students write the winning names in the pictures so that everyone has the same information.

VARIATION: Instead of making up creative names for the stores, have students choose names of actual stores in their community. For example: *CVS for the drugstore or Kay Jewelers for the jewelry store.*

4. ASK DIRECTIONS AT THE MALL.

SETUP: (1) Point out that this conversation uses the Conversation Tip strategy from the Preview page. (2) Have students close their books as they listen to the audio program for the first time. Then have students open their books and read along as they listen to the audio program again. Finally, play the audio a third time, pausing after each line for students to repeat chorally. (3) As students practice the conversation in pairs, circulate to give individual feedback on pronunciation

VARIATIONS AND EXPANSIONS: (1) Have students listen to the conversation on the audio program and place dots over the stressed words (as in the conversation chants). Review the stress marks with the class. Practice the conversation chorally, paying special attention to word stress. (2) Invite pairs of

students to perform the conversations for the class. (3) To help students internalize the language, write the conversation on the board. Phrase by phrase, erase portions of the conversation and have students practice it, filling in the blanks. See to what extent you can erase the conversation with students still able to recall it.

5. HOW ABOUT YOU?

SETUP: (1) Have students work in pairs to take turns asking and answering the questions. (2) Set a time limit; tell students they have ten minutes to discuss these questions. (3) Circulate to listen in and to answer students' questions as needed.

VARIATIONS AND EXPANSIONS: (1) Invite students to share their ideas with the class, and write them on the board. (2) Have pairs of students choose one kind of store (for example: *sporting goods*). Have them ask other students in the school: "What (sporting goods) store do you recommend?" Have them tally their results and report back to the class. For example: *Ten students recommend Sports Authority, and four recommend Paragon for sportswear.* They can even post their findings on the school bulletin board and title the findings: (*Your school name)'s Most Recommended Stores.* (3) For homework, have students look up the following kinds of stores in the yellow pages: hardware store, shoe store, sporting goods store, toy store. In class, have them report two names they found for each kind of store.

USE YOUR ENGLISH!

SETUP: Have students do this activity as a homework assignment. (1) To prepare students for this assignment, have the class brainstorm the names of shopping malls in your area. Write them on the board. Talk about transportation and directions to these malls so that students feel confident they can get there. (2) Have students choose one mall to visit with their conversation partners. (3) Tell students to write down the information they learn from their excursion. For example: *At the North Gate Mall, there are many stores: a drugstore, a clothing store, a shoe store, a music store.* At the beginning of the next class, students can share this information in small groups or simply hand in their reports to you.

EXPANSION: In the follow-up class discussion, ask: "Which malls do you recommend? Why?"

Lesson 2: Buying Shoes

Pages 84–85

1. AT THE SHOE STORE

SETUP: (1) Write the word *shoes* on the board. Ask the class: "What kinds of shoes do you wear?" Write their responses on the board. (2) Have students work individually or in pairs to look at the picture and complete the matching exercise. (3) Go over the answers with the class. Then play the audio program, pausing between items, and have students repeat chorally. (4) Brainstorm other vocabulary in the picture (for example: *shoe box, laces, shoe polish*). Write the words on the board, and have students add the new words to the list in their books; alternatively, tell students to write at least ten new words in their vocabulary notebooks.

VARIATIONS AND EXPANSION: (1) Say or write a word or phrase, and have students point to the item in the picture. (2) Point to an item in the picture, and have students say the word or phrase. (3) Have students work in pairs to take turns pointing to and identifying items in the picture. (4) Make true/false statements about the kinds of shoes that students are wearing. Have students correct your false statements. For example:

> Teacher: *Bich Hang is wearing sandals.*
> Student 1: *True.*
> Teacher: *Tim is wearing cowboy boots.*
> Student 2: *False! He's wearing sneakers.*

2. WHAT'S HAPPENING?

SETUP: (1) Read the questions aloud. Call on volunteers for their responses. Encourage students to give complete-sentence answers. (2) Write students' responses on the board in the correct present progressive or simple present form. For example: *She is shopping for high heels. Yes, she likes the shoes she is trying on. Her friend is feeling frustrated. The salesperson is feeling tired.*

EXPANSION: For homework, have students write a story about the woman who is trying on so many shoes.

3. HOW ABOUT YOU?

SETUP: (1) Model the pronunciation of the questions. (2) Have students work in pairs to take turns asking and answering the questions. (3) Set a time limit; tell students they have only five minutes to discuss these questions. (4) Circulate to listen in and to answer students' questions as needed.

VARIATIONS AND EXPANSIONS: (1) Invite students to tell the class one thing they learned about their partners in this discussion. (2) Write these additional questions on the board for students to discuss in pairs: *What shoes do you wear to work? What shoes do you wear to school? What shoes do you wear dancing? What shoes do you wear at home? What shoes do you wear in warm weather? What shoes do you wear in cold weather?* (3) Have students copy the questions from the board and write complete-sentence answers for homework.

4. WHAT SIZE DO YOU WEAR?

SETUP: (1) Point out that this conversation uses the Conversation Tip strategy from the Preview page. (2) Set the context by pointing to the man looking at cowboy boots in the picture on page 84. (3) Have students close their books as they listen to the audio program for the first time. Then have students open their books and read along as they listen to the audio program again. Finally, play the audio a third time, pausing after each line for students to repeat chorally. (4) As students practice the conversation in pairs, circulate to give individual feedback on pronunciation.

VARIATIONS AND EXPANSIONS: (1) Have students listen to the conversation on the audio program and place dots over the stressed words (as in the conversation chants). Review the stress marks with the class. Practice the conversation chorally, paying special attention to word stress. (2) Invite pairs of students to perform the conversation for the class. (3) Have pairs of students write a shoe store conversation of their own. Have volunteer pairs perform their conversations for the class.

5. CONVERSATION CHANT: BUYING SHOES

SETUP: (1) Play the audio program. Tell students to read along as they listen to the chant. As you play the audio program, make hand motions or clap to reinforce the stress on the dotted syllables. (2) Play the audio program again, pausing after each line, and have students repeat each line. (3) Have the class chant chorally.

VARIATIONS: (1) Once students are familiar with the chant, divide the class into two groups. The indented chant lines represent a second voice. Have one group chant the lines that start at the left margin, and have the other group chant the indented lines. (**2**) Have students clap or make a hand motion to indicate where the stress falls as they chant. (**3**) Have groups switch and chant the opposite lines. (**4**) Write these questions on the board: *What kinds of shoes are comfortable? What kinds of shoes are practical? What kinds of shoes are beautiful?* Have students discuss these questions in pairs and then present their ideas to the class.

6. FIND SOMEONE WHO . . .

SETUP: (**1**) Model (or ask for volunteers to model) the questions students will need to ask. For example: *What size shoes do you wear? Do you wear shoes at home? Do you wear high heels to work?* (**2**) Have students circulate around the classroom asking and answering the questions. Tell the class they have five minutes to complete their charts. (**3**) Ask the class questions about the chart, such as "Who wears size 6 shoes?" and call on volunteers to answer.

VARIATIONS AND EXPANSIONS: (**1**) Encourage students to add one more sentence to the list. For example: _____ *wears sneakers to work.* (**2**) For homework, have students write affirmative and negative sentences about themselves using the ideas in this activity. For example: *I wear size 11 shoes. I never wear shoes at home.* (**3**) Have students choose one question and survey other students in the school hallways. Have students report their findings to the class. For example: *Four students wear size 6, and twelve students wear size 10.*

USE YOUR ENGLISH!

SETUP: Have students do this activity as a homework assignment. (**1**) To prepare students for this independent conversation, model the conversation with a volunteer, using the questions in the box. (**2**) Tell students to write down the information they learn from their conversation partners. For example: *My conversation partner shops for shoes at Shoe Barn. She recommends Shoe Barn because the prices are good.* At the beginning of the next class, students can share this information in small groups or simply hand in their reports to you.

EXPANSION: Have the class brainstorm other questions they can ask their conversation partners, such as: *What kind of shoes do you usually wear? What are your favorite shoes?*

Lesson 3: Shopping for Clothing

Pages 86–87

1. IN THE MEN'S DEPARTMENT

SET UP: (**1**) Write the phrase *men's clothing* on the board. Ask the class: "What kinds of clothing do men wear?" Write students' ideas on the board. (**2**) Have students work individually or in pairs to look at the picture and complete the matching exercise. (**3**) Go over the answers with the class. Then play the audio program, pausing between items, and have students repeat chorally. (**4**) Have the class brainstorm other vocabulary in the picture (for example: *hat, belt, bathrobe, fitting room*). Write the words on the board, and have students add the new vocabulary to the list in their books; alternatively, tell students to write at least twelve new words in their vocabulary notebooks.

VARIATIONS AND EXPANSIONS: (**1**) Say or write a word or phrase, and have students point to the item in the picture. (**2**) Point to an item in the picture, and have students say the word or phrase. (**3**) Have students work in pairs to take turns pointing and identifying items in the picture.

2. WHAT CAN THEY BUY?

SETUP: (**1**) Set the context: Two customers are in the men's department and are looking for something. (**2**) Write on the board language that students can use to complete the conversations. For example:

Salesperson: *How about these (sports jackets)? What size do you wear?*
Customer: *Can I try it on?*

(**3**) Have students work in pairs to complete the conversations. Circulate to listen in and to answer students' questions as necessary. (**4**) Have each pair choose one of their conversations to perform for the class.

EXPANSION: Write the following questions on the board: *What kind of clothing do you wear at work? What kind of clothing do you wear to a job interview? What kind of clothing do you wear at home?* Divide the class into pairs of mixed gender. Have the women interview the men and write down their partner's responses. Have them submit their writing to you for correction and comment.

3. IN THE WOMEN'S DEPARTMENT

SETUP: (**1**) Write the phrase *women's clothing* on the board. Ask the class: "What kinds of clothing do women wear?" Write their ideas on the board. (**2**) Have students work individually or in pairs to look at the picture and complete the matching exercise. (**3**) Go over the answers with the class. Point out that *panty hose* refers to the item to the right of the number 2. Panty hose are a set of stockings with panty underwear attached. *Stockings* (the items to the left of the number 2) cover only the legs and are attached to a separate garter belt. (**4**) Play the audio program, pausing between items, and have students repeat chorally. (**5**) Have the class brainstorm other vocabulary in the picture (for example: *shopping bag, sweater, dress*). Write the words on the board, and have students add the new vocabulary to the list in their books; alternatively, tell students to write at least ten new words in their vocabulary notebooks.

VARIATIONS AND EXPANSIONS: (**1**) Say or write a word or phrase, and have students point to the item in the picture. (**2**) Point to an item in the picture, and have students say the word or phrase. (**3**) Write the following questions on the board: *What kind of clothing do you wear at work? What kind of clothing do you wear to a job interview? What kind of clothing do you wear at home?* Divide the class into pairs of mixed gender. Have the men interview the women and write down their partner's responses. Have them submit their writing to you for correction and comment.

4. WHAT'S IN THE PICTURE?

SETUP: (**1**) Have students close their books and work individually to write a list of everything they remember from the picture in Exercise 3. Set a two-minute time limit for this part of the activity. (**2**) Have students work in small groups to share the items on their lists. As students share lists, have them add any new ideas. Circulate to listen in and to check students' spelling and pronunciation.

EXPANSION: Have the groups return to the picture and write down any items that are not already on their lists.

5. ROLE PLAY

SETUP: (**1**) Write on the board possible language that students can use for their clothing store conversations. For example:

> *May I help you? Yes. I'm looking for _____.*
> *What size do you wear? I wear size _____.*

> *Can I try it on? Yes. The fitting rooms are over there.*
> *How does it fit? It fits well. It doesn't fit well.*
> *How much is it? It's _____.*

(**2**) Have students work in pairs to write their conversations. Circulate around the class answering questions and correcting the writing where necessary. (**3**) Have the pairs present their role plays to the class. After each presentation, ask: "What does the customer want?" "What does the salesperson do?" and call on volunteers to answer.

VARIATIONS: (**1**) Bring props to class for students to use in their role plays (shirts, hats, a jacket, a belt, etc.). (**2**) Have students submit their written conversations to you for correction before they perform the conversations in the following class.

USE YOUR ENGLISH!

SETUP: Have students do this activity as a homework assignment. (**1**) To prepare students for this independent conversation, model the conversation with a volunteer, using the questions in the box. (**2**) Tell students to write down the information they learn from their conversation partners. For example: *My conversation partner shops for men's clothing at Target. He recommends Target because the clothes are fashionable and the prices are good.* At the beginning of the next class, students can share this information in small groups or simply hand in their reports to you.

EXPANSION: Have students visit a men's or a women's clothing store and write a list of the kinds of clothing they see. Have them report their findings to the class.

Lesson 4: Shopping for Jewelry
Pages 88–89

1. JEWELRY

SETUP: (**1**) Write the word *jewelry* on the board. Have the class brainstorm names of different kinds of jewelry. Write their ideas on the board. (**2**) Have students work individually or in pairs to look at the picture and complete the matching exercise. (**3**) Go over the answers with the class. Then play the audio program, pausing between items, and have students repeat chorally. Have the class brainstorm other vocabulary in the picture (for example: *customer, salesperson, jewelry set*). Write the words on the board, and have students add the new vocabulary to the list in their books; alternatively, tell them to write at least ten new words in their vocabulary notebooks.

VARIATIONS AND EXPANSIONS: (**1**) Say or write a word or phrase, and have students point to the item in the picture. (**2**) Point to an item in the picture, and have students say the word or phrase. (**3**) Have students in pairs take turns pointing to and identifying items in the picture. (**4**) Draw two large intersecting circles on the board. Label one circle *men* and the other circle *women*. At the intersection of the two circles, write *both*. Have students categorize the jewelry according to whether men/women/or both customarily wear it. In a multicultural setting, students can make their own charts and then compare them in small groups of mixed cultural backgrounds.

Language and Culture Notes: (**1**) Wedding bands are simple rings, usually gold, that both the husband and the wife wear on the left third finger. These rings are presented during the wedding ceremony. (**2**) An engagement ring is a fancier ring with a precious stone (as in the picture) that a woman wears from the time her engagement is announced. (**3**) In the United States, it is customary for the husband and wife to buy their wedding bands together because they both wear them. (**4**) Traditionally, men present their girlfriends with an engagement ring when they propose marriage. These days, couples will often shop for an engagement ring together (as in the picture) or forego getting an engagement ring altogether.

2. WHAT'S HAPPENING?

SETUP: (**1**) Read the questions aloud. Call on volunteers for the responses. (**2**) Write students' responses on the board in complete sentences using the correct form of the present progressive to model the correct grammar (for example: *They're shopping for a diamond ring.*).

EXPANSION: For homework, have students write a story about one of the customers in the picture on page 88 and submit it to you for correction and comment.

3. ROLE PLAY

SETUP: (**1**) Write on the board possible language that students can use for their jewelry store conversations. For example:

> *Can I help you? Yes. I'm looking for* _____.
> *Can I try it/them on? Of course!*
> *How do you like it/them? I like it/them. I love it/them!*
> *How much is it?/How much are they?*
> *It's* _____./*They're* _____.

(**2**) Have students work in groups of three to write their conversations. Circulate around the class answering questions and correcting the writing where necessary. (**3**) Have the groups present their role plays to the class. After each presentation, ask: "What do the customers want?" "What does the salesperson do?" and call on volunteers to answer.

VARIATIONS: (**1**) Bring costume jewelry to class for students to use in their role plays. (**2**) Have students submit their written conversations to you for correction before they perform the conversations in the following class.

4. WHAT'S YOUR FAVORITE PIECE OF JEWELRY?

SETUP: (**1**) Model the activity. Ask a student: "What's your favorite piece of jewelry?" and write the student's response on the board using the same template as in the book. For example: *Linda—family ring*. Then ask the student: "Why do you like it?" and take notes on the side of the template (for example: *grandmother's ring*). (**2**) Have students stand up and circulate around the classroom to take turns asking one another the questions. Set a time limit; tell students they have five minutes to complete the chart. (**3**) Have students report their findings back to the class.

EXPANSION: Have students take turns telling the class about a special piece of jewelry they have and why it is so important to them. Limit these presentations to one minute each.

5. HOW MANY?

SETUP: (**1**) Model the pronunciation of the questions for the class. (**2**) Have students work in groups of four to five to look around at their classmates and answer the questions. (**3**) Read each question aloud again and have a student from each group report on their findings. For example:

Teacher: How many classmates are wearing necklaces?
Student 1:   We think twelve classmates are wearing necklaces.
Student 2:   We think eleven classmates are wearing necklaces.

Then have all the students in the class who are wearing necklaces stand up so that the class may count them. Do the same with the rest of the questions.

EXPANSION: Make true/false statements about what jewelry students are wearing. Have students correct your false statements. For example:

Teacher: Gilmar is wearing a watch.
Student 1:   True.
Teacher: Eloisa is wearing silver earrings.
Student 2:   False! She's wearing gold earrings!

6. WHO AM I?

SETUP: (**1**) Explain the new word: *accessories* (things people wear that are not clothing, such as jewelry, belts, hats, and glasses). (**2**) Give students three minutes to compose their sentences. For example: *My clothes are black, blue, and yellow. I'm wearing silver earrings and a necklace.* (**3**) Collect the papers, mix them up, and then have each student select one. Make sure no student has received his or her own description. (**4**) Have students read the descriptions to the class. (**5**) Have the class guess who the person is.

USE YOUR ENGLISH!

SETUP: Have students do these activities as homework assignments. (**1**) To prepare students for this independent conversation, model the conversation with a volunteer, using the questions in the box. Tell students to write down the information they learn from their conversation partners. For example: *My conversation partner has a special necklace from her grandmother. She wears it only for special occasions. When she wears it, she remembers her grandmother.* At the beginning of the next class, students can hand in their reports to you. (**2**) Have students survey five other students inside or outside the school and then report their findings to the class. For example: *Three students never shop for jewelry. One student shops at Alpha*

Omega because they have nice jewelry. One student shops at the Wal-Mart because the prices are good there.

EXPANSION: Have students brainstorm other questions they can ask their conversation partners, such as *Where do you shop for jewelry? What stores do you recommend?*

Lesson 5: Sales and Advertisements
Pages 90–91

1. SALES AND ADVERTISEMENTS

SETUP: (**1**) Have students work individually or in pairs to look at the pictures and complete the matching exercise. (**2**) Go over the answers with the class. Then play the audio program, pausing between items, and have students repeat chorally.

VARIATION AND EXPANSIONS: (**1**) Check students' comprehension. Ask the following questions: "What does Rashid want to buy?" "How does he find out about the used-car sale?" "Who does he buy the car from?" "What happens to the car after he buys it?" Call on volunteers for their responses. (**2**) Have students rewrite the story on a separate piece of paper, adding more details. Write the following questions on the board to get students to think about the story details: *What day of the week is it? What kind of car does Rashid want? Why does he need to get a car? What does the car look like? What price did he pay?* An example of a partial story with more detail:

Rashid needs to buy a car for his new job. He wants to get a used car because it will be less expensive. On Saturday he gets up early to read the ads in the newspaper. He sees there is a big used-car sale. He takes the bus to the dealership. There he meets a very nice salesperson . . .

Have students share their writing in pairs and then submit it to you for correction and comment. (**3**) Have pairs of students write the conversation between Rashid and the salesperson and then perform it for the class.

Language and Culture Note: *Ad* is a common shortened version of the word *advertisement*.

2. RASHID'S MISTAKE

SETUP: Call on a volunteer to read each question aloud. Ask other volunteers to respond.

EXPANSIONS: (1) Write the following questions on the board: *Do you have a car? Is it new or used? What is a good way to buy a car?* Have students discuss the questions in pairs. (2) For homework, have students write their responses to the questions.

3. WHAT'S HAPPENING?

SETUP: (1) Set the context: One morning, Angela sees an ad in the newspaper for a clearance sale. (2) Remind students to model their story on Rashid's story in Exercise 1, using the simple present tense. (3) Divide the class into pairs. Have students look at the pictures and take turns telling Angela's story. Set a time limit of four minutes.

VARIATION AND EXPANSION: (1) In a round-robin, have students tell you the story again, this time with as many details as possible. For example:

Student 1: *One morning, Angela sees an ad in the newspaper for a clearance sale.*
Student 2: *She decides to go with her baby boy.*
Student 3: *She drives to the store.*
etc.

(2) For homework, have students write the story adding more details.

Language and Culture Note: At the end of a season or when items are no longer in fashion, stores have "clearance sales" to sell off the old inventory as quickly as possible.

4. HOW ABOUT YOU?

SETUP: (1) Model the pronunciation of the questions. (2) Have students work in pairs to take turns asking and answering the questions. (3) Set a time limit; tell students they have only five minutes to discuss these questions. (4) Circulate to listen in and to answer students' questions as necessary.

VARIATION AND EXPANSION: (1) Invite students to report what they learned about their partners. (2) Have students write down their partners' responses in complete sentences and submit them for correction.

5. A RAINCHECK

SETUP: (1) Set the context: Berta wants to buy some towels on special. (2) Have students listen to the audio program while looking at the picture. Play the audio program again while the students read along. Play the audio a third time, pausing after each sentence for students to repeat chorally. (3) As students practice the conversation in pairs, circulate to give individual feedback on pronunciation.

VARIATIONS AND EXPANSIONS: (1) Have students listen to the conversation on the audio program and place dots over the stressed words (as in the conversation chants). Review the stress marks with the class. Practice the conversation chorally, paying special attention to word stress. (2) Invite pairs of students to perform the conversation for the class. (3) To help students internalize the language, write the conversation on the board. Phrase by phrase, erase portions of the conversation and have students practice it, filling in the blanks. See to what extent you can erase the conversation with students still able to recall it.

Language and Culture Note: Most states in the United States require stores to offer rainchecks when they sell out of an item that is on sale. A raincheck is a guarantee that the customer can buy the item at the sale price even when the sale is over. The only time a raincheck is not required is when the store makes clear in the advertisement that the item on sale is available "in limited quantities."

6. WHAT'S ON SALE?

SETUP: (1) Model the pronunciation of the questions. (2) Have students ask and answer the questions in pairs. (3) Set a time limit; tell students they have only five minutes to discuss these questions. (4) Circulate to listen in and to answer students' questions as necessary.

VARIATIONS: (1) Answer the questions as a class. Ask volunteers to read each question aloud, and call on other volunteers to answer. (2) For homework, have student write their responses in complete sentences and submit their work to you for correction.

7. A YARD SALE

SETUP: (1) Set the context: The picture shows a yard sale. This family is selling old items that they no longer want or need. (2) Model the pronunciation of the questions for the class. (3) Have students ask and answer the questions in small groups of three to four. (4) Set a time limit; tell students they have only ten minutes to discuss these questions. (**5**) Circulate to listen in and to answer students' questions as necessary.

VARIATIONS: (**1**) Answer the questions as a class. Have volunteers read each question aloud, and call on other volunteers to answer. (**2**) For homework, have student write their responses in complete sentences and submit their answers to you for correction.

Language and Culture Notes: (**1**) In the United States, a yard sale is a traditional way for people to sell old and unwanted items. Yard sales are usually advertised on community bulletin boards and in the classified ads of local newspapers. Most yard sales occur on weekends. This type of sale is often referred to as a "garage sale." (**2**) When a yard/garage sale is prompted by a move, the sale is called a "moving sale."

8. CROSS-CULTURAL EXCHANGE

SETUP: (**1**) Model the pronunciation of the questions for the class. (**2**) Have students work in groups of three to four to take turns asking and answering the questions. Circulate to listen in and to answer questions as necessary. (**3**) Invite students to report what they learned in their groups. For example: *In Spain, people don't have yard sales. They give the things they don't want to people they know. In the United States, many people give things they don't want to charities like the Salvation Army.*

VARIATION AND EXPANSION: (**1**) If you have a multicultural ESOL setting, mix students from different cultural backgrounds in each group. (**2**) Have students visit various Web sites to see how people sell personal items on the Internet. Two possible sites are eBay and craigslist.

USE YOUR ENGLISH!

SETUP: Have students do this activity as a homework assignment. (**1**) To prepare students for this independent conversation, model the conversation with a volunteer, using the questions in the box. (**2**) Tell students to write down the information they learn from their conversation partners. For example: *My conversation partner likes to shop at sales. He shops at Target and Macy's because they have good sales.* At the beginning of the next class, students can share this information in small groups or simply hand in their reports to you.

EXPANSION: Have the class brainstorm other questions that students can ask their conversation partners, such as *Do you like to go to yard sales? Why or why not?*

Lesson 6: Shopping in the 21st Century
Pages 92–93

1. SHOPPING

SETUP: (**1**) Have students work individually or in pairs to look at the pictures and complete the matching exercise. (**2**) Go over the answers with the class. Then play the audio program, pausing between items, and have students repeat chorally.

VARIATIONS AND EXPANSIONS: (**1**) Say or write a word or phrase, and have students point to the item in the pictures. (**2**) Point to an item in the pictures, and have students say the word or phrase.

2. HOW DO THEY LIKE TO SHOP?

SETUP: Read each question aloud and call on volunteers to answer. Many of the questions are open-ended: Students should guess at reasons that Alice, Lena, and Robert like to shop at home. For example: *It's convenient. It's easy to compare prices. The prices are better.*

EXPANSION: Ask the class: "Is it a good idea to shop on the home-shopping channel? Why or why not?" "Is it a good idea to shop from catalogs? Why or why not?" "Is it a good idea to shop online? Why or why not?" "Is it a good idea to pay for purchases with a credit card? Why or why not?" Write students' ideas on the board so the whole class can see and remember different ideas. For example:

Shopping on the Home-Shopping Channel

<u>Good</u>	<u>Bad</u>
easy	*too easy*
more fun	*make bad decisions*

Then, for homework, have students write a response to this question: *What is the best way to shop? Why?* Have students turn in their answers to you for correction and comment.

3. HOW ABOUT YOU?

SETUP: (1) Model the pronunciation of the questions. (2) Have students take turns asking and answering the questions in pairs. (3) Set a time limit; tell students they have only ten minutes to discuss these questions. (4) Circulate to listen in and answer students' questions as necessary.

EXPANSION: Have students use these questions to interview someone outside the class. Have students write the interviewee's responses to the questions and submit the answers to you. For example:

1. *Anza shops online. She buys books and electronics online.*
2. *Anza doesn't watch a home-shopping channel.*
3. *Anza looks at catalogs. She loves the Lands' End and Shopper's World catalogs.*

4. WHAT ARE THEY SAYING?

SETUP: (1) Set the context: This is a telephone conversation between a customer-service representative and a person shopping from a catalog. (2) Have students work individually to match the questions and answers. Circulate to answer students' questions as necessary. (3) Pair students up to compare their answers.

VARIATIONS: (1) Model the questions and answers before students do the exercise. (2) After students match the questions and answers, have a pair of students perform the conversation for the class.

5. ROLE PLAY

SETUP: (1) Have students work in pairs to write their own phone conversations using the questions and answers in Exercise 4 as a model. (2) Circulate around the class answering questions and correcting students' writing where necessary. (3) Have the pairs present their role plays to the class.

VARIATIONS: (1) Bring catalogs to class for students to use in their role plays. (2) Have students submit their written conversations to you for correction before they perform the conversations in the following class.

6. A SHOPPING SURVEY

SETUP: (1) Model the pronunciation of the questions. (2) Divide the class into small groups of three or four. Have students take turns asking

and answering the questions and taking notes about their classmates' answers. Then tell students to count up their results and report them to the class. Circulate to listen in and to answer students' questions as necessary. (3) Write this model sentence on the board: *Four students often use a credit card number online.* Underline *often* and remind the class that adverbs of frequency usually come before the verb. Erase the word *often* and write in the word *sometimes*. Read the sentence aloud again. Then erase the word and write in *never* and read the new sentence aloud. (4) Read each question aloud and have a student from each group report on their response. For example:

> *Teacher:* How often do you watch the home-shopping channel?
>
> *Student 1:* In our group, two students often watch the home-shopping channel. Two students never watch the home-shopping channel.
>
> *Student 2:* In our group, all four of us never watch the home-shopping channel.

VARIATIONS AND EXPANSIONS: (1) Have students add one more question to their surveys. For example: *How often do you shop online?* (2) Have students survey five other students in the school and report their findings to the class. For example: *Four students sometimes buy clothing from catalogs. One student never buys clothing from catalogs.*

USE YOUR ENGLISH!

SETUP: Have students do this activity as a homework assignment. (1) To prepare students for this activity, have them brainstorm the numbers of the home-shopping channels in their area. (2) Tell students to write down the time and channel they watch and the items that are being sold. For example: *8:30 P.M., Channel 59. They are selling watches, necklaces, and skin cream.* At the beginning of the next class, have students share this information in small groups.

VARIATION: Lead a class discussion. Ask the class the following questions, and call on volunteers to respond: "What items does the home-shopping channel sell in the morning? In the afternoon? In the evening?" "What do you think? Are their customers different at different times of day? Who are their customers in the morning? In the afternoon? In the evening?"

Listening Practice

1. QUESTIONS AND ANSWERS

SETUP: (**1**) Tell students to read through the sentences silently. (**2**) Play the audio program. (**3**) Review the answers with the class. If there is confusion about any answers, replay the audio program.

VARIATION AND EXPANSION: (**1**) Have students first listen and then read the answers. (**2**) After finishing the whole activity, have students compose questions for the uncircled answers. (**3**) Have students listen to the audio program again and take dictation on the questions. Write the questions on the board so students can correct their sentences, or have students self-correct by referring to the Audioscript in the back of the book.

2. WHERE ARE THEY?

SETUP: (**1**) Have students first read the questions and answers. Then play the audio program. (**2**) Review the answers with the class. If there is confusion about any answers, replay the audio program.

VARIATION: Have students first listen with their books closed and then read the questions and answers.

3. PLACING AN ORDER

SETUP: (**1**) Have students first look carefully at the pictures. Point out the circled items on the catalog page for the sweater. (**2**) Play the audio program, pausing after each line to give students a few minutes to write their response before playing the next question. (**3**) When students are finished with all the questions, check answers with the whole class. Ask volunteers to read the correct sentence aloud and write it on the board. If there is any confusion about any of the answers, play the audio program again.

VARIATION: Have students take dictation on the questions, using their own paper, and then write their responses in the book after the dictation is corrected. Write the questions on the board so students can correct their dictations, or have students self-correct by referring to the Audioscript in the back of the book.

Review

1. WHAT KIND OF STORE IS IT?

SETUP: (**1**) Have the class brainstorm different kinds of stores before they compose their lists. Write their ideas on the board (for example: *drugstore, hardware store, department store*). (**2**) Have students choose one place and write three things you can buy there (for example: *shampoo, soap, medicine*). Circulate around the classroom to answer questions as necessary. (**3**) Collect the papers, mix them up, and then have each student select one. Make sure no student has received his or her own list. (**4**) Have students read the lists to the class. (**5**) Have the class guess what kind of store it is.

EXPANSION: Bring to class various advertisements and store flyers. Show students the ads. Make sure the store name is not on the paper you show the class. Have students identify the kind of store and even the store name if they can.

2. WHAT'S YOUR PARTNER WEARING?

SETUP: (**1**) Have the class brainstorm words for clothing and jewelry and for all the colors. Write their ideas on the board for reference. (**2**) Divide the class into pairs. (**3**) Tell students they have fifteen seconds to look at their partners. (**4**) Have pairs sit back-to-back and write a list of what their partners are wearing. Encourage students to write details about the clothing and accessories such as their color and material. (**5**) After two minutes, have students turn around and compare their lists to what they see.

VARIATION: Walk behind the class so no one can see you and ask the class: "What am I wearing today?" Have students describe what you are wearing. Have students take turns standing behind the class while the rest of them try to remember details about their clothes and jewelry.

3. WHAT DO PEOPLE WEAR?

SETUP: (**1**) Model the questions for the class. (**2**) Divide the class into small groups of three or four. Circulate around the class to listen in and to answer questions as necessary. Encourage students to list more than three items in each category. (**3**) Read each question aloud and have a student from each group report on the group's response. For example:

Teacher: What do women wear?
Student 1: Dresses, skirts, blouses.
Student 2: High heels.

Write students' idea on the board to make a master list for each category.

VARIATION: In a multicultural ESOL classroom, group students according to their cultural background. When students share their lists, draw contrasts in the differing cultural responses.

4. SHOPPING

SETUP: (1) Have students work in pairs to complete the conversations. Circulate around the class answering questions and correcting the writing where necessary. (2) Pair up the pairs so that students work in groups of four. Have the two pairs in each group take turns presenting their role plays.

Assessment

Page 96

PART 1: QUESTIONS

SETUP: Have students work individually to write the questions. Challenge students not to look at the previous lessons but to construct their questions from memory.

VARIATION: Have students write their questions on a separate sheet of paper to hand in to you for correction at the end of the assessment.

PART 2: SPEAKING

SETUP: (1) Divide the class into pairs, and have students take turns asking and answering their questions. (2) Circulate to listen in and to answer students' questions as necessary.

VARIATION: Have students write their partners' responses to their questions and hand them in for correction at the end of the assessment.

PART 3: LISTENING

SETUP: (1) Have students first read the answers silently. Then play the audio program. (2) Check answers with the whole class by asking volunteers to read the correct sentence aloud. If there is any confusion about any of the answers, replay the audio program.

VARIATIONS AND EXPANSION: (1) Have students write the number of the question and the letter of their response on a separate sheet to hand in to you for correction at the end of the assessment. (2) The class can also review the answers together. (3) As an added challenge, have students compose questions for the uncircled answers.

PART 4: WRITING

SETUP: (1) Set the context by asking students: "What is happening in each picture?" Lead a brief brainstorming session about what the people in the pictures could be saying. (2) Have students work individually to write their conversations. Circulate as students are writing to answer questions as necessary.

VARIATIONS: (1) Have students write their conversations on a separate piece of paper to hand in to you for correction. (2) Have students share their conversations with a partner. Then ask volunteer pairs to perform one of their conversations for the class.

Preview

Page 97

PREVIEW QUESTIONS

SETUP: (**1**) Have the class look at the photographs. Read each question aloud, and call on individual students to respond. (**2**) Write students' responses on the board so they can see the various possible responses. For example:

1. *First picture: Maybe they're at the beach. Second picture: Maybe they're on the street.*
2. *It's warm and sunny in the first picture. It's cold and snowy in the second picture.*
3. *It depends on where the picture was taken. In New York, it's probably June or July in the first picture. In New York, it's probably December or January in the second picture.*
4. *It's spring or summer in the first picture. It's winter in the second picture.*

CONVERSATION TIP

SETUP: (**1**) Explain that in English it is common and appropriate to give extra information when answering a question. (**2**) Have students read the conversations silently. (**3**) Model the conversations with a volunteer. (**4**) These conversations introduce students to the simple past tense and the future with *will*. Write the verb *bought* on the board and label it as *simple past.* Ask the class: "What is the present form of *bought?*" Write *buy* next to *bought.* Explain that this is the simple past form of the irregular verb *buy.* Write the question *Will you be home tonight?* on the board. Under the question, write the responses *Yes, I will* and *No, I won't.* Underline the verbs in all three sentences and explain that this is the simple future tense. (**5**) Have students practice the conversations in pairs. (**6**) Circulate to correct pronunciation.

EXPANSION: (**1**) Prompt students with other questions. Have students answer the question and then give extra information. For example:

Teacher: Where are you from, Chang?
Student 1: I'm from Jinan, China. It's a city in the north.

Teacher: Do you like living here, Rupinder?
Student 2: Yes, I do. I like the opportunities here.

(**2**) Have students work in pairs to practice the conversations with their own information.

CONVERSATION CHANT: A SURPRISE PARTY

SETUP: (**1**) The dots over the words indicate where the stress falls. As you play the audio program, make hand motions or clap to reinforce the stress on the dotted syllables. (**2**) Have students listen once through as they read along. (**3**) Play the audio program again, pausing after each line, and have students repeat. (**4**) Have the class chant chorally.

VARIATIONS AND EXPANSIONS: (**1**) Have students clap or make a hand motion to indicate where the stress falls as they chant. (**2**) Have groups switch and chant the opposite lines.

Lesson 1: Months, Years, and Birthdays

Pages 98–99

1. MONTHS AND YEARS

SETUP: (**1**) Have students read along as they listen to the audio program. Play the audio program again, pausing after each line so students can repeat chorally. (**2**) Review numbers on page 169. Have the class chorally count the numbers 1–20, 30, 40, 50, 60, 70, 80, 90, and 100. (**3**) Review how to read years. Explain that between 1000 and 2000, the years are read in two digits (for example: *1492—fourteen ninety-two; 1776—seventeen seventy-six; 1999—nineteen-ninety-nine*). The convention for the current millennium is to say "two thousand" (for example: *2009—two thousand and nine*). (**3**) Call on a volunteer to read each question aloud. Ask individual students to respond.

VARIATION: Before students ask and answer the questions, have them focus on the verb tenses. Have them underline the verb in each question. Then write the past, present, and future forms of the verb *to be* on the board.

Past	_Present_	_Future_
I was	_I am_	_I will be_
You were	_You are_	_You will be_
He/She/It was	_He/She/It is_	_He/She/It will be_
We were	_We are_	_We will be_
They were	_They are_	_They will be_

Read the verb forms aloud and have the class listen and repeat.

2. WHEN'S YOUR BIRTHDAY?

SETUP: (**1**) Go over the way to say dates in English. Explain that ordinal numbers are used in dates (for example: _March 2nd, October 23rd_). Tell the class to turn to the list of ordinal numbers on page 169 in their books. Read the numbers aloud and have students repeat chorally. (**2**) Set the context: Two friends are talking about their birthdays. (**3**) Have students close their books as they listen to the audio program for the first time. Then have students open their books and read along as they listen to the audio program again. Finally, play the audio again, pausing after each line so students can repeat chorally. (**4**) As students practice the conversation in pairs, circulate to give individual feedback on pronunciation.

VARIATIONS AND EXPANSIONS: (**1**) Have students listen to the conversation on the audio program and place dots over the stressed syllable (as in the conversation chants). Review the stress marks with the class. Practice the conversation chorally, paying special attention to word stress. (**2**) Invite pairs of students to act out the conversation for the class. (**3**) Pass out blank cards to pairs of students. Have students write each line from the conversation on a different card. Have the pairs mix up their cards and then put them in order again. (**4**) Give students additional chances to practice listening to and saying dates. Show the class a calendar. Say a date and have students write down the date they hear. Write the date on the board for students to check their answers. Once students seem able to correctly identify dates, have them take turns calling out a date and having their classmates write down the date they hear. Provide correction by writing the date on the board.

3. HOW OLD . . . ?

SETUP: Call on a volunteer to read each question aloud. As a class, discuss the answers.

VARIATIONS AND EXPANSIONS: (**1**) Review the present and future forms of _to be_. Write the forms on the board:

Present	_Future_
she is	_she will be_
_it is_	_it will be_

Have students refer to the forms of _be_ as they answer the questions. (**2**) Write these questions on the board: _When's your birthday? What year were you born?_ Have students ask and answer the questions in pairs. Tell students that this information is often considered private; they can make up the information or they can reply with "I'd rather not say." (**3**) For homework, have students write their answers to the questions.

4. HARRY'S SURPRISE PARTY

SETUP: (**1**) Have students work individually or in pairs to look at the picture and complete the matching exercise. (**2**) Go over the answers with the class. Then play the audio program, pausing between items, and have students repeat chorally. (**3**) With the class, brainstorm other vocabulary in the pictures (for example: _excited, nervous, balloons_). Write the words on the board, and have students add the new vocabulary to the list in their books; alternatively, tell students to write at least ten new words in their vocabulary notebooks.

VARIATIONS AND EXPANSIONS: (**1**) Say or write a word or phrase, and have students point to the picture. (**2**) Point to the picture, and have students say the word or phrase. (**3**) Have students work in pairs to take turns pointing to and identifying items in the picture. (**4**) Ask the class: "What kind of party is this?" (Answer: _It's a surprise birthday party._)

5. WHAT'S HAPPENING?

SETUP: (**1**) Set the context by pointing to the picture in Exercise 4. (**2**) Have students close their books as they listen to the audio program for the first time. Then have students open their books and read along as they listen to the audio program again. Finally, play the audio a third time, pausing after each line for students to repeat chorally. (**3**) Divide the class into groups of three. Have one student read the first "Friends" line, another student read the "Harry" line, and the third student read the next "Friends" line. (**4**) As students practice the conversation, circulate to give individual feedback on pronunciation.

VARIATIONS AND EXPANSIONS: (**1**) Have students listen to the conversation on the audio program and place dots over the stressed words (as in the conversation chants). Review the stress marks with the class. Practice the conversation chorally, paying special attention to word stress. (**2**) Invite groups of students to perform the conversation for the class.

6. HOW ABOUT YOU?

SETUP: (**1**) Point out that this is an opportunity to practice the Conversation Tip in the Preview on page 97. Encourage students to give extra information when they answer the questions. (**2**) Model the pronunciation of the questions. (**3**) Have students work in pairs to take turns asking and answering the questions. (**4**) Set a time limit; tell students they have only ten minutes to discuss these questions. (**5**) Circulate to listen in and to answer students' questions as necessary.

VARIATIONS AND EXPANSIONS: (**1**) Invite students to tell the class one thing they learned about their partners. (**2**) Take notes as students talk in pairs. Then write incomplete sentences on the board, and have students circulate to ask one another questions to find out whose name completes each sentence. For example:

_____ *doesn't like birthday parties.*
_____ *was in New York last year on her birthday.*
_____ *likes to eat dinner with his family on his birthday.*

(**3**) If you are in a monocultural classroom, change question 4 to read *How does your family celebrate birthdays?* (**4**) In a multicultural classroom, invite students to sing their customary birthday song to the class.

LANGUAGE AND CULTURE NOTE: In the United States, family and friends present the birthday person with a cake as they sing "Happy Birthday to You!" On the cake, there is usually a candle representing each year the person has lived—and sometimes one extra candle for good luck. The person blows the candles out as he/she makes a secret wish. The friends and family then applaud.

7. MAKE A BIRTHDAY CARD!

SETUP: (**1**) Distribute one slip of paper to each student. (**2**) Have students write their names on the papers. (**3**) Collect the papers, mix them up, and then have each student select one. Make sure no student has received his or her own name. (**4**) Have the class

brainstorm common phrases on birthday cards as you write their ideas on the board. For example: *Happy Birthday! Many happy returns! A birthday wish for you.* (**5**) Distribute paper and colored pencils or markers for students to use to make their birthday cards. (**6**) Set a time limit; tell students they have only ten minutes to make their cards. (**7**) Have students give their cards to one another.

VARIATIONS AND EXPANSION: (**1**) Have students make their birthday cards for homework. (**2**) Suggest that students look at birthday cards on the Internet to get ideas or even compose a birthday card using a "make your own card" Web site. (**3**) Bring old birthday cards (or printed-out Internet birthday cards) to class for students to read before they make their own cards.

USE YOUR ENGLISH!

SETUP: Have students do this activity as a homework assignment. (**1**) To prepare students for this independent conversation, have the class brainstorm places to buy birthday cards. Write students' ideas on the board. (**2**) Tell students to write down what they said in their conversations with their conversation partners. For example: *I usually buy birthday cards at the stationery store in the mall.* At the beginning of the next class, students can share this information in small groups.

EXPANSION: Have the class brainstorm questions that they can ask their conversation partners. For example: *When's your birthday? What do you like to do on your birthday? Where were you last year on your birthday? Where do you buy birthday cards?*

Lesson 2: Dates and Holidays

Pages 100–101

1. HOLIDAYS IN THE UNITED STATES

SETUP: (**1**) Write *Holidays in the United States* on the board. Have the class brainstorm the names of American holidays. Write their ideas on the board. (**2**) Model the pronunciation of the holidays and have students repeat chorally. (**3**) Have students work individually or in pairs to look at the pictures and complete the matching exercise. (**4**) Go over the answers with the class. Then play the audio program, pausing after each item, and have students repeat chorally. (**5**) With the class, brainstorm other vocabulary in the pictures (for example: *kiss, march, pray, give*). Write the words on the board, and have students add the new vocabulary to the list in their books; alternatively, tell students to write at least twelve new words in their vocabulary notebooks.

VARIATIONS AND EXPANSIONS: (**1**) Say or write a word or phrase, and have students point to the picture. (**2**) Point to a picture, and have students say the word or phrase. (**3**) Have students work in pairs to take turns pointing to and identifying items in the pictures.

Language and Culture Notes:
- **New Year's Eve** is December 31. It is customarily celebrated at a large party with dancing and champagne. People "count down" the last seconds of the old year and then blow noise makers and kiss one another at midnight, saying "Happy New Year!"
- **Valentine's Day** is celebrated on February 14. Saint Valentine is the patron saint of romantic love. It is customary for men to give women flowers or chocolates. In schools, children give one another small cards called valentines.
- **Independence Day** is celebrated July 4. In 1776, on July 4, the English colonists declared independence from England. After that declaration, the colonists fought in the revolutionary war of independence until 1783. The holiday is celebrated with parades, displays of patriotism (American flags), and fireworks in the evening.
- **Halloween** is celebrated on the evening of October 31. Children dress up in *costume*s and go knocking on neighbors' doors. When the neighbor opens the door, the children say "Trick or treat!" Customarily, children receive candy or coins.
- **Thanksgiving** is celebrated on the fourth Thursday of November. It commemorates a harvest dinner shared between the early colonial settlers and the Native Americans. The traditional food for this meal includes turkey, potatoes, stuffing, sweet potatoes, and cranberry sauce.
- **Christmas** is celebrated December 25. It is a Christian holiday that celebrates the birth of Jesus. Children believe that Santa Claus (or Saint Nick) travels the world on Christmas Eve (the night of December 24) to distribute gifts to children. He flies

through the sky on a snow sleigh pulled by flying reindeer. He lands on rooftops and enters houses through their chimneys. He stuffs children's stockings hanging by the fireplace with small gifts and peppermint candy canes. He may leave additional gifts under the family Christmas tree.

2. CELEBRATING HOLIDAYS

SETUP: Call on a volunteer to read each question aloud. As a class, discuss the answers. If students are unfamiliar with American holidays, you can use the Language and Culture notes for Exercise 1 to answer any questions that may come up.

VARIATIONS AND EXPANSIONS: (**1**) Have students ask and answer questions 3 and 4 in pairs. Circulate to listen in and to answer questions as necessary. (**2**) Write this additional question on the board for the class discussion: *What other holidays are celebrated in the United States?* Possible answers:

Memorial Day: to remember those who died in war. It is celebrated on the last Monday of May.
Veterans Day: to remember those who served in war. It is celebrated November 11.

(**3**) For homework, have students write a report on one holiday that they celebrate. In their writing, have them answer the following questions: *What is the name of the holiday? When is it? How do people in your country celebrate it?* Have students submit their writing to you for correction and comment.

Language and Culture Note: The calendar dates of some holidays vary from year to year. Thanksgiving is celebrated on the fourth Thursday of November, so its calendar date varies. The following holidays are officially celebrated on Mondays so that workers may enjoy a three-day weekend.

Martin Luther King Day (third Monday in January)
Presidents' Day (third Monday in February)
Memorial Day (last Monday in May)
Labor Day (first Monday in September)
Columbus Day (second Monday in October)

3. HOLIDAY GREETINGS

SETUP: (**1**) Have students work in pairs to write the holiday names next to the greetings. (**2**) Circulate to listen in and to answer students' questions as necessary. (**3**) Have the pairs add two more holidays celebrated in the United States and the greetings associated with those holidays. If students aren't familiar with other holidays celebrated in the United States, you can supply them with additional ideas. For example:

Christmas: *Merry Christmas! Happy Holidays!*
Hanukkah: *Happy Hanukkah! Happy Holidays!*
Happy Saint Patrick's Day: *Happy Saint Patty's Day!*

(**4**) Invite students to report their answers to the class.

EXPANSION: Have pairs of students choose a holiday celebrated in the United States and research it on the Internet. Have each pair give a five-minute report to the class about the holiday. Make sure they answer the following questions:

What is the name of the holiday?
When is it?
How do people celebrate it?

4. FAVORITE HOLIDAYS

SETUP: (**1**) Model the questions that students will need to ask to gather the information for their charts. For example: *What's your favorite holiday? What's your favorite holiday food? What's your favorite holiday activity?* (**2**) You may want to provide students with additional support by giving possible answers to question 3, using gerunds, and writing them on the board. For example:

What's your favorite holiday activity? Eating. Singing. Giving presents.

Point out the *-ing* form of the verbs. Encourage students to use this form in their answers about their favorite holiday activities. (**3**) Divide the class into groups of four. Have students work in their groups to take turns asking and answering questions and filling in the chart. (**4**) Ask the class: "What's your favorite holiday?" and have a spokesperson from each group answer. Ask about the other details in a similar fashion.

EXPANSION: Have students survey four other students in the school and report their findings to the class.

5. HOLIDAY SONGS AND GREETINGS

SETUP: (**1**) Write the phrase *Happy New Year* on the board. Ask the class: "How do you say this in your language?" (**2**) Call on volunteers to teach the class the phrase in their native language. Have the class repeat after the student chorally. If you have a monocultural classroom, skip this part of the activity. (**3**) Invite students to volunteer to sing one of

their favorite holiday songs in their native language. If other students know the song, encourage them to join in.

VARIATIONS AND EXPANSIONS: (**1**) For homework, have students translate several lines of a favorite holiday song from their native language into English. Have students teach their translated lines to the class. (**2**) Play popular American holiday songs, such as "America the Beautiful" (Fourth of July), "Dreidel, Dreidel, Dreidel!" (Hanukkah), "Jingle Bells" (Christmas), and "Auld lang syne" (New Year's Eve). You can download these songs from the Internet. Have students listen and identify the holiday that corresponds to the song.

6. WHAT'S THE HOLIDAY?

SETUP: (**1**) Have students brainstorm different holidays. Write their ideas on the board. (**2**) Have students choose one holiday and write about its food, activity, or a common greeting on a slip of paper. (**3**) Circulate around the classroom to answer questions as necessary. (**4**) Collect the papers, mix them up, and then have each student select one. Make sure no student has received his or her own paper. (**5**) Have students read the writing to the class. (**6**) Have the class guess the holiday that it belongs to.

EXPANSION: Have students write three things about the holiday: a food, an activity, and a greeting.

USE YOUR ENGLISH!

SETUP: Have students do this activity as a homework assignment. (**1**) To prepare students for this independent activity, brainstorm with the class how they can find this information (for example: doing an Internet search on "national holidays," looking at a calendar). (**2**) Write students' ideas on the board. (**3**) Tell students to write down the information they learn with their conversation partners. At the beginning of the next class, students can share this information in small groups or simply hand in their reports to you.

Culture Notes: (**1**) The legal national holidays that are observed by U.S. government offices are:

New Year's Day (January 1)
Martin Luther King Day (third Monday in January)
Presidents' Day (third Monday in February)
Memorial Day (last Monday in May)
Independence Day (July 4)

Labor Day (first Monday in September)
Columbus Day (second Monday in October)
Veterans' Day (November 11 every year)
Thanksgiving Day (fourth Thursday in November)
Christmas Day (December 25)

(**2**) States sometimes observe local holidays. For example: The state governments of Massachusetts and Maine celebrate Patriots Day (April 17). This is not a holiday in other states.

Lesson 3: Weather Report

Pages 102–103

1. THE WEATHER

SETUP: (**1**) Have students work individually or in pairs to look at the picture and complete the matching exercise. (**2**) Go over the answers with the class. Then play the audio program, pausing between items, and have students repeat chorally. (**3**) With the class, brainstorm other vocabulary in the picture (for example: *storm, thunder*). Write the words on the board, and have students add the new vocabulary to the list in their books; alternatively, tell students to write at least twelve new words in their vocabulary notebooks.

VARIATIONS AND EXPANSIONS: (**1**) Say or write a word, and have students point to the item in the picture. (**2**) Point to an item in the picture, and have students say the word. (**3**) Have students work in pairs to take turns pointing to and identifying items in the picture.

Language Note: A meteorologist is often known as a "weatherman" (or "weatherwoman") or a "weather forecaster."

2. THE WEATHER REPORT

SETUP: (**1**) Draw an X on the board and label the four points *North, East, South*, and *West*. Then add the intermediary lines and write the intermediary directions of *Northeast, Southeast, Southwest*, and *Northwest*. Model the pronunciation of these new words. (**2**) Test students' ability to locate intermediary directions on a map. Point to areas on the map on page 102 and ask students: "What is this?" (Answer: *That's the Northeast.*) (**3**) Call on

a volunteer to read each question aloud. Call on other volunteers for their responses.

VARIATION AND EXPANSION: (**1**) Before the class asks and answers the questions, write the following forms of the verb *to be* on the board for students' reference. For example:

Past	*Present*	*Future*
it was	*it's*	*it will be*

(**2**) Photocopy today's newspaper weather map, and distribute the maps in class. Have students work in pairs to read the weather map and write today's weather forecast for different sections of the country. Have students submit their writing to you for correction and comment.

3. CELSIUS OR FAHRENHEIT?

SETUP: (**1**) Read the boxed information aloud to the class. For example: "To change from Celsius to Fahrenheit, use this equation: Fahrenheit equals nine-fifths times the Celsius temperature, plus 32. In the first example, you want to know how much 20 degrees Celsius is in Fahrenheit."

- Write the math problem on the board, and use the appropriate mathematical language to explain it: "20 times nine-fifths equals 36. 36 plus 32 equals 68 degrees Fahrenheit."
- "To change from Fahrenheit to Celsius, use this equation: Celsius equals five-ninths times the Fahrenheit temperature, minus 32. In the second example, you want to find out how much 68 degrees Fahrenheit is in Celsius."
- Write the math problem on the board, and use the appropriate mathematical language to explain it. "68 minus 32 equals 36. And 36 times five-ninths equals 20."

(**2**) Have students work individually to answer the questions. (**3**) Circulate to answer students' questions as necessary. (**4**) Divide the class into small groups of three or four, and have students compare their answers. (**5**) Invite students to share their answers with the class.

VARIATION: If the math is too complicated to tackle in your class, skip questions 1 and 2 and instead write the following conversion chart on the board and ask students questions, such as "If it's 25 degrees Celsius, what is the Fahrenheit temperature?" Then have students continue working in small groups to ask and answer questions 3 and 4.

Degrees Celsius	Degrees Fahrenheit
40	104
35	95
30	86
25	77
20	68
15	59
10	50
0	32
−5	23
−10	14
−15	5
−20	−4
−25	−13

4. TOMORROW'S WEATHER FORECAST

SETUP: (**1**) Set the context: A meteorologist is giving the weather report. (**2**) Have students close their books as they listen to the audio program for the first time. Then have students open their books and read along as they listen to the audio program again. Finally, play the audio a third time, pausing after each line for students to repeat chorally. (**3**) Ask: "Are they having nice weather?" (**4**) Have students work in pairs and take turns reading the forecast aloud. (**5**) Circulate to give individual feedback on pronunciation.

VARIATIONS: When the pairs are finished, ask a student to read the weather forecast aloud for the class.

5. ROLE PLAY

SETUP: (**1**) Write various dates on the board, making sure to spread the dates throughout the year so students can describe a range of weather. For example: *January 10, March 23, June 30, August 5, October 4, December 1.* (**2**) Have each student choose a date and work individually to prepare his or her own weather forecasts. (**3**) Circulate, answering questions and correcting students' writing where necessary. (**4**) Invite students to the front to present their weather forecasts to the class. Make sure they write the date for the forecast before they begin.

VARIATIONS: (**1**) Instead of having students present in front of the whole class, have them present their role plays in small groups of three or four. Circulate to give feedback. (**2**) Have students submit their written conversations to you for correction before they present their weather forecasts in the following class.

USE YOUR ENGLISH!

SETUP: (**1**) To prepare students for this independent activity, ask the class: "What TV channels give weather reports? At what times?" Write students' ideas on the board. Have each student choose a channel and time to watch the weather report. (**2**) Tell students to write down the information they learn. For example: *Tomorrow will be cold and snowy. The high temperature will be 30 degrees Fahrenheit.* At the beginning of the next class, students can share this information in small groups or simply hand in their reports to you.

Lesson 4: Good and Bad Weather

Pages 104–105

1. WEATHER

SETUP: (**1**) Have students work individually or in pairs to look at the pictures and complete the matching exercise. (**2**) Go over the answers with the class. Then play the audio program, pausing between items, and have students repeat chorally. (**3**) With the class, brainstorm other vocabulary in the pictures (for example: *dry, hot, wet*). Write the vocabulary on the board, and have students add the words to the list in their books; alternatively, tell students to write at least twelve new words and phrases in their vocabulary notebooks.

VARIATIONS AND EXPANSIONS: (**1**) Say or write a word, and have students point to the picture. (**2**) Point to a picture, and have students say the word. (**3**) Have students work in pairs to take turns pointing to and identifying items in the pictures.

2. WHAT'S HAPPENING IN THE PICTURES?

SETUP: (**1**) Have students work in pairs to look at the pictures and complete the matching exercise. (**2**) Go over the answers with the class.

VARIATIONS AND EXPANSIONS: (**1**) Have students write an additional sentence for each picture and share it with the class or submit it to you for correction and comment. For example: *A Sunny Day: The sun is shining. A man is lying under a tree. It's a perfect summer day.* (**2**) Bring in pictures of people in different weather conditions, and distribute them to pairs of students. Have students write a title and a description of their picture. Then place all the pictures at the front of the room, and invite each pair of students to read their description. Have the class listen and then identify the picture that was described.

3. GOOD WEATHER / BAD WEATHER

SETUP: (**1**) Point out that this is an opportunity to practice the Conversation Tip from the Preview page on page 97. Encourage students to give extra information when they answer one another's questions. (**2**) Model the questions for the class, and have students listen and repeat. (**3**) Have students work in pairs to take turns asking and answering the questions. (**4**) Circulate to listen in and to answer students' questions as necessary.

VARIATIONS AND EXPANSIONS: (**1**) Tell students to write a brief report on their partners' responses and submit it to you for correction. (**2**) For homework, have students write responses to the questions and submit their writing to you for correction.

4. FIND SOMEONE WHO . . .

SETUP: (**1**) Ask volunteers to model the questions that students will need to ask. For example: *Do you like snowy days? Do you like to read on rainy days? Do you like to be outside in all kinds of weather?* (**2**) Have students walk around the room asking and answering the questions. Tell the class they have five minutes to complete their charts. (**3**) Have students report their information to the class.

VARIATIONS AND EXPANSIONS: (**1**) Encourage students to add one more sentence to the list. For example: _____ *likes to take long walks on snowy days.* (**2**) For homework, have students write affirmative and negative sentences about themselves using the ideas in this activity. For example: *I don't like snowy days. I like to read on rainy days.* (**3**) Have students choose one question, survey twenty other students in the school, and then report their findings to the class. For example: *Six students like snowy days, and fourteen don't.*

5. CONVERSATION CHANT: SAILORS LOVE THE WIND

SETUP: (**1**) Introduce the new vocabulary: *sailor* and *sail.* Draw a sailboat on the board and a stick figure

of a sailor. Point to the sail and say: "This is a sail." Point to the sailor and say: "This is a sailor." (**2**) Play the audio program. Tell students to read along as they listen to the chant. As you play the audio program, make hand motions or clap to reinforce the stress on the dotted syllables. (**3**) Play the audio again, pausing after each line, and have students repeat. (**4**) Have the class chant chorally.

USE YOUR ENGLISH!

SETUP: Have students do this activity as a homework assignment. (**1**) To prepare students for this independent activity, have them brainstorm ways they can find out about the weather in other countries (in the newspaper, on the Internet). Write their ideas on the board. (**2**) Tell students to write down the names of two or three countries—or even the names of two or three regions—that have similar weather to their own location. For example: *Texas and southern Italy have the same weather as Spain.* At the beginning of the next class, students can share this information in small groups or simply hand in their reports to you.

Lesson 5: The Seasons

Pages 106–107

1. THE SEASONS

SETUP: (**1**) Have students work individually or in pairs to look at the pictures and complete the matching exercise. (**2**) Go over the answers with the class. Then play the audio program, pausing between items, and have students repeat chorally. (**3**) Have the class brainstorm other vocabulary in the pictures (for example: *leaves, waves, make a snowman, sunbathe*). Write the words and phrases on the board, and have students add the new vocabulary to the list in their books; alternatively, tell students to write at least ten new words and phrases in their vocabulary notebooks.

VARIATIONS AND EXPANSIONS: (**1**) Say or write a word or phrase, and have students point to the picture. (**2**) Point to an item in a picture, and have students say the word or phrase. (**3**) Have students work in pairs to take turns pointing to and identifying items and actions in the pictures. (**4**) Make false statements about the pictures, and have students correct you. For example:

Teacher: *They're raking leaves in the spring.*
Student: *No, that's not right. They're raking leaves in the fall.*

2. SPRING, SUMMER, FALL, WINTER

SETUP: (**1**) Call on students to read each question aloud, and ask other volunteers to answer it. (**2**) If students come up with new vocabulary, write the words on the board and have students add the new words to the list in their books or in their vocabulary notebooks. (**3**) Point out that question 2 is in the present progressive tense, so the response also should be in the present progressive. For example:

> *In the spring picture, they're planting a new garden. In the summer picture, people are playing volleyball.*

EXPANSION: Have pairs of students write a paragraph describing one of the pictures in Exercise 1. Then invite the pairs to read their descriptions to the class. Have the class listen and identify the picture being described.

3. HOW ABOUT YOU?

SETUP: (**1**) Model the questions for the class. (**2**) For questions 1 and 5, explain that some countries have only two seasons a year: a dry season and a rainy season. If your students currently live in their native country, skip question 5. (**3**) Have students work in pairs to take turns asking and answering the questions. (**4**) Set a time limit; tell students they have ten minutes to discuss the questions. (**5**) Circulate to give individual feedback on pronunciation and to answer students' questions as necessary.

VARIATION: For homework, have students write responses to the questions and submit their writing to you for correction and comment.

4. FIND SOMEONE WHO . . .

SETUP: (**1**) Model (or have volunteers model) the questions that students will need to ask. For example: *Do you rake leaves in the fall? Do you like to plant a garden in the spring? Do you go to the beach in the summer?* (**2**) Have students walk around the room asking and answering the questions. Tell the class they have seven minutes

to complete their charts. (**3**) Have students report their information to the class.

VARIATIONS AND EXPANSIONS: (**1**) Encourage students to add one more sentence to the list. For example: _____ *likes to drive in the snow.* (**2**) For homework, have students write affirmative and negative sentences about themselves using the ideas in this activity. For example: *I never rake leaves in the fall. I like to plant a garden in the spring.* (**3**) Have students choose one question, survey twenty other students in the school, and then report their findings to the class. For example: *Eleven students go to the beach in the summer, and nine don't.*

5. HOW ABOUT YOU?

SETUP: (**1**) Point out that this is an opportunity to practice the Conversation Tip from the Preview on page 97. Encourage students to give extra information when they answer one another's questions. (**2**) Model the questions for the class. (**3**) Have students work in pairs to take turns asking and answering the questions. (**4**) Set a time limit; tell students they have ten minutes to discuss the questions. (**5**) Circulate to give individual feedback on pronunciation and to answer students' questions as necessary.

VARIATIONS AND EXPANSIONS: (**1**) For student reference, write the following skeletal responses:

1. *I like _____.*
2. *I was born in _____. I like/don't like _____.*
3. *Last _____ I was _____.*
4. *I like to eat _____ in the _____. I like to drink _____ in the _____.*

(**2**) Invite students to report what they learned about their partners. For example: *Lee likes the leaves and wind in fall. He was born in the winter. He doesn't like the winter.*

6. YOUR FAVORITE SEASON

SETUP: (**1**) Copy the chart onto the board. Have a student ask you the two questions, and give your response. For example: *Summer is my favorite season. I like to go to the beach.* Have the student fill in the chart on the board in note form. For example:

Name	Favorite Season	Why?
Mrs. King	summer	likes to go to the beach

(2) Have students circulate around the room to ask four classmates the questions. Set a time limit; tell students they have five minutes to complete the chart. **(3)** Circulate to listen in and to answer students' questions as necessary.

VARIATIONS AND EXPANSION: (1) Ask the class: "How many students like winter/spring/summer/fall best?" Count the raised hands and write the number on the board each time. **(2)** With the class, brainstorm the good and bad of each season. Ask the class: "What's good about winter?" "What's bad about winter?" Write their ideas in two columns on the board. For example: ***Good****: It's not so busy.* ***Bad****: Heating my home is expensive.* Repeat this procedure by asking questions about spring, summer, and fall. **(3)** For homework, have students write a paragraph about their favorite season of the year, saying why they like it best.

USE YOUR ENGLISH!

SETUP: Have students do this activity as a homework assignment. **(1)** To prepare students for this independent conversation, model the conversation with a student, using the questions in the box. **(2)** Tell students to write down the information they learn from their conversation partners. For example: *My conversation partner plays soccer in the spring. He goes to the beach in the summer. In the fall, he goes to the mountains. In the winter, he shovels snow.* At the beginning of the next class, students can hand in their reports to you.

EXPANSION: Have the class brainstorm other questions they can ask their conversation partners. For example: *What's your favorite season? Why? What season were you born in? Where were you last spring? Last summer? Last fall? Last winter?*

Lesson 6: Taking a Trip

Pages 108–109

1. TAKING A TRIP

SETUP: (1) Ask the class: "What do you take with you on a trip?" Write their ideas on the board (for example: *a camera, a map, a suitcase*). **(2)** Have students work individually or in pairs to look at the picture and complete the matching exercise. **(3)** Go

over the answers with the class. Then play the audio program, pausing between items, and have students repeat chorally. **(4)** Have the class brainstorm other vocabulary in the picture (for example: *bathing suit, T-shirts*). Write the words on the board, and have students add the new vocabulary to the list in their books; alternatively, tell students to write at least ten new words or phrases in their vocabulary notebooks.

VARIATIONS AND EXPANSIONS: (1) Say or write a word or phrase, and have students point to the item in the picture. **(2)** Point to an item in the picture, and have students say the word or phrase. **(3)** Have students work in pairs to take turns pointing to and identifying items in the picture.

2. WHAT'S IN THE PICTURE?

SETUP: Call on volunteers to read each question aloud. Discuss the answers with the class. For example:

1. *She's packing a camera, film, a passport, a sun hat, and sunscreen.*
2. *She's traveling by plane. I know because she has a plane ticket.*
3. *I think she's going to Tahiti because she's packing beach clothes and a passport.*

VARIATIONS: (1) Have students ask and answer the questions in pairs. **(2)** For homework, have students write their answers to the questions.

3. WHAT ARE THEY SAYING?

SETUP: (1) Set the context: Yumiko is talking about her trip. **(2)** Teach the meaning of the new phrase *go sightseeing* (*to travel around and see the important places in a city or country*). **(3)** Have students close their books as they listen to the audio program for the first time. Then have students open their books and read along as they listen to the audio program again. Finally, play the program a third time, pausing after each line for students to repeat chorally. **(4)** As students practice the conversation in pairs, circulate to give individual feedback on pronunciation.

VARIATIONS: (1) Have students listen to the conversation on the audio program and place dots over the stressed words (as in the conversation chants). Review the stress marks with the class. Practice the conversation chorally, paying special attention to word stress. **(2)** Invite two students to perform the conversation for the class. **(3)** Write the conversation on the board. Phrase by phrase, erase portions of the conversation and have students in pairs practice saying it, filling in the blanks. See to what extent you can erase the conversation with students still able to recall it.

4. ROLE PLAY

SETUP: (**1**) Have students work in pairs to choose a destination country on the maps at the back of their books (pages 161–167). (**2**) Have students write their conversation. (**3**) Circulate around the class, answering questions and correcting students' writing where necessary. (**4**) Have the pairs present their role plays for the class. (**5**) Write the question *Where is he/she going?* on the board. Have students watch their classmates' role plays and write down their answer to the question. After each role play, call on students to give their answer to the question. If the response is not correct, have the pair perform their role play again.

VARIATION: Have students submit their written work to you for correction before they present the conversations in the following class.

5. WHO IS IT?

SETUP: (**1**) Have students look at the maps on pages 161–167 to decide on a place they want to visit. (**2**) Have students write the name of the place on a slip of paper. For example: *I want to go to Hawaii.* (**3**) Circulate around the classroom to answer questions as necessary. (**4**) Collect the papers, mix them up, and then have each student select one. Make sure no student has received his or her own paper. (**5**) Have students read the papers to the class. (**6**) Have the class guess who wrote it.

VARIATION: Have students write two reasons they want to visit that place. For example: *I want to go to Hawaii because I like the beach and I like to surf.*

6. PACKING ABC GAME

SETUP: (**1**) Write the letters *A, B, C* on the board in a vertical column. Ask students: "What's the next letter?" Continue with student input to write the whole alphabet on the board in widely spaced vertical columns. (**2**) Model the activity. Read the first sentence, point to the letter *A* on the board, and write the word *airline ticket* extending from the letter. Read the second line, point to the letter *B* on the board, and write the word *bathing suit* extending from the letter *B*. Ask the class: "What word begins

with *C*?" (Possible answer: *camera*). Write their ideas on the board. For example:

> *Airline ticket*
> *Bathing suit*
> *Camera*

(**3**) The letters *q, x, y,* and *z* are particularly difficult, as few common English words begin with these letters. Underline or circle these letters on the board, and tell students they don't need to find a word beginning with them. (**4**) Divide the class into groups of four. Tell students they have ten minutes to brainstorm words. (**5**) Circulate to answer questions as necessary. (**6**) Invite students to report their ideas to the class. Write their ideas into your alphabet on the board.

EXPANSION: Write different destinations on the board (for example: *Alaska, New York City, Kyoto, Mount Kilimanjaro, Kenya*). Have students work in small groups to write up a list of all the things they would pack for each destination. Invite students to tell you their ideas, and write a master list under each destination on the board.

7. CONVERSATION CHANT: TAKING A TRIP

SETUP: (**1**) Play the audio program. Tell students to read along as they listen to the chant. As you play the audio program, make hand motions or clap to reinforce the stress on the dotted syllables. (**2**) Play the audio again, pausing after each line, and have students repeat. (**3**) Have the class chant chorally.

VARIATIONS: (**1**) Once students are familiar with the chant, divide the class into two groups. The indented chant lines represent a second voice. Have one group chant the questions that start at the left margin, and have the other group chant the responses that are indented. (**2**) Have students clap or make a hand motion to indicate where the stress falls as they chant. (**3**) Have students circle all the words and syllables that rhyme. Call on volunteers to read the rhyming pairs aloud and then write them on the board.

USE YOUR ENGLISH!

SETUP: Have students do this activity as a homework assignment. (**1**) To prepare students for this independent conversation, have the class brainstorm the question they might ask their conversation partners For example: *Where do you want to go on a trip?* (**2**) Tell students to write down the information they learn from their conversation partners. For example: *My conversation partner wants to go to Patagonia to* *see the mountains*. At the beginning of the next class, students can hand in their reports to you.

EXPANSION: Have each student choose a place to visit and get information about that place on the Internet. Students can download pictures and answer simple questions about the place, such as *Where is it? What's the weather like?* In class, students can meet in small groups to share their information.

Listening Practice

Page 110

1. HOLIDAYS

SETUP: (1) Tell students to read the questions and answers silently. (2) Play the audio program. (3) Review the answers with the class. If there is confusion about any answers, play the audio program again.

VARIATIONS AND EXPANSIONS: (1) Have students first listen and then read the questions and answers. (2) Invite pairs of students to write another conversation about a different holiday (for example: Thanksgiving, New Year's Day, or Independence Day). Have students watch their classmates' role plays and then answer when you ask this question: "What holiday is it?"

2. A WEATHER REPORT

SETUP: (1) Tell students to read the question and answers silently. (2) Play the audio program. (3) Review the answers with the class. If there is confusion about any answers, replay the audio.

VARIATIONS AND EXPANSIONS: (1) Have students first listen and then read the answers. (2) Photocopy the map of the United States on page 161. Show students where Florida and Montana are located on their maps—Florida is the southeast peninsula, and Montana is in the northwest. As students listen, have them write the weather words they hear (*sunny and hot, cold, rainy*) into the map and then retell the weather report in pairs.

3. WHERE ARE THEY?

SETUP: (1) Play the audio program, pausing after each item to allow students time to write the numbers.

(2) When students have numbered all three scenes, call on volunteers to read their answers to the class.

EXPANSION: After students finish the listening practice, have them work in pairs to write their own conversation for one of the three scenes and then present their conversations to the class. Have students listen to their classmates' conversations and then answer when you ask this question: "Where are they?"

Review

Page 111

1. TALKING ABOUT THE CALENDAR

SETUP: (1) Model the questions for the class. (2) Have students ask and answer the questions in pairs. (3) Circulate to listen in and to answer students' questions as necessary.

VARIATION: After the pair work, call on individual students to answer the questions.

2. WHAT HOLIDAY IS IT?

SETUP: (1) Have students brainstorm the names of different holidays before they compose their sentences. Write their ideas on the board (for example: *Valentine's Day, Independence Day, Memorial Day*). (2) Have students choose one holiday and answer the two questions. For example: *It is in summer. People watch patriotic parades and fireworks.* Circulate around the classroom to answer questions as necessary. (3) Collect the papers, mix them up, and then have each student select one. Make sure no student has received his or her own paper. (4) Have students read the papers to the class and tell the class to guess what holiday it is.

VARIATION: If you are in a non-English-speaking country, students can also write about their native holidays. The only requirement is that students all know the same holidays so that they may guess one another's descriptions.

3. WEATHER REPORT

SETUP: (1) Have students work in pairs to write up a weather forecast for the area. (2) Set a time limit; tell students they have ten minutes to

write and practice their weather reports.
(3) Have one student in each pair stand up and present the weather report to the class. Have students watch their classmates' role plays and answer when you ask these questions: "What's the weather report for today? What's the weather forecast for tomorrow?"

VARIATIONS: (1) Have the pairs choose different locations for their weather reports—a region in their native country or in the United States. When they present their weather reports, have them write the name of their location on the board and, if necessary, show the class where it is located on one of the maps in the back of the book (pages 161–167). (2) Photocopy the weather map in today's newspaper and distribute the copies in class. Have each pair choose a different section of the country to report on. Have the pairs write their weather report for their section of the country and then present it to the class.

4. MAKE A LIST!

SETUP: (1) Write the following questions on the board to guide students' group work: *Where are you going? When are you going? What are you packing?* (2) Have students work in groups of three or four to choose one person to write as the group brainstorms their answers to the questions. Set a ten-minute time limit for this part of activity. (3) Call on students to share their trip ideas with the class.

VARIATIONS: If students choose exotic locations, have them locate their destinations on the maps in the back of the book (pages 161–167).

5. HOW ABOUT YOU?

SETUP: (1) Point out that this is an opportunity to practice the Conversation Tip from the Preview on page 97. Encourage students to give extra information when they answer one another's questions. (2) Model the pronunciation of the questions. (3) Have students ask and answer the questions in pairs. (4) Set a time limit; tell students they have only seven minutes to discuss these questions. (5) Circulate to listen in and to answer students' questions as necessary.

VARIATION AND EXPANSION: (1) Ask students to tell the class one thing they learned about their partners. (2) For homework, have students write their own answers to the questions.

Assessment

Page 112

PART 1: QUESTIONS

SETUP: Have students work individually to write the questions. Challenge students not to look at the previous lessons but to construct their questions from memory.

VARIATION: Have students write their questions on a separate sheet of paper to hand in at the end of the assessment for correction.

PART 2: SPEAKING

SETUP: (1) Divide the class into pairs, and have students take turns asking and answering their questions. (2) Circulate to listen in and to answer students' questions as necessary.

VARIATION: Have students write their partners' responses to their questions and hand them in at the end of the assessment for correction.

PART 3: LISTENING

SETUP: (1) Have students first read the answers silently. Then play the audio program. (2) Check answers with the whole class by asking volunteers to read the correct sentences aloud. If there is confusion about any of the answers, replay the audio program.

VARIATIONS AND EXPANSION: (1) Have students write the number of the question and the letter of their response on a separate sheet to hand in to you for correction at the end of the assessment. (2) As an added challenge, have students compose questions for the uncircled answers.

PART 4: WRITING

SETUP: (1) Ask the class: "What are the people doing in the pictures?" Lead a brief brainstorming session about what the people could be saying. (2) Have students work individually to write their conversations. Circulate as students are writing, and answer questions as necessary.

VARIATIONS: (1) Have students write their conversations on a separate piece of paper to hand in to you for correction. (2) Have students share their conversations with a partner. Then ask volunteer pairs to perform one of their conversations for the class.

YOUR HEALTH

Preview

Page 113

PREVIEW QUESTIONS

SETUP: (**1**) Have the class look at the photograph. Read each question aloud, and call on individual students to respond. (**2**) For questions 2 and 3, write students' responses on the board so they can see the various possible responses. For example:

2. *They're talking. They're laughing. The doctor is asking the woman questions.*
3. *A: How are you feeling today?*
   B: I feel great. My knees don't hurt anymore!

CONVERSATION TIP

SETUP: (**1**) Write on the board: *I'm glad to hear that. I'm sorry to hear that.* Tell students they can say these phrases when they hear good or bad news. (**2**) Have students read the conversations silently. (**3**) Act out the conversations with a volunteer. (**4**) Have students practice the conversations in pairs. (**5**) Circulate to correct pronunciation.

EXPANSION: (**1**) Demonstrate the Conversation Tip in open conversations by asking individual students: "How are you feeling today?" Depending on their reply, say "I'm glad to hear that" or "I'm sorry to hear that." (**2**) Have students work in pairs to practice the conversations with their own information.

CONVERSATION CHANT: WHAT'S WRONG WITH JOE?

SETUP: (**1**) The dots over the words indicate where the stress falls. As you play the audio program, make hand motions or clap to reinforce the stress on the dotted syllables. (**2**) Have students listen once through as they read along. (**3**) Play the audio program again, pausing after each line, and have students repeat. (**4**) Have the class chant chorally.

VARIATIONS AND EXPANSIONS: (**1**) Once students are familiar with the chant, divide the class into two groups. The indented chant lines represent a second voice. Have one group chant the lines that start at the left margin, and have the other group chant the lines that are indented (**2**) Have students clap or make a hand motion to indicate where the stress falls as they chant. (**3**) Have groups switch and chant the opposite lines. (**4**) Substitute various students' names for the names in the conversation chant, keeping in mind the number of syllables in the names. (**5**) Have students circle all the words that rhyme. Call on volunteers to read the rhyming pairs aloud and then write them on the board.

Lesson 1: Staying Healthy

Pages 114–115

1. THE HUMAN BODY

SETUP: (**1**) Write *the human body* on the board. Have the class brainstorm parts of the body. Write their ideas on the board. (**2**) Point to the picture, and set the context: These people are in an exercise class. (**3**) Have students work individually or in pairs to look at the picture and complete the matching exercise. (**4**) Go over the answers with the class. Then play the audio program, pausing between items, and have students repeat chorally. (**5**) Have the class brainstorm other vocabulary in the picture (for example: *shoulders, eyes, ears, nose*). Write the words on the board, and have students add the new vocabulary to the list in their books; alternatively, tell students to write at least twelve new words in their vocabulary notebooks.

VARIATION AND EXPANSION: (**1**) You may want students to draw lines in the picture pointing to each body part and write the name of the body part on the line so that it is easier to study the vocabulary. (**2**) Have students draw a human body and label as many parts of the body as they can. Then have students work in pairs to compare their pictures and information. Finally, have students submit their work to you for correction.

2. WHAT'S THIS?

SETUP: (**1**) Model the activity for the class. Point to a part of your body, and ask: "What's this?" or "What are these?" When a student calls out the correct response, say: "That's right!" and continue by asking another question. (**2**) Have students work in groups of three or four to do the activity. Circulate to correct pronunciation and to answer questions as necessary.

VARIATIONS: (**1**) To avoid social taboos or student embarrassment, point to parts of the bodies in the picture, instead of pointing to your own body. (**2**) To avoid embarrassment, group students by gender, so that women work with women and men work with men.

Language and Culture Note: It is acceptable to point to parts of your own body, but not acceptable to point to parts of another person's body.

3. HEALTHY HABITS

SETUP: (**1**) Model the pronunciation of the questions. (**2**) Have students ask and answer the questions in groups of three or four. Some possible answers are:

1. *Fruit, vegetables, and fish.*
2. *Walking, riding a bike, and running.*
3. *Six hours may be enough, but eight hours is better.*

(**3**) Set a time limit; tell students they have ten minutes to discuss these questions. (**4**) Circulate to listen in and to answer questions as necessary. (**5**) When the time is up, invite a spokesperson from each group to report their ideas.

EXPANSION: Draw two large columns on the board. Label one column *Healthy* and the other column *Unhealthy*. Call out foods and ask individual students to categorize them as *healthy* or *unhealthy*. Write students' ideas into the columns on the board. For example:

Healthy	*Unhealthy*
grapes	*french fries*
lettuce	*chicken nuggets*
fish	*ice cream*

4. DO YOU HAVE HEALTHY HABITS?

SETUP: (**1**) Model (or ask volunteers to model) the questions for the class. For example: *How often do you sleep eight hours a night? How often do you exercise?* (**2**) Divide the class into small groups of three to four students. Have students work in their groups to ask and answer the questions and tally their group's responses. Set a five-minute time limit for this part of the activity. (**3**) Copy the chart from page 115 onto the board. Invite a spokesperson from each group to report their numbers to the class. For example: *One student sleeps eight hours a night every night. Three students sleep eight hours a night three times a week.* Tally the numbers in the chart.

VARIATIONS AND EXPANSIONS: (**1**) Have each group add one more question to their survey. For example: *How often do you eat fast food?* (**2**) Tell students to briefly interview their schoolmates in the hallways or in their classes and write down the information. Then have them report the results in class in small groups. Suggest that students tally the results and make a bar graph illustrating the information.

5. CONVERSATION CHANT: EXERCISE EVERY DAY!

SETUP: (**1**) Play the audio program. Tell students to read along as they listen to the chant. As you play the audio program, make hand motions or clap to reinforce the stress on the dotted syllables. (**2**) Play the audio program again, pausing after each line, and have students repeat. (**3**) Have the class chant chorally.

USE YOUR ENGLISH!

SETUP: Have students do this activity as a homework assignment. (**1**) To prepare students for this independent conversation, model a conversation with a volunteer, using the questions in the box. (**2**) Tell students to write down the information they learn from their conversation partners. For example: *My conversation partner sleeps five hours a night! On the weekends, he sleeps more. He exercises every day. He walks to work and back.* At the beginning of the next class, students can share this information in small groups or simply hand in their reports to you.

EXPANSION: Have the class brainstorm other questions they can ask their conversation partners. For example: *How often do you eat fruit? How often do you eat vegetables? How often do you eat fast food?*

Lesson 2: What's the Matter?

Pages 116–117

1. AILMENTS

SETUP: (**1**) Have students work individually or in pairs to look at the pictures and complete the matching exercise. (**2**) Go over the answers with the class. Then play the audio program, pausing between items, and have students repeat chorally. (**3**) Have the class brainstorm other vocabulary in the pictures. Encourage students to look at the pictures and focus on the actions illustrated for each person (for example: *singing, eating too much, hearing loud music*). Have students add the phrases to the list in their books; alternatively, tell students to write at least ten new words and phrases in their vocabulary notebooks.

VARIATIONS AND EXPANSIONS: (**1**) Say or write a word or phrase, and have students point to the item in the pictures. (**2**) Point to an item in the pictures, and have students say the word or phrase. (**3**) Have students work in pairs to take turns pointing to and identifying items in the picture.

2. WHAT'S THE MATTER?

SETUP: (**1**) Have students turn to page 171 to see the names of the internal organs. Tell students to point to words they want to learn to pronounce, and model the pronunciation for those words only. Try to avoid introducing all the words to prevent students from getting overwhelmed. (**2**) Write the following conversation on the board:

Doctor: *Where does it hurt?*
Patient: *Here.*
Patient: *Maybe it's your* _____ .

Read the conversation aloud. Then read it again, pointing to your chest when you say "Here." Have students suggest possible organs that could hurt there, such as heart, trachea, esophagus. Read the conversation again several times, calling on students to say "Here" and to point to a different parts of the body. Have the class suggest possible organs each time. (**3**) Write the following skeletal model on the board:

A: *What's the matter?*
B: *She/He has a/an* _____ .

(**4**) Model the activity with a volunteer. (**5**) Invite another student to come up to the front of the class and act out an ailment. Ask the class: "What's the matter?" Continue until everyone has had an opportunity to act out an ailment.

VARIATIONS: (**1**) Write the ailments on slips of paper. Have students take turns coming up to the front of the class, selecting a slip of paper, and acting out the ailment. (**2**) Have students do this activity in groups. Circulate to answer questions as necessary.

3. HOW ARE THEY DOING?

SETUP: (**1**) Introduce and practice the first conversation before going on to the second one. (**2**) Set the context for both conversations: Two friends are talking. (**3**) Have students close their books as they listen to the audio program for the first time. Then have students open their books and read along as they listen to the audio program again. Finally, play the audio a third time, pausing after each line for students to repeat chorally. (**4**) As students practice each of the conversations in pairs, circulate to give individual feedback on pronunciation.

VARIATIONS: (**1**) Have students listen to the conversations on the audio program and place dots over the stressed words (as in the conversation chants). Review the stress marks with the class. Practice the conversations chorally, paying special attention to word stress. (**2**) Invite pairs of students to perform the conversations for the class.

4. HOW ARE YOU DOING?

SETUP: (**1**) Write the following skeletal conversational model on the board:

A: *How are you doing?*
B: _____ .
A: *I'm sorry to hear that. I hope you feel better soon. / I'm glad to hear that.*

Have students stand and move around the room to talk to four classmates. Set a time limit of five minutes for this activity. (**2**) Circulate to listen in and to answer questions as necessary. (**3**) Ask individual students: "What did you find out? How are your classmates feeling today?"

EXPANSION: Have the class brainstorm questions that have the same meaning as *How are you doing?* and *How are you feeling?* For example: *How are you?* and *How's it going?* Write students' ideas on the board and encourage the class to vary their questions in their brief conversations.

5. MAKING AN APPOINTMENT

SETUP: (**1**) Have students work individually or in pairs to match the questions and the answers. (**2**) Go over the answers with the class. Then play the audio program, pausing between items, and have students repeat chorally. (**3**) Have students work in pairs to practice the conversation. Circulate to correct pronunciation.

VARIATION AND EXPANSION: (**1**) Invite a pair of students to perform the conversation for the class. (**2**) Brainstorm with students other questions that the receptionist may ask. For example: *What's your date of birth? What's your phone number?*

6. ROLE PLAY

SETUP: (**1**) Have students work in pairs to write their own phone conversations. (**2**) Circulate around the class answering questions and correcting the writing where necessary. (**3**) Have the pairs present their role plays to the class. After each presentation, ask: "What's the matter? When's the appointment?" and call on volunteers to answer.

VARIATION AND EXPANSION: (**1**) Bring props to class for students to use in their role plays (for example: a thermometer, tissues, a telephone). (**2**) Have students submit their written conversations to you for correction before they perform the conversations in the following class.

USE YOUR ENGLISH!

SETUP: Have students do this activity as a homework assignment. (**1**) To prepare students for this independent activity, brainstorm with the class ways that they can find this kind of information. For example, on the Internet, students can do a keyword search with the words *doctors* (or *physicians*) *in* (location). In the yellow pages, students can find the information under the category *Physicians*. (**2**) Tell students to write down the information they learn. At the beginning of the next class, have students hand in their reports to you.

Lesson 3: The Drugstore

Pages 118–119

1. AT THE DRUGSTORE

SETUP: (**1**) Write *drugstore* on the board. Have the class brainstorm items they can get at a drugstore.

Write their ideas on the board (for example: *medicine, soap, makeup*). (**2**) Have students work individually or in pairs to look at the picture and complete the matching exercise. (**3**) Go over the answers with the class. Then play the audio program, pausing between items, and have students repeat chorally. (**4**) With the class, brainstorm other vocabulary in the pictures (for example: *toothpaste, soap, combs*). Write the words on the board, and have students add the new vocabulary to the list in their books; alternatively, tell students to write at least twelve new words in their vocabulary notebooks.

VARIATIONS AND EXPANSIONS: (**1**) Say or write a word or phrase, and have students point to the picture. (**2**) Point to a picture, and have students say the word or phrase. (**3**) Have students work in pairs to take turns pointing and identifying items in the picture.

2. WHAT CAN YOU BUY THERE?

SETUP: Call on a volunteer to read each question aloud. Ask other volunteers to respond.

VARIATIONS: (**1**) Have students work in groups of three or four to write a list of all the things they see in the picture. Which group has the longest list? (**2**) For homework, have students write their answers to the questions and turn in their writing for correction.

3. WHAT'S IN THIS MEDICINE CABINET?

SETUP: (**1**) Model the pronunciation of the questions. (**2**) Have students work in pairs to ask and answer the questions. (Answers: *cough syrup, cold medicine, sunscreen, nail polish, toothpaste, antacid, vitamins, aspirin*) (**3**) Tell students they have only ten minutes to discuss these questions. (**4**) Circulate to listen in and to answer students' questions as necessary.

VARIATION: You can do this activity as a class, pointing to each item in the book and calling on students to respond.

4. WHAT ITEMS ARE NECESSARY IN A MEDICINE CABINET?

SETUP: (**1**) Divide the class into groups of three or four students. Have one student in each group be the secretary. (**2**) Tell students they have only four minutes to brainstorm their list. (**3**) Ask a spokesperson from each group to report to the class. Write all the groups' ideas on the board, and encourage students to check their spelling.

VARIATIONS AND EXPANSIONS: (1) For homework, have students go home, look in their medicine cabinets, and write a list of what they see. (2) Bring over-the-counter medicines to class. Show the class a product, pointing out the expiration date. Explain: "Medicine gets old. When it expires, we should throw it away." Hand out different kinds of over-the-counter medicine to the class, and ask students to find the expiration date on each container. Circulate to check their answers. Have students exchange products and find the expiration on the new container.

Language and Culture Note: In the United States, drugstores sell more than medicine. They also sell many health and beauty products. Many of the medicines in a drugstore are available without a prescription. These are called "over-the-counter" medicines. Other medicines cannot be sold unless the customer has a prescription from a doctor.

5. WHAT DO YOU RECOMMEND FOR HEADACHES?

SETUP: (1) Set the context: A customer is asking a pharmacist for a recommendation. (2) Have students close their books as they listen to the audio program for the first time. Then have students open their books and read along as they listen to the audio program again. Finally, play the audio a third time, pausing after each line for students to repeat chorally. (3) As students practice the conversation in pairs, circulate to give individual feedback on pronunciation

VARIATIONS AND EXPANSIONS: (1) Have students listen to the conversation on the audio program and place dots over the stressed words (as in the conversation chants). Review the stress marks with the class. Practice the conversation chorally, paying special attention to word stress. (2) Phrase by phrase, erase portions of the conversation and have students practice it, filling in the blanks. See to what extent you can erase the conversation with students still able to recall it.

6. ROLE PLAY

SETUP: (1) Have students work in pairs to write their own conversations. Circulate around the class answering questions and correcting the writing where necessary. (2) Have the pairs present their role plays to the class. After each

presentation, ask: "What does the customer want?" and call on volunteers to answer.

VARIATION: Have students submit their written work to you for correction before they perform the conversations in the following class.

USE YOUR ENGLISH!

SETUP: Have students do this activity as a homework assignment. (1) To prepare students for this independent conversation, model a conversation with a student volunteer, using the questions in the box. (2) Tell students to write down the information they learn from their conversation partners. For example: *My conversation partner recommends Reeve for headaches. He says mint tea is good for a stomachache.* At the beginning of the next class, students can hand in their reports to you; alternatively, have students give oral presentations to the class.

Lesson 4: Going to the Doctor

Pages 120–121

1. DOCTOR VISITS

SETUP: (1) Have students work individually or in pairs to look at the pictures and complete the matching exercise. (2) Go over the answers with the class. Then play the audio program, pausing between items, and have students repeat chorally. (3) With the class, brainstorm other vocabulary in the pictures (for example: *scale, eye chart, examination table*). Write the words and phrases on the board, and have students add them to the list in their books; alternatively, tell students to write at least ten new words and phrases in their vocabulary notebooks.

VARIATIONS AND EXPANSIONS: (1) Say or write a word or phrase, and have students point to the picture. (2) Point to a picture, and have students say the word or phrase. (3) Have the class brainstorm the actions in the pictures (for example: *weighing, checking blood pressure, giving a shot, listening to the heart and lungs, giving a urine sample, getting a blood test*). Write students' ideas on the board. Have students write this list down for reference while they do Exercise 2.

2. WHAT ARE THEY DOING?

SETUP: Call on volunteers to read each question aloud. Discuss the answers with the class. For example:

1. *She is weighing the patient. The patient is taking an eye exam. The nurse is checking the patient's blood pressure. The nurse is giving the boy an injection. The doctor is listening to the baby's heart and lungs. The patient is giving a urine sample. The nurse is taking a blood test.*
2. *I go to the doctor when I'm sick. I go to the doctor for my annual checkup.*

VARIATION: For homework, have students write their answers to the questions.

3. YOU SHOULD SEE THE DOCTOR

SETUP: (1) Have the class look at the list of doctors in the Medical Arts Building Directory. Model the pronunciation of each medical profession and explain what it is, for example: "An allergist helps patients who have bad allergies." "An obstetrician takes care of pregnant women and delivers babies." "An ophthalmologist is an eye doctor." "A pediatrician takes care of children." (2) Have students read the conversations silently. Answer any questions students may have about unfamiliar vocabulary. (3) Have students work in pairs to read the conversations aloud and complete them. (4) Circulate to give individual feedback on pronunciation and to answer questions as necessary. (5) Call on various pairs to present one of the conversations to the class.

EXPANSION: Have the class brainstorm the names of other kinds of doctors and what they do. Write their ideas on the board. Tell students to choose five new words and write them in their vocabulary notebooks.

4. AT THE DOCTOR'S OFFICE

SETUP: (1) Set the context: A patient is arriving at a doctor's office. (2) Have students close their books as they listen to the audio program for the first time. Then have students open their books and read along as they listen to the audio program again. Finally, play the audio a third time, pausing after each line for students to repeat chorally. (3) As students practice the conversation in pairs, circulate to give individual feedback on pronunciation.

VARIATIONS AND EXPANSION: (1) Have students listen to the conversation on the audio program and place dots over the stressed words (as in the conversation chants). Review the stress marks with the class. Practice the conversation chorally, paying special attention to word stress. (2) Invite two students to perform the conversation for the class. (3) Write the following sentences on the board, and have students work in pairs to write their own role plays starting with one of these sentences:

I'm here to see the obstetrician.
My son has an appointment with Dr. Garcia.
I have an appointment with the eye doctor.

5. CAN YOU RECOMMEND A GOOD PEDIATRICIAN?

SETUP: (1) Model the questions for the class. (2) Have students work in groups of three to take turns asking and answering the questions. (3) Invite a spokesperson from each group to report on their recommendations. Write the names of the recommended doctors on the board.

EXPANSIONS: (1) Have students ask other students in the school question 2 and report their recommendations to the class. (2) Write these questions on the board: *Where do you go to see a doctor? Do you go to a health clinic? The emergency room? A doctor's office?* Have students discuss these questions in pairs. After a few minutes, have students report the kinds of places they visit to see a doctor.

USE YOUR ENGLISH!

SETUP: (1) To prepare students for this independent activity, brainstorm with the class how they can find this kind of information. For example, on the Internet, students can do a keyword search with the words *medical arts buildings* in (location). In the yellow pages, students can find the information under the category *Medical centers*. Students can also ask their neighbors: "Is there a medical building in our area?" (2) Tell students to write down the address of the medical building. At the beginning of the next class, have students hand in their reports to you. (3) Tell students to write down the information they learn. At the beginning of the next class, have students hand in their reports to you.

EXPANSIONS: (1) Have students go to the medical building, look at the building directory, and write down the kinds of doctors who have offices there. (2) Have students ask their conversation partners: "Can you recommend a good general practitioner? An ophthalmologist? An allergist? A pediatrician?"

Lesson 5: Going to the Dentist

Pages 122–123

1. AT THE DENTIST'S OFFICE

SETUP: (**1**) Have students work individually or in pairs to look at the picture and complete the matching exercise. (**2**) Go over the answers with the class. Then play the audio program, pausing between items, and have students repeat chorally. (**3**) Have the class brainstorm other vocabulary in the picture (for example: *dentist chair, lips, tooth*). Write the words on the board, and have students add the new vocabulary to the list in their books; alternatively, tell students to write at least ten new words and phrases in their vocabulary notebooks.

VARIATIONS AND EXPANSIONS: (**1**) Say or write a word or phrase, and have students point to the picture. (**2**) Point to a picture, and have students say the word or phrase. (**3**) Have students work in pairs to take turns pointing to and identifying actions in the pictures.

2. WHAT'S HAPPENING?

SETUP: (**1**) Point to the two patients in the picture and ask: "What are their names?" Call on volunteers to name each patient. This will make it easier to answer questions 3 and 4. (**2**) Read each question aloud to the class. (**3**) Call on volunteers to respond. For example:

1. *He's cleaning the patient's teeth.*
2. *He's giving an anesthetic to the patient.*
3. *(Jim) is afraid, but (Amy) isn't.*
4. *(Amy) is comfortable, but (Jim) isn't.*

VARIATION: For homework, have students write their answers to the questions and turn in their work for correction.

3. HOW DO YOU LIKE YOUR DENTIST?

SETUP: (**1**) Model the questions for the class. (**2**) Have students work in pairs to take turns asking and answering the questions. Circulate to give individual feedback on pronunciation and to answer students' questions as necessary.

VARIATIONS AND EXPANSIONS: (**1**) Have students tell the class one thing they learned about their partner. (**2**) For homework, have students write their answers to questions 1 and 5.

Language and Culture Note: In the United States, dentists recommend that patients have their teeth cleaned by a dental hygienist every six months. During that visit, the dentist briefly visits the patient to make sure his or her teeth look healthy. If there is a problem, the patient will schedule a visit with the dentist.

4. CROSS-CULTURAL EXCHANGE

SETUP: (**1**) Set the context: This is the story of the tooth fairy. Write the term *tooth fairy* on the board. (**2**) Read the story aloud, or have a volunteer read it to the class. (**3**) Model the pronunciation of the questions for the class. (**4**) Have students work in groups of three to ask and answer the questions. Set a ten-minute limit for this discussion. Circulate to answer students' questions as necessary. (**5**) Invite individual students to explain to the class their culture's beliefs about losing baby teeth.

VARIATIONS AND EXPANSION: (**1**) Students can discuss the questions in pairs. (**2**) In a monocultural classroom, also encourage students to talk about the special traditions their families have about losing baby teeth. (**3**) For homework, have students write their culture's beliefs about losing baby teeth. They can turn in their writing for correction in the next class.

Language and Culture Note: In the United States, most young children believe in the tooth fairy. They believe that if they put a tooth under their pillow, the tooth fairy will come at night while they are sleeping and take the tooth away. The tooth fairy will leave behind some money for the child. Some children believe the tooth fairy is building a castle with all the beautiful baby teeth.

5. CONVERSATION CHANT: I LIKE MY DENTIST.

SETUP: (**1**) Play the audio program. Tell students to read along as they listen to the chant. As you play the audio program, make hand motions or clap to reinforce the stress on the dotted syllables. (**2**) Play the audio program again, pausing after each line, and have students repeat. (**3**) Have the class chant chorally.

VARIATIONS AND EXPANSION: (**1**) Have students clap or make a hand motion to indicate where the stress falls as they chant. (**2**) Write this question on the board: *What do you do to take care of your teeth?* (Possible responses: *I brush my teeth twice a day. I use dental floss every day. I see a dental hygienist* *twice a year. I don't eat candy. I don't snack too often.*) Have students discuss the question in pairs and then share their ideas with the class.

USE YOUR ENGLISH!

SETUP: Have students do this activity as a homework assignment. (**1**) To prepare students for this independent conversation, model a conversation with a volunteer, using the questions in the box. (**2**) Tell students to write down the information they learn from their conversation partners. For example: *There are many dentists in my conversation partner's neighborhood. He goes to Dr. Smith because Dr. Smith has office hours on Saturday.* At the beginning of the next class, students can hand in their reports to you; alternatively, they can present their findings orally.

EXPANSION: Have the class brainstorm other questions they can ask their conversation partners. For example: *How do you like your dentist? When do you go to the dentist?*

Lesson 6: The Hospital

Pages 124–125

1. AT THE HOSPITAL

SETUP: (**1**) Have students work individually or in pairs to look at the picture and complete the matching exercise. (**2**) Go over the answers with the class. Then play the audio program, pausing between items, and have students repeat chorally. (**3**) Have the class brainstorm other vocabulary in the picture (for example: *leg cast, get-well cards, cart*). Write the words on the board, and have students add the new vocabulary to the list in their books; alternatively, tell students to write at least ten new words or phrases in their vocabulary notebooks.

VARIATIONS AND EXPANSIONS: (**1**) Say or write a word or phrase, and have students point to the item in the picture. (**2**) Point to an item in the picture, and have students say the word or phrase. (**3**) Make false statements about the picture, and have students correct you. For example:

Teacher: *The patient in the private room has a heart monitor.*
Student: *False. A patient in the double room has a heart monitor.*

2. WHAT'S IN THE PICTURE?

SETUP: (**1**) Point to the three patients and ask: "What are their names?" Call on volunteers to name each patient. This will make it easier to answer question 1. (**2**) Have a volunteer read each question aloud to the class. Call on other volunteers to respond. For example:

1. *(Joyce) has a broken leg. (James) has heart trouble. Maybe (Bob) has a stomach problem.*
2. *The nurses are talking. One nurse is taking care of a patient.*
3. *The aide is delivering clean laundry.*
4. *She's eating and watching TV.*
5. *(James) is very sick.*
6. *The doctor is listening to the patient's breathing with a stethoscope.*

VARIATION: For homework, have students write their answers to the questions and turn in their work for correction.

3. VISITING HOURS

SETUP: (**1**) Set the context: Someone wants to visit a patient in the hospital. (**2**) Have students close their books as they listen to the audio program for the first time. Then have students open their books and read along as they listen to the audio program again. Finally, play the audio a third time, pausing after each line for students to repeat chorally. (**3**) As students practice each of the conversations in pairs, circulate to give individual feedback on pronunciation.

VARIATION: Invite a pair of students to perform the conversation for the class.

Language and Culture Note: Most hospitals in the United States have restricted visiting hours. Visitors can see patients only during certain hours.

4. ROLE PLAY

SETUP: (**1**) Have students work in pairs to write their own conversations. (**2**) Circulate around the class answering questions and correcting students' writing where necessary. (**3**) Have the pairs present their role plays to the class. After each presentation, ask: "Who does the visitor want to visit?" and call on volunteers to answer

VARIATIONS AND EXPANSIONS: (**1**) Have the class brainstorm other questions that the receptionist might ask before letting the visitor enter. For example: *Are you a relative of the patient?* (**2**) Have students submit their written work to you for correction before they perform the conversations in the following class.

5. HOSPITAL SIGNS

SETUP: (1) Model the pronunciation of each sign for the class. (2) Have students read the conversations silently. Answer any questions students may have. (3) Have students work in pairs to read the conversations aloud and complete them. (4) Circulate to give individual feedback on pronunciation and to answer questions as necessary. (5) As students finish completing the conversations, join pairs to form groups of four to compare answers

VARIATION AND EXPANSION: (1) Invite pairs of students to role-play the conversations for the class. (2) Have the class brainstorm other signs they see in hospitals (for example: *Stairway, Exit, Information, Parking*).

Language and Culture Notes: An *outpatient* is someone who is visiting the hospital for the day for a procedure or doctor visit, but is not staying in a bed overnight. An *admitted* patient is staying in a hospital bed overnight.

USE YOUR ENGLISH!

SETUP: Have students do this activity as a homework assignment. (1) To prepare students for this independent conversation, model a conversation with a volunteer, using the questions in the box. (2) Tell students to write down the information they learn from their conversation partners. For example: *My conversation partner lives near Columbia Presbyterian Hospital. He went to a hospital once. He had appendicitis.* At the beginning of the next class, students can share this information in small groups or simply hand in their reports to you.

EXPANSION: Have the class brainstorm other questions they can ask their conversation partners. For example: *What hospital do you recommend? Why?*

Listening Practice

Page 126

1. HOW ARE YOU DOING?

SETUP: (1) Tell students to read through the questions and answers silently. (2) Play the audio program. (3) Review the answers with the class. If there is confusion about any answers, replay the audio program.

VARIATION: Have students first listen and then read the questions and answers.

2. MAKING AN APPOINTMENT

SETUP: (1) Set the context: Patients are calling Dr. Lander's office to schedule appointments. (2) Have students read the information in the appointment book and then listen to the audio program. (3) If students are uncertain about their answers, play the audio program again.

EXPANSION: Have pairs of students write the conversation between Jane Smith and the receptionist at Dr. Lander's office. Circulate to answer questions and to correct students' writing. Invite one or two pairs of students to perform their role plays for the class.

3. FOLLOW THE SIGNS!

SETUP: (1) Pause the audio program after each conversation so that students have time to number the signs. (2) Review the answers once students have numbered all five signs. Call on volunteers to read their answers to the class. (3) If necessary, replay the audio program.

Review

Page 127

1. STAYING HEALTHY

SETUP: Read the question aloud. Call on students for their ideas. Some possible answers are:

> *Eat a lot of fruits and vegetables.*
> *Sleep eight hours a night.*
> *Don't drink a lot of coffee.*
> *Don't eat too many sweet foods.*
> *Exercise often.*

VARIATION: For homework, have students write their own answer to the question.

2. MEDICINE

SETUP: (1) Model the questions. (2) Divide the class into groups of three students. (3) Circulate and listen in as students ask and answer the questions. (4) In the follow-up discussion, ask a spokesperson from each group to report what medicines the group members recommended for each ailment.

EXPANSIONS: (**1**) Have students add one more ailment (for example: *backache*). (**2**) Have students work in the same groups again, but this time asking and answering this question stem: "What natural remedy do you recommend for . . . ?" Have students report their ideas to the class.

3. MAKE A LIST!

SETUP: (**1**) Divide the class into groups of three or four students. (**2**) Have students choose one member to write the words down as the group brainstorms vocabulary. Set a five-minute time limit for the brainstorming. (**3**) Call out each topic, and have groups take turns calling out an item that belongs to that topic. Write the items on the board so students can check their spelling. Have everyone check each item off as it is mentioned so there are no duplications.

4. AT THE DOCTOR'S OFFICE

SETUP: (**1**) Divide the class into pairs, and tell students to complete the conversation. (**2**) Circulate to answer questions as necessary. (**3**) Invite each pair up to the front of the class to perform their role play for the class.

Assessment

Page 128

PART 1: QUESTIONS

SETUP: Have students work individually to write the questions. Challenge students not to look at the previous lessons but to construct their questions from memory.

VARIATION: Have students write their questions on a separate sheet of paper to hand in for correction at the end of the assessment.

PART 2: SPEAKING

SETUP: (**1**) Divide the class into pairs, and have students take turns asking and answering their questions. (**2**) Circulate to listen in and to answer students' questions as necessary.

VARIATION: Have students write their partners' responses to their questions and hand them in at the end of the assessment for correction.

PART 3: LISTENING

SETUP: (**1**) Have students first read the answers silently. Then play the audio program. (**2**) Check answers with the whole class by asking volunteers to read the correct sentence aloud. If there is confusion about any of the answers, replay the audio program.

VARIATIONS AND EXPANSION: (**1**) Have students write the number of the question and the letter of their response on a separate sheet to hand in to you for correction at the end of the assessment. (**2**) As an added challenge, have students compose questions for the uncircled answers.

PART 4: WRITING

SETUP: (**1**) Ask the class: "What is the woman in the picture doing?" Lead a brief brainstorming session about what she could be saying. (**2**) Have students work individually to write their conversation. Circulate as students are writing, and answer questions as necessary.

VARIATIONS: (**1**) Have students write their conversations on a separate piece of paper to hand in to you for correction. (**2**) Have students share their conversations with a partner. Then ask volunteer pairs to perform one of their conversations for the class.

YOUR WORK

Preview

Page 129

PREVIEW QUESTIONS

SETUP: Have the class look at the photograph. Read each question aloud, and call on individual students to respond. Possible answers may be:
1. *They're construction workers.*
2. *They're wearing helmets (hard hats), boots, jeans, and safety ropes.*
3. *They're building a building.*

CONVERSATION TIP

SETUP: (**1**) Write *Could you explain that?* on the board. Tell students they can ask for clarification when they don't understand a word or concept. (**2**) Have students read the conversation silently. (**3**) Act out the conversation with a volunteer. (**4**) Have students practice the conversation in pairs. (**5**) Circulate to correct pronunciation.

EXPANSION: Write the following skeletal model on the board:

> *I'm sorry. _____? Could you explain that?*

Prompt students with other statements or questions. For example: *Do you have a hard hat? He's wearing a face shield. Do you have a pair of welding gloves*? Have students respond to you using the Conversation Tip. For example:

Teacher: Do you have a hard hat?
Student: I'm sorry. A hard hat? Could you explain that?
Teacher: Of course. It's a helmet that construction workers wear. Here's one in the picture.

CONVERSATION CHANT: A BAD INTERVIEW

SETUP: (**1**) The dots over the words indicate where the stress falls. As you play the audio program, make hand motions or clap to reinforce the stress on the dotted syllables. (**2**) Have students listen once through as they read along.

(**3**) Play the audio program again, pausing after each line, and have students repeat. (**4**) Have the class chant chorally.

EXPANSION: Write this question on the board: *Why is it a bad interview?* Call on volunteers to answer the question. (Answer: *It's a bad interview because they aren't listening to each other*.)

Lesson 1: Workers and Their Work

Pages 130–131

1. WHAT DO THEY DO AT WORK?

SETUP: (**1**) Write *jobs* on the board. Have the class brainstorm types of jobs that people have. Write students' ideas on the board (for example: *doctor, teacher, nurse*). (**2**) Say the number, point to each occupation word in the book, and model the pronunciation for the class. Have students repeat chorally. (**3**) Have students work individually or in pairs to look at the pictures and complete the matching exercise. (**4**) Go over the answers with the class. Then play the audio program, pausing between items, and have students repeat chorally. (**5**) If students are keeping vocabulary notebooks, have them write the words for at least ten workers and their jobs in their notebooks.

VARIATIONS: (**1**) Say or write a phrase, and have students point to the picture. (**2**) Point to a picture, and have students say what the person does on his or her job. (**3**) Have students work in pairs to take turns pointing to and identifying actions in the pictures.

2. JOBS

SETUP: (**1**) Write the following skeletal model on the board:

> *Number _____. He/She is a/an (occupation).*

Read question 1 to the class and call on volunteers to respond, referring to the model on the board if necessary. (**2**) For question 2, write the following skeletal model on the board:

> *Number _____. He/She (verb)s _____.*

Read question 2 aloud to the class and call on volunteers to respond, referring to the model on the board if necessary. Write down the verbs as students say them so that you can model their correct spelling. Point out that *catch* and *teach* both add *-es* for the third-person singular form.

VARIATIONS AND EXPANSIONS: (**1**) Before the class discusses the questions, write the simple present forms of the verbs *drive* and *catch* on the board. Underline the final *-s* endings. For example:

I drive a tractor.	*I catch fish.*
You drive a tractor.	*You catch fish.*
He drive<u>s</u> a tractor.	*He catch<u>es</u> fish.*
She drive<u>s</u> a tractor.	*She catch<u>es</u> fish.*
They drive a tractor.	*They catch fish.*

Point out that you added an *-e* to the third-person singular *-s* of *catch*, and remind students that this adds a syllable to the word. Contrast the pronunciation of *catch* and *catches*. Explain: "Add *-es* to the third-person singular of verbs that end in *-ch, -sh, -x,* and *-s.*" Write some of the other verbs in this exercise on the board (*build, cut, deliver, give, pack, take care of, teach*), and invite volunteers up to the board to write out the simple present forms. Review the pronunciation of all the verb forms, with special emphasis on the *-s* of the third-person singular. (**2**) Make false statements about the occupations in the pictures, and have students correct you. For example:

Teacher: A barber builds with wood.
Student: No, that's not right. A barber cuts hair.

(**3**) Have the class brainstorm other things the workers do in their jobs. For example:

A manicurist gives pedicures. A farm worker picks fruit.

(**4**) For homework, have students write two sentences for each picture, answering the two questions. For example:
1. *She's a manicurist. She gives manicures.*

3. INTERESTING JOBS

SETUP: (**1**) Model the questions for the class. (**2**) Write the following skeletal model on the board:

I think a (farm worker)'s job is interesting.
I don't think a (packer)'s job is interesting.

(**3**) Have students work in groups of four to ask and answer the questions. Circulate to answer students' questions as necessary. (**4**) Call on students and ask them to tell the class one thing they learned about one of their partners. For example: *Lino thinks a farm worker's job is interesting.*

VARIATION AND EXPANSION: (**1**) Instead of asking and answering the questions in groups, have students work individually to write two lists, one of *interesting jobs* and one of *not interesting jobs*. Then have students compare their lists in pairs. Finally, have students report one thing they learned about their partner. (**2**) Draw two large intersecting circles on the board. Label one circle *indoor jobs* and the other circle *outdoor jobs*. At the intersection of the two circles, write *both*. Ask the class: "Is being a farmer worker an indoor job? Is it an outdoor job? Is it both?" Write the class response into the diagram. If students have differing opinions, write the item in all the places they indicate. Continue asking questions until students have categorized all the jobs. For example: ***indoor jobs:*** *teacher, packer, barber;* ***outdoor jobs:*** *farm worker, mail carrier;* ***both:*** *carpenter, security guard.*

4. WHAT ARE THEY SAYING?

SETUP: (**1**) Set the context: A manicurist and her client are talking. (**2**) Have students close their books as they listen to the audio program for the first time. Then have students open their books and read along as they listen to the audio program again. Finally, play the program a third time, pausing after each line for students to repeat chorally. (**3**) As students practice the conversation in pairs, circulate to give individual feedback on pronunciation.

VARIATIONS AND EXPANSION: (**1**) Have students listen to the conversation on the audio program and place dots over the stressed words (as in the conversation chants). Review the stress marks with the class. Practice the conversation chorally, paying special attention to word stress. (**2**) Invite pairs of students to perform the conversation for the class. (**3**) Pass out blank cards to pairs of students. Have students write each line from the conversation on a different card, mix up their cards, and then put them in order again.

Language and Culture Note: In the United States, it is common and appropriate for people to talk about their jobs. The most common question about work is: *What do you do?* which means "What's your job?" or "How do you make a living?" Note the following exchange from the conversation:

Angela: What do you do?
Nancy: I'm a bank teller.

5. HOW ABOUT YOU?

SETUP: (**1**) Model the questions for the class. (**2**) Have students work in pairs to take turns asking and answering the questions. (**3**) Set a time limit; tell students they have only seven minutes to discuss these questions. (**4**) Circulate to listen in and to answer students' questions as necessary.

VARIATIONS AND EXPANSIONS: (**1**) If there are students who do not have a job, have them talk about a job they had in the past or a job they would like to have. (**2**) Take notes as students talk in pairs. Then write incomplete sentences on the board, and have students circulate to ask one another the three questions in this exercise to find out whose name completes each sentence. For example:

> _____ is a security guard.
> _____ takes care of sick people.
> _____ doesn't like her job.

(**3**) For homework, have students write responses to the questions and turn in their writing to you during the next class.

6. THE FUTURE

SETUP: (**1**) Write the following conversation model on the board:

A: *What job would you like to have in the future?*
B: *I would like to be a(n) _____.*

(**2**) Model the conversation with a volunteer. (**3**) Have students ask and answer the question in groups of four. (**4**) Set a time limit; tell students they have only ten minutes to discuss this question and complete their charts. (**5**) Circulate to listen in and to answer students' questions as necessary. (**6**) When the time is up, invite a spokesperson from each group to report to the class about their members.

EXPANSIONS: (**1**) Take notes as students tell the class about their future hopes. Then write incomplete sentences on the board, and have students circulate to ask one another the question in the exercise to find out whose name completes each sentence. For example:

> _____ would like to be a teacher.
> _____ would like to be a nurse.
> _____ would like to be a barber.

(**2**) For homework, have students write a paragraph about what job they would like to have in the future and why they want that job. Have students submit their writing to you for correction and comment.

7. GUESS WHO!

SETUP: (**1**) Have students write their job (or the job they would like to have) on a slip of paper. (**2**) Collect the slips of papers, mix them up, and then have each student select one. Make sure no student has received his or her own paper. (**3**) Have each student read a paper to the class. (**4**) Have the class guess who wrote it.

VARIATION: Have students write answers to the following four questions to give more identifying information on their slips of paper:

> *What job do you have?*
> *What do you do at your job?*
> *Do you like your job?*
> *What job would you like to have in the future?*

USE YOUR ENGLISH!

SETUP: Have students do this activity as a homework assignment. (**1**) To prepare students for this independent conversation, model a conversation with a volunteer, using the questions in the box. (**2**) Tell students to write down the information they learn about their conversation partners. For example: *My conversation partner is a taxi driver. He doesn't like his job. He drives a taxi at night. He would like to be a truck driver.* (**3**) At the beginning of the next class, students can hand in their reports to you.

Lesson 2: Life at Work

Pages 132–133

1. WORK CLOTHES AND EQUIPMENT

SETUP: (**1**) Have students work individually or in pairs to look at the pictures and complete the matching exercise. (**2**) Go over the answers with the class. Then play the audio program, pausing after each item, and have students repeat chorally. (**3**) Have the class brainstorm other vocabulary in the pictures (for example: *whistle, bathing suit, sunglasses*). Write the words on the board, and have students add the new vocabulary to the list in their books; alternatively, tell students to write at least ten new words in their vocabulary notebooks.

VARIATIONS AND EXPANSIONS: (**1**) Say or write a word or phrase, and have students point to the pictures.

(2) Point to a picture, and have students identify all the equipment. **(3)** To practice this new vocabulary, play a drawing game. Write the names of the work equipment on slips of paper. Have students take turns coming up to the front of the classroom, taking a slip of paper, and drawing the item on the board. The rest of the class guesses the item. To keep the pace moving, set a time limit of one minute for each turn.

2. WHAT DO THEY WEAR AT WORK?

SETUP: **(1)** Call on a volunteer to read each question aloud. **(2)** Explain that *wear* refers to clothes. For example:

> *Question 1. A police officer wears a uniform.*
> *Question 2. A police officer uses a night stick*
> *and a gun.*

(3) Call on volunteers to respond to the questions.

VARIATION AND EXPANSION: **(1)** Have students ask and answer these questions in pairs. **(2)** For homework, have students write two sentences about each worker answering questions 1 and 2. For example: *A custodian wears a uniform. He uses a broom and a lot of keys.*

3. HOW ABOUT YOU?

SETUP: **(1)** Model the questions for the class. **(2)** Have students work in groups of three to take turns asking and answering the questions. **(3)** Set a time limit; tell students they have only eight minutes to discuss these questions. **(4)** Circulate to listen in and to answer students' questions as necessary. **(5)** Invite students to report what they learned in their groups.

VARIATION AND EXPANSION: **(1)** Students can also do this activity in pairs. **(2)** Bring to class downloaded images of work uniforms from the Internet. Show the class the pictures and have students guess the type of work that each person in the pictures does.

4. DAY JOB OR NIGHT JOB?

SETUP: **(1)** Set the context: This is Rick's routine. **(2)** Have students read along as they listen to the audio program. Play the audio program again, pausing after each line for students to repeat chorally. **(3)** Write this question on the board: *Does Rick have a day job or a night job?* Have students work in pairs to decide their answer to that question (*He could have either a day job or a night job*) and then write times

into the clocks in the pictures. Have the pairs tell the class about Rick's work routine. For example:

> *Rick drives to work at 10:30 at night.*
> *He clocks in at 11:00.*

VARIATIONS AND EXPANSION: **(1)** After students have read about Rick's day, ask the following questions: "What does Rick study? Why does he study?" Call on students to respond with their own ideas. **(2)** To review the verb forms, write the sentences from the book about Rick on the board, but draw a blank line in place of the verbs. Have students come up to the board and complete the sentences. **(3)** Have students work in pairs to write a story about one of the workers on page 132 of their books. For example:

> *Jesse is a lifeguard.*
> *He drives to work at 8:00 in the morning.*
> *He works as a lifeguard.*
> *He drinks a lot of water on break.*
> *He leaves work at 6:00.*

5. HOW ABOUT YOU?

SETUP: **(1)** Model the questions for the class. **(2)** Have students work in pairs to take turns asking and answering the questions. **(3)** Circulate to listen in and to answer students' questions as necessary.

VARIATION AND EXPANSION: **(1)** Invite students to explain to the class why their partner is studying English. **(2)** Take notes as you circulate, and listen in on student conversations. Then write incomplete sentences on the board, and have students circulate to ask one another the questions in the exercise to find out whose name completes each sentence. For example:

> _____ *works from 11:00 to 7:00.*
> _____ *drives to work.*
> _____ *speaks English at work.*
> _____ *is studying English to get a better job.*

6. CONVERSATION CHANT: A DAY JOB OR A NIGHT JOB?

SETUP: **(1)** Play the audio program. Tell students to read along as they listen to the chant. As you play the audio program, make hand motions or clap to reinforce the stress on the dotted syllables. **(2)** Play the audio program again, pausing after each line, and have students repeat. **(3)** Have the class chant chorally.

VARIATIONS: **(1)** Once students are familiar with the chant, divide the class into two groups. The indented chant lines represent a second voice. Have one group chant the lines that start at the left margin, and have the other group chant the lines that are indented. (2) Have students clap or make a hand motion to indicate where the stress falls as they chant. (3) Have students circle the words that rhyme. Call on volunteers to read the rhyming pairs aloud and then write them on the board. (4) Write these questions on the board, and have students discuss their answers in pairs: *What time of day do you like to work? Why?* After a few minutes, call on volunteers to report to the class what they learned about their partners.

USE YOUR ENGLISH!

SETUP: Have students do this activity as a homework assignment. (1) Tell students to write down their ideas from the list they made with their conversation partners. For example: *Jobs that require uniforms: police officer, custodian, nurse, doctor, orderly, server at McDonald's.* (2) At the beginning of the next class, students can share their ideas in small groups or simply hand in their reports to you.

Lesson 3: Looking for a Job

Pages 134–135

1. HELP WANTED ADS

SETUP: (1) Set the context: These are classified ads that you can find in the Help Wanted section of a newspaper. Show the class the Help Wanted section of the local newspaper. (2) Give students five minutes to silently read through the ads in their books. (3) Have students work individually or in pairs to look at the ads and complete the matching exercise. (4) Go over the answers with the class. Then play the audio program, pausing between items, and have students repeat chorally. (5) If students are keeping vocabulary notebooks, have them write at least ten words and their abbreviations in their notebooks.

VARIATION: Write the abbreviations on the board, and call on different students to tell you the full words or phrases.

2. WHAT DO THE ADS MEAN?

SETUP: (1) Point out that this exercise gives students an opportunity to practice the Conversation Tip question from the Preview: *Could you explain that?* Write the question on the board. As students answer

the questions in groups of three, encourage them to ask for clarification when they don't understand something. (2) Circulate to answer questions as necessary while students talk in their groups. (3) Set a time limit of ten minutes for students to discuss the questions. (4) Read the questions aloud, and call on individual students for the answers.

VARIATION AND EXPANSION: (1) Have students work individually to answer the questions and then meet in groups to compare their answers. (2) Have students work in pairs to write up an ad for one of their own jobs or for a dream job. Have each pair join another pair to share their ideas.

3. HELP WANTED IN YOUR COMMUNITY

SETUP: (1) Explain that *job opening* means there's a job available. (2) Write the following question on the board: *Do you know of any job openings?* (3) Have students ask and answer this question in groups of four. (4) Set a four-minute time limit for the group discussion. (5) Circulate and answer students' questions as necessary. (6) Ask the class the same question, and have students tell the class of any job openings they know of.

EXPANSION: Bring in help wanted ads from the newspaper and from the Internet. Have students work in pairs to choose one interesting job and rewrite the ad in full words. Then invite the pairs to the front of the class to tell the class about the job opening that they chose.

4. REPLYING TO A HELP WANTED AD

SETUP: (1) Have students work in pairs to complete the conversation. (2) Circulate to correct students' pronunciation and to answer questions as necessary. (3) Invite pairs up to the front of the class to present their role plays.

VARIATIONS AND EXPANSIONS: (1) If students are uncertain about what to write to complete the phone conversation, they can refer to the nurse, packer, security guard, or carpenter help wanted ads on page 134 and use one of those as the basis for their phone conversation. (2) Have pairs of students also write a help wanted ad for the job they mention in their role play. (3) Pass out blank cards to pairs of students. Have students write each completed line from the conversation on a different card, mix up their cards, and then put them in order again. Then have the pairs trade their sets of cards with another pair and put each other's cards in order again.

USE YOUR ENGLISH!

SETUP: Have students do this activity as a homework assignment. (**1**) To prepare students for this assignment, brainstorm with the class the best newspapers and Internet sites for finding jobs. (For newspapers, local papers are best. For the Internet, have students try a keyword search with words such as *job listings, job banks,* or *employment opportunities* and the name of the locality.) (**2**) Tell students to find three ads for job openings to bring to class. (**3**) At the beginning of the next class, students can meet in groups of three to share the information they have gathered. Have each group tell the class about the three most interesting job openings they found.

Lesson 4: Job Applications

Pages 136–137

1. CARMEN'S APPLICATION

SETUP: (**1**) Have students read through the application silently for two minutes. (**2**) Ask volunteers to read aloud the written information on each line of the application. (**3**) Answer any questions students may have about abbreviations (*Rd. stands for Road; R.N. stands for Registered Nurse; H.S. stands for High School*). Also clarify any new vocabulary that appears on the application form (for example, *references are people who know the applicant well and can attest to his or her good work performance*). (**4**) Call on students to read each question aloud. Ask other volunteers to respond.

VARIATIONS AND EXPANSIONS: (**1**) Ask students to locate and point to the following information. Circulate around the classroom to make sure students are able to point to the information in the application:

employer
date of application
first name of applicant
address of applicant
applicant's high school
two people the applicant worked with

(**2**) Ask the class these additional comprehension questions: "When did Carmen work? Is she working now? How do you know?" Call on students to respond.

Language and Culture Note: Note that in the Education section, the first line is more recent and the second line is older. This is the custom for filling out forms in the United States. Applicants write down their most recent experience first and then work back chronologically.

2. CARMEN'S JOB INTERVIEW

SETUP: (**1**) Write the following schema for question formation on the board so students have an easier time composing correct questions:

Question Word	Helping Verb	Subject	Base Verb	Object?
Where	*did*	*you*	*go*	*to college?*
When	*do*	*you*	*want*	*to begin?*
X	*Can*	*you*	*work*	*2nd shift?*

(**2**) Have students work in pairs to write all six questions. (**3**) Circulate to answer questions and to correct grammar as necessary. (**4**) Once students have composed their questions, have the pairs role-play Carmen's job interview.

VARIATIONS AND EXPANSIONS: (**1**) After the pairs have written their questions, ask them to report their ideas to the class. Write a master list on the board. Have students refer to the questions on the board as they do their job interview role plays in pairs. (**2**) If some students finish much sooner than others, they can write out Carmen's job interview role play and hand it in to you. (**3**) Invite two or three pairs to the front of the class to perform their role plays. After each role play, ask the class: "Did Carmen get the job? Was it a good interview? Why or why not?" Call on individual students to respond.

Language and Culture Note: There are several questions that an employer in the United States cannot ask in an interview because the answer could bias the employer and result in discrimination. These are questions that define the applicant's age, color, gender, national origin, race, religion, creed, or whether the applicant has a disability. For example, the following questions are not permissible in an interview:

Where were you born?
Are you a U.S. citizen?
What is your age?
Are you married?
Do you have children?
What race are you?
What is your religion?

How much do you weigh?
Do you have any disabilities?
What's your medical history?

3. YOUR JOB APPLICATION

SETUP: (1) Have students work individually to fill out the job application. (2) Remind students to write their most recent work experience and education first, and then work back chronologically. (3) Tell students they can make up the personal information such as address and phone number, and the phone numbers of their references. (4) Circulate to answer questions as necessary. (5) Once students finish their applications, pair them up to read each other's forms.

VARIATION: If students are uncertain about what job they want to apply for, they can choose among the jobs posted in the help wanted ads on page 134.

4. YOUR JOB INTERVIEW ROLE PLAY

SETUP: (1) Point out that this exercise gives students an opportunity to practice the Conversation Tip question from the Preview. Write this question on the board: *Could you explain that?* Encourage students to ask for clarification when they don't understand something during their job interview role plays. (2) Write the following phrases on the board: *job opening, employer name,* and *job requirements.* Tell the partners that before each interview, they must be sure to decide on these facts about the job opening. (3) As students interview their partners, circulate to answer questions as necessary. (4) Set a time limit of twenty minutes for students to complete both partners' interviews.

VARIATIONS AND EXPANSIONS: (1) Write on the board (or photocopy) your master list of job interview questions from Exercise 2 so students can use those questions in their role plays. (2) Have each student compose a classified ad for the job they are seeking and give it to the job interviewer before they begin their role plays. (3) Invite pairs of students to the front of the class to perform their job interview role plays. After each role play, ask the class: "Did he/she get the job? Was it a good interview? Why or why not?" Call on individual students to respond. (4) For homework, have students write their "dream job interview" and hand in their writing to you at the beginning of the next class.

USE YOUR ENGLISH!

SETUP: Have students do this activity as a homework assignment. (1) To prepare students for this assignment, brainstorm with the class about where they can get job applications (large retailers, any businesses that have a help wanted sign posted, and large corporation Web sites on the Internet) and how they can ask for an application (for example: *May I have a job application?*). (2) Tell students to find at least one job application form to bring to class. (3) At the beginning of the next class, students can meet in groups of three for five minutes to compare their applications. (4) Ask a spokesperson from each group to report on the similarities between their applications. Write their ideas on the board so that by the end of the class discussion, you have a list of the information most frequently requested on a job application form.

Lesson 5: Safety at Work

Pages 138–139

1. SAFETY CLOTHING, SIGNS, AND EQUIPMENT

SETUP: (1) Write *safety equipment* on the board. Have the class brainstorm equipment that workers use to stay safe (for example: *helmet, sunglasses, hat, boots*). (2) Have students work individually or in pairs to look at the pictures and complete the matching exercise. (3) Go over the answers with the class. Then play the audio program, pausing between items, and have students repeat chorally. (4) Have the class brainstorm other vocabulary in the illustrations (for example: *detour, jackhammers, supervisor*). Write the words on the board, and have students add the new vocabulary to the list in their books; alternatively, tell students to write at least ten new words and phrases in their vocabulary notebooks.

VARIATIONS AND EXPANSIONS: (1) Say or write a word or phrase, and have students point to the picture. (2) Point to a picture, and have students say the word or phrase. (3) Have students work in pairs to take turns pointing to and identifying actions in the pictures.

2. SAFETY ON THE JOB

SETUP: Read the questions aloud, and call on volunteers to give their answers.

EXPANSION: Download safety sign images from the Internet. Show the class each sign, and ask: "What does this sign mean?" and "Where is this kind of sign located?" Call on students for their ideas.

3. CROSS-CULTURAL EXCHANGE

SETUP: Read the questions aloud, and call on one or more volunteers to answer each question.

VARIATIONS AND EXPANSIONS: (**1**) Model the questions for the class, and then have students ask and answer them in groups of four. (**2**) Write this additional question on the board: *What safety equipment do you have at work?* Have students discuss it along with the questions in the book, either as a class or in groups.

4. SAFETY VIOLATIONS

SETUP: (**1**) Set the context by pointing to the picture and having students cover the printed conversation as they listen to the audio program for the first time. (**2**) Have students uncover the conversation and read along as they listen to the audio program again. Finally, play the audio a third time, pausing after each line for students to repeat chorally. (**3**) As students practice the conversation in pairs, circulate to give individual feedback on pronunciation. (**4**) Call on volunteers to name each character in the picture. This will make it easier to answer the questions. (**5**) Read each question aloud to the class, and call on volunteers to respond.

VARIATIONS: (**1**) Have students listen to the conversation on the audio program and place dots over the stressed words (as in the conversation chants). Review the stress marks with the class. Practice the conversation chorally, paying special attention to word stress. (**2**) Invite a pair of students to perform the conversation for the class.

5. ROLE PLAY

SETUP: (**1**) Set the context: Point to the picture in Exercise 4. Then read the first line of the conversation, pointing to the worker in the picture who is operating the machine. Say: "This is Worker 1. He is laughing at a joke or funny story told by Worker 2." (**2**) Have students work in groups of three to write their own conversation. (**3**) Circulate

around the class answering questions and correcting the writing where necessary. (**4**) Have the groups present their role plays to the class.

EXPANSION: Have the class brainstorm other safety violations at the workplace. Write their ideas on the board. Have students work in small groups of two or three to choose one situation and write a conversation about that safety violation to role-play for the class. After each group presents their role play, ask the class: "What is the safety violation in this role play?" and call on a student to respond.

USE YOUR ENGLISH!

SETUP: Have students do this activity as a homework assignment. (**1**) Tell students to make a list of the safety signs they and their conversation partners see. They should write down what the actual signs say. (**2**) At the beginning of the next class, students can share their lists with the class.

EXPANSION: Have students draw on the board one or two of the signs they saw. Ask the class: "What does the sign mean? What do you think? Where is the sign located?"

Lesson 6: Leaving a Job
Pages 140–141

1. LAYOFFS

SETUP: (**1**) Have students work individually or in pairs to look at the pictures and complete the matching exercise. (**2**) Go over the answers with the class. Then play the audio program, pausing between lines, and have students repeat chorally.

VARIATION: Have students point to the pictures and retell the story in pairs.

LANGUAGE NOTE: The word *layoff* is a noun, and the corresponding verb is *lay off*. An employer *lays off* an employee. An employee *is* (or *gets*) *laid off*.

2. HOW'S BUSINESS IN YOUR CITY?

SETUP: Read the questions aloud to the class, and call on volunteers to respond.

VARIATIONS AND EXPANSIONS: (**1**) Have students ask and answer the questions in groups of four. While students are working, circulate to answer questions as necessary. (**2**) For homework, have students write their answers to the questions.

3. YOU'RE FIRED!

SETUP: (**1**) Set the context: Henry is at work, but he's not working. (**2**) Divide the class into pairs. Have students look at the pictures and answer the questions. Set a time limit of four minutes for this activity. (**3**) Read each question aloud, and call on students to respond.

EXPANSION: Have students write Henry's story on a separate piece of paper, adding details. Write the following questions on the board to get students thinking more about the story: *What's Henry's job? Where does he work? Does Henry like his job? Does Henry like to work hard? Why doesn't he pay attention to the customers? Why is his boss angry? What does his boss say to him?* An example of a partial story with more detail:

> *Henry works in a large department store. He is a salesperson. He helps customers shop in the store. Usually his store is very quiet, but not today. Today there is a big sale in the store. It is very busy.*

Language and Culture Notes: (**1**) In the United States, an employee can be fired if there is a "just cause" such as not performing one's job responsibilities. (**2**) An employer *fires* an employee. An employee *is* (or *gets*) *fired*.

4. LEAVING A JOB

SETUP: (**1**) Have students work individually or in pairs to look at the pictures and complete the matching exercise. Tell students they will use some numbers more than once. (**2**) Go over the answers with the class. Then play the audio program, pausing between items, and have students repeat chorally.

5. GOOD REASONS TO LEAVE A JOB

SETUP: Call on individual students to read the questions aloud to the class. Ask other volunteers to respond.

VARIATION AND EXPANSIONS: (**1**) Have students answer the questions in pairs. Circulate to listen in and to answer students' questions as necessary. (**2**) Have groups of three students choose one of the situations in Exercise 4 and write a conversation among three of the characters. Have each group present their role play to the class. After each presentation, ask the class: "Which situation is the role play about—situation 1, 2, or 3?" and call on a volunteer to answer. (**3**) Point to each picture in Exercise 4, and ask the class: "What's next?" For each picture, have students discuss their ideas for the story line. Rephrase what students say to make sure they all agree on what happens next in the story. Then call on individual students to tell parts of the story as you write their sentences on the board. Write a correct version of what students dictate so that only correct language is modeled. The result is a "cooperative" story about the next step in each story line.

6. CONVERSATION CHANT: OUT OF WORK

SETUP: (**1**) To be sure students recognize the past tense verbs in this conversation chant, have them circle all the verbs. Then call on students to name the past tense verbs as you write them on the board. Point to each of the verbs on the board, and ask the class: "What is the present tense form of this verb?" If students are uncertain, supply the answer (*spoke—speak; got—get; lost—lose; did—do; asked—ask*). (**2**) Play the audio program. Tell students to read along as they listen to the chant. As you play the audio program, make hand motions or clap to reinforce the stress on the dotted syllables. (**3**) Play the audio program again, pausing after each line, and have students repeat. (**4**) Have the class chant chorally.

VARIATIONS: (**1**) Once students are familiar with the chant, divide the class into two groups. Have one group chant the lines that start at the left margin, and have the other group chant the lines that are indented. (**2**) Have students clap or make a hand motion to indicate where the stress falls as they chant. (**3**) Have students circle the words that rhyme. Call on volunteers to read the rhyming pairs aloud and then write them on the board.

Language and Culture Note: *A leave* is an arrangement between an employer and an employee where the employee doesn't work for a period of time but is able to return to his or her job at a later date. *A leave with pay* (or *a paid leave*) means the employee receives income while *on leave*. *A leave without pay* (or *an unpaid leave*) means that the employee does not receive any income while away from the job.

USE YOUR ENGLISH!

SETUP: Have students do this activity as a homework assignment. (**1**) To prepare students for this independent conversation, model the conversation with a volunteer, using the questions in the box. (**2**) Tell students to write what their conversation partner says in two different lists: *Good Reasons to Leave a Job* and *Bad Reasons to Leave a Job*. (**3**) At the beginning of the next class, students can hand in their reports to you.

EXPANSION: Have the class brainstorm other questions they can ask their conversation partners. For example: *What do you think? Is business good or bad in our city? Are any companies hiring new employees? Are any companies laying off employees?*

Listening Practice

Page 142

1. I'M CALLING ABOUT THE JOB.

SETUP: (**1**) Set the context: Jim is looking for a job. (**2**) Tell students to read through the questions and answers silently. (**3**) Play the audio program. (**4**) Review the answers with the class. If there is confusion about any answers, replay the audio program.

VARIATION: Have students first listen and then read the sentences.

2. WHAT DO YOU DO?

SETUP: (**1**) Tell students to read through the questions and answers silently. (**2**) Play the audio program. (**3**) Review the answers with the class. If there is confusion about any answers, play the audio program again.

VARIATION: Have students first listen and then read the sentences.

3. QUESTIONS AND ANSWERS

SETUP: (**1**) Have students read the answers and then listen to the audio program. (**2**) If students are uncertain about any of their answers, replay the audio program.

VARIATIONS AND EXPANSIONS: (**1**) Have students first listen and then read the answers. (**2**) After finishing the activity, have students compose questions for the uncircled answers. (**3**) Have students listen to the audio program again and take dictation on the questions. Write the questions on the board so students can correct their work, or have students self-correct by referring them to the Audioscript in the back of their books.

Review

Page 143

1. MAKE A LIST!

SETUP: (**1**) Have students work in pairs to generate a list of jobs. Set a five-minute time limit for this part of the activity. (**2**) Group three pairs together, and have students compare their lists.

VARIATION: Have students compare their lists as a class by asking students to take turns reading a job from their lists. Write the job on the board as students check their spelling. Continue until students have no more jobs to mention.

2. AT WORK

SETUP: (**1**) Model the questions for the class. (**2**) Have students take turns asking and answering the questions in pairs. Set a seven-minute limit for this discussion. (**3**) Circulate around the classroom listening in on students' conversations and answering questions as necessary.

EXPANSION: For homework, have students write a paragraph about their partners using information they learned from this activity.

3. HELP WANTED ADS

SETUP: (**1**) Have the class brainstorm interesting jobs. Write their ideas on the board. (**2**) Have students work in pairs to choose one job and write an ad for it in full-word form (without abbreviations). (**3**) Have pairs read their ads aloud to the class.

VARIATION: Have students write another version of their ads in abbreviations using Exercise 1 on page 134 as a guide. Then have the pairs write their ads on the board. Call on other students in the class to read the ads aloud, deciphering the abbreviations.

4. APPLYING FOR A JOB

SETUP: (**1**) Have students work in pairs to compose a phone conversation about a help wanted ad. (**2**) Circulate to answer questions as necessary. (**3**) Invite students to present their conversations to the class. After each role play, ask the class: "What is the job opening?" and call on a student to respond.

VARIATIONS: (**1**) Students can base their conversation on one of the help wanted ads in Exercise 3. (**2**) Challenge students not to look back at the phone conversation model on page 135.

5. SAFETY AT WORK

SETUP: (**1**) Have students work in groups of three or four to make their lists. Set a six-minute time limit for this part of activity. (**2**) Pair up two groups, and have students compare their lists. Alternatively, have a spokesperson from each group read their list aloud to the class.

6. LEAVING A JOB

SETUP: (**1**) Model the question for the class. (**2**) Have students circulate around the classroom asking four classmates the question. (**3**) Set a five-minute time limit for this activity.

VARIATION: Have students survey other students in the school and report their findings to the class.

Assessment

Page 144

PART 1: QUESTIONS

SETUP: Have students work individually to write the questions. Challenge students not to look at the previous lessons but to construct their questions from memory.

VARIATION: Have students write their questions on a separate sheet of paper and hand them in for correction at the end of the assessment.

PART 2: SPEAKING

SETUP: (**1**) Divide the class into pairs, and have students take turns asking and answering their questions. (**2**) Circulate to listen in and to answer students' questions as necessary.

VARIATION: Have students write their partners' responses to their questions and hand them in for correction at the end of the assessment.

PART 3: LISTENING

SETUP: (**1**) Have students first read the answers silently. Then play the audio program. (**2**) Check answers with the whole class by asking volunteers to read the correct sentence aloud. If there is confusion about any of the answers, replay the audio program.

VARIATIONS AND EXPANSION: (**1**) Have students write the number of the question and the letter of their response on a separate sheet to hand in to you for correction at the end of the assessment. (**2**) As an added challenge, have students compose questions for the uncircled answers.

PART 4: WRITING

SETUP: (**1**) Ask the class: "What are the people doing in the picture?" Lead a brief brainstorming session about what the people could be saying. (**2**) Have students work individually to write their conversations. Circulate as students are writing, and answer questions as necessary.

VARIATIONS: (**1**) Have students write their conversations on a separate piece of paper to hand in to you for correction. (**2**) Have students share their conversations with a partner. Then ask volunteer pairs to perform one of their conversations for the class.

Preview

Page 145

PREVIEW QUESTIONS

SETUP: Have the class look at the photograph. Read each question aloud, and call on individual students to respond. For example:

1. *They're at a park.*
2. *They're having a picnic.*
3. *I think it's the weekend because the parents aren't working.*

CONVERSATION TIP

SETUP: (**1**) Write on the board: *So do I. I do, too.* Tell students these are ways to express agreement about what you like. For example:

A: I like ice cream.
B: So do I. / I do, too.

(**2**) Write on the board: *Neither do I.* Tell students this is a way to express agreement about what you don't like. For example:

A: I don't like soda.
B: Neither do I.

(**3**) Write on the board: *I don't. I do.* Tell students these are ways to express disagreement. For example:

A: I like coffee.
B: I don't.
A: I don't like tea.
B: I do!

(**4**) Have students read the conversations silently.
(**5**) Act out the conversations with a volunteer.
(**6**) Have students practice the conversations in pairs.
(**7**) Circulate to correct pronunciation.

EXPANSION: (**1**) Prompt students with other statements. For example: "I like chocolate." "I don't like vegetables." Call on individual students to react to your statements by agreeing or disagreeing. (**2**) Tell students to write three sentences about things they like or don't like. Then have students work in pairs to take turns telling their partners about their likes and dislikes, with their partners agreeing or disagreeing.

CONVERSATION CHANT: I LOVE TO FLY

SETUP: (**1**) The dots over the words indicate where the stress falls. As you play the audio program, make hand motions or clap to reinforce the stress on the dotted syllables. (**2**) Have students listen once through as they read along. (**3**) Play the audio program again, pausing after each line, and have students repeat. (**4**) Have the class chant chorally.

VARIATIONS AND EXPANSIONS: (**1**) Once students are familiar with the chant, divide the class into two groups. The indented chant lines represent a second voice. Have one group chant the lines that start at the left margin, and have the other group chant the lines that are indented. (**2**) Have students clap or make a hand motion to indicate where the stress falls as they chant. (**3**) Have groups switch and chant the opposite lines. (**4**) Have students circle all the words that rhyme. Call on volunteers to read the rhyming pairs aloud and then write them on the board. (**5**) Write on the board: *So _____ I. Neither _____ I.* Explain that the helping verb (auxiliary verb) goes in the blank. Have students underline all the verbs in the conversation chant. Ask students to call out the verbs from the first six lines, and write them on the board (*love—do, don't like—do, 'm—am*). Explain that *do* is the helping verb for *love, do* is the helping verb for *don't like*, and that *am* is the helping verb for *'m*. Ask students for other helping verbs (*can, will, did*), and explain that the same structure works for these helping verbs. For example:

I loved the movie.
So did I.
I can ski.
So can I.
I'll leave later.
So will I.

Language and Culture Note: It is common and appropriate to use the phrase *I love* + noun or *I love to* + verb when talking about things one enjoys very much. Note these sentences from the conversation chant: *I love to fly. I love the mountains. I love to ski. I love the sea.*

Lesson 1: Going Out

Pages 146–147

1. PEOPLE AND PLACES

SETUP: (**1**) Have students work individually or in pairs to look at the pictures and complete the matching exercise. (**2**) Go over the answers with the class. Then play the audio program, pausing between items, and have students repeat chorally. (**3**) Have the class brainstorm other places to go (for example: *a festival, a restaurant*) and other people to go with (*co-workers, neighbors*). Write the words on the board, and have students add the new vocabulary to the list in their books; alternatively, tell students to write at least ten new words in their vocabulary notebooks.

VARIATIONS: (**1**) Say: "They are at a/an (*art museum*)," and have students point to the appropriate picture. Repeat with other statements about where the people are. (**2**) Point to a picture, and ask: "Where are they?" Call on a student to respond. (**3**) Have students work in pairs to take turns pointing to and identifying the locations of the pictures.

2. GOOD PLACES TO GO

SETUP: (**1**) Read the questions aloud, and call on volunteers to respond. (**2**) Write students' ideas on the board. (**3**) If students express interest in knowing more about these locales, talk about their locations and hours of operation.

EXPANSIONS: (**1**) Bring several copies of the local newspaper to class. Have pairs of students look in the arts and entertainment section of the paper to find an advertisement or a listing for each of the following venues: a movie theater, a concert, a theater, an art museum, and a nightclub. Have the pairs report their findings to class. (**2**) Take the class on a field trip. Have the class brainstorm places to visit in your community. The places should be possible to visit during your regular class hours. Write students' ideas on the board. Have groups of three students choose one destination and investigate the logistics of the trip (for example: transportation, admission costs, food costs, time required) and then present their information to the class. Have the class vote on the best destination for a class field trip. Choose a time and date for the field trip. Write any complicated instructions (for example: directions, admission fees, etc.) on papers to distribute to all students several days in advance of the trip.

3. HOW ABOUT YOU?

SETUP: (**1**) Model the questions. (**2**) Have students work in groups of three or four to take turns asking and answering the questions. (**3**) Tell students they have only eight minutes to discuss these questions. (**4**) Circulate to listen in and to answer students' questions as necessary.

VARIATION AND EXPANSION: (**1**) Have a spokesperson from each group report the group's recommendations to the class. (**2**) Have students write a specific question, such as *What nightclub do you recommend?* or *What's a good place to take children?* and survey students in the school hallways before or after class, or during break time. Have students tally their results and report their findings to the class. They can even post their findings on the school bulletin board and title the findings: (*Your school name*)'*s Most Recommended Places to Go.* (**3**) For homework, have students write full-paragraph answers to the questions.

4. INVITATIONS

SETUP: (**1**) Set the context: Mary gets two invitations. (**2**) For each conversation, have students close their books as they listen to the audio program for the first time. Then have students open their books and read along as they listen to the audio program again. Finally, play the audio a third time, pausing after each line for students to repeat chorally. (**3**) As students practice each of the conversations in pairs, circulate to give individual feedback on pronunciation.

VARIATIONS AND EXPANSIONS: (**1**) Have students listen to the conversations on the audio program and place dots over the stressed words (as in the conversation chants). Review the stress marks with the class. Practice the conversations chorally, paying special attention to word stress. (**2**) Invite pairs of students to perform the conversations for the class. (**3**) Pass out blank cards to pairs of students. Have students write each line from both conversations on a different card. Have the pairs mix up their cards and then separate out the two conversations and put them in order again.

5. ROLE PLAY

SETUP: (**1**) Brainstorm with the class some possible invitations to make. For example: *Would you like to go to the movies / to a concert / to the amusement park?* (**2**) Have students work in pairs to write their own phone conversations. (**3**) Circulate around the class answering questions and correcting students' writing where necessary. (**4**) Have the pairs present their role plays to the class. After each presentation, ask: "What was the invitation?" and call on a volunteer to respond.

VARIATIONS AND EXPANSIONS: (**1**) If students need more guidance in how to compose their conversations, write these skeletal model conversations for accepting and declining an invitation on the board:

A: *Would you like to* _____ *?*
B: *Sure!*

A: *Would you like to* _____ *?*
B: *Oh, I'm sorry. I already have plans.*

(**2**) Have students submit their written work to you for correction before they perform the conversations in the following class.

USE YOUR ENGLISH!

SETUP: Have students do this activity as a homework assignment. (**1**) Tell students to talk with their conversation partners about interesting places to take a visitor. Tell them to write a list of the ideas that come up during their conversations. For example:

> *Interesting Places to Take a Visitor*
> *The Heritage Museum*
> *The Ice Cream Factory*
> *Lake Winnipesauke*

(**2**) At the beginning of the next class, students can share their ideas in small groups or simply hand in their reports to you.

EXPANSION: Have students do an Internet search with the key words *best of* (*their locality*) to learn about other interesting places to see in the area.

Lesson 2: Free Time

Pages 148–149

1. FREE-TIME ACTIVITIES

SETUP: (**1**) Have students work individually or in pairs to look at the pictures and complete the matching exercise. (**2**) Go over the answers with the class. Then play the audio program, pausing between items, and

have students repeat chorally. (**3**) Have the class brainstorm other free-time activities (for example: *collecting stamps, playing cards*). Write the words and phrases on the board, and have students add the new vocabulary to the list in their books; alternatively, tell students to write at least ten new words and phrases in their vocabulary notebooks.

VARIATIONS AND EXPANSIONS: (**1**) Say or write a word or phrase, and have students point to the pictures. (**2**) Point to a picture, and have students say the word or phrase. (**3**) Have students work in pairs to take turns pointing to and identifying the pictures.

2. WHAT DO THEY DO IN THEIR FREE TIME?

SETUP: (**1**) Model the pronunciation of each question for the class. (**2**) Have students work in pairs to answer the questions. (**3**) Circulate to answer questions as necessary.

VARIATIONS: (**1**) Before the class discusses the questions, write the simple present forms of the verbs *dance* and *watch* on the board. Underline the final *-s* endings. For example:

I dance.	*I watch TV.*
You dance.	*You watch TV.*
He dances.	*He watches TV.*
She dances.	*She watches TV.*
They dance.	*They watch TV.*

- Point out that you add an additional syllable with the *-s* in the third-person singular form of *dance*. Contrast the pronunciation of *dance* and *dances*. Tell the class: "We add an extra syllable to verbs that end in *-x, -s, -ch, -sh, -ce,* and *-se*." Ask the class: "What other verbs in this exercise add a syllable in the third-person singular?" (*exercise, watch*)
- Point out you added an *-e* to the third-person singular *-s* to *watch*. Explain: "We add *-es* to the third-person singular of verbs that end in *-ch, -sh, -x, -s,* and *-o*." Ask students: "What other verb in this exercise adds *-es* in the third-person singular?" (*go*) Ask: "Does the *-es* in *goes* add another syllable?" (*no*)

Write the other verbs in this exercise on the board (*play, read, sing*), and invite volunteers to come to the board to write out the simple present forms. Review the pronunciation of all the verbs, with special emphasis on the *-s* of the third-person singular. (**2**) Write on the board the following three questions: *What does she do in her free time? What does he do in his free time? What do they do in their* *free time?* Underline the subjects and the possessive adjectives. Point out that the possessive adjective "agrees" with the subject. (**3**) For homework, have students write sentences about the characters in the pictures. For example:

1. *They dance in their free time.*
2. *She plays the guitar in her free time. He sings in his free time.*

3. CONVERSATION CHANT: FREE-TIME FUN

SETUP: (**1**) Play the audio program. Tell students to read along as they listen to the chant. As you play the audio program, make hand motions or clap to reinforce the stress on the dotted syllables. (**2**) Play the audio program again, pausing after each line, and have students repeat. (**3**) Have the class chant chorally.

VARIATIONS: (**1**) Once students are familiar with the chant, divide the class into two groups. The indented chant lines represent a second voice. Have one group chant the lines that start at the left margin, and have the other group chant the lines that are indented. (**2**) Have students clap or make a hand motion to indicate where the stress falls as they chant. (**3**) Have students circle all the words that rhyme. Call on volunteers to read the rhyming pairs aloud and then write them on the board.

Language and Culture Note: Another way to disagree with someone is with the phrase *Not me.* Note this excerpt from the conversation chant:

A: *I love to go camping.*
B: *Not me.*

4. HOW OFTEN . . . ?

SETUP: (**1**) Model the questions. For example: *How often do you watch TV?* (**2**) Have students work in groups of three or four to take turns asking and answering the questions. Circulate to listen in and to answer students' questions as necessary. (**3**) Set a time limit; tell students they have ten minutes to complete the chart. (**4**) Write the following skeletal model on the board for student reference:

(Three)	students	often	(watch TV).
		sometimes	
		never	

(**5**) Invite students to report their findings to the class. For example: *In our group, three students often watch TV. And one student sometimes watches TV.*

VARIATIONS AND EXPANSIONS: (**1**) Encourage students to add one more question to the list (for example: *How often do you sing?*). (**2**) For homework, have students write sentences about themselves answering the questions in this activity. For example: *I sometimes watch TV. I often exercise.* (**3**) Have students choose one question, survey twenty other students in the school, and then report their findings to the class. For example: *Nineteen students often watch TV, and one never watches TV.*

5. FREE TIME

SETUP: (**1**) Point out that this conversation uses the Conversation Tip strategy from the Preview on page 145. (**2**) Set the context: Two people are talking about what they like to do in their free time. (**3**) Have students close their books as they listen to the audio program for the first time. Then have students open their books and read along as they listen to the audio program again. Finally, play the audio a third time, pausing after each line for students to repeat chorally. (**4**) As students practice the conversation in pairs, circulate to give individual feedback on pronunciation.

VARIATIONS AND EXPANSIONS: (**1**) Have students listen to the conversation on the audio program and place dots over the stressed words (as in the conversation chants). Review the stress marks with the class. Practice the conversation chorally, paying special attention to word stress. (**2**) Have the pairs practice the conversation with their own information. Circulate to listen in and to answer questions as necessary. (**3**) Invite pairs of students to perform their original conversations for the class.

6. HOW ABOUT YOU?

SETUP: (**1**) Give students three minutes to write their lists of things they like to do in their free time. Circulate to answer students' questions as necessary. (**2**) Write this question on the board: *What do you like to do in your free time?* (**3**) Have students work in pairs to ask and answer the question. (**4**) Have students write their partner's information in the appropriate circle in their books. When the partners find they both like to do something, they both write it in the middle list in their books. (**5**) Set a time limit; tell students they have only ten minutes to complete their diagrams.

(6) Circulate to listen in and to answer students' questions as necessary.

VARIATION AND EXPANSION: (**1**) Write these two skeletal model conversations on the board for student reference:

A: What do you like to do in your free time?
B: I like to _____.
A: So do I!

A: What do you like to do in your free time?
B: I like to _____.
A: I don't! / Not me!

(2) Have the partners report back to the class about the things they both like to do. For example: *We both like to play soccer. And we both like to exercise.*
(3) Take notes as students talk in pairs. Then write incomplete sentences on the board, and have students circulate to ask one another questions to find out whose name completes each sentence. For example:

_____ *doesn't like to go camping.*
_____ *likes to dance.*
_____ *likes to read.*
_____ *doesn't like to watch TV.*

(4) For homework, have each student write a paragraph about what their partner likes to do in his/her free time.

USE YOUR ENGLISH!

SETUP: Have students do this activity as a homework assignment. (**1**) To prepare students for this independent activity, brainstorm with the class about places where students can find the best arts and entertainment information (for example: certain local newspapers or a local paper's Web site). Write students' ideas on the board. (**2**) Tell students to write down the plan they make with their conversation partners. For example: *We plan to go to a Taiko drumming concert at Open Space on Saturday night at 8:00. On Sunday afternoon, we plan to go to the library book sale.* At the beginning of the next class, students can share this information in small groups or simply hand in their written plans to you.

VARIATION: If students are not close friends with their conversation partners, they don't need to make plans with them. Instead, they can do this planning activity with their own friends and family and then report their weekend plans to the class.

Lesson 3: TV and Movies
Pages 150–151

1. TV SHOWS

SETUP: (**1**) Have students work individually or in pairs to look at the picture and complete the matching exercise. (**2**) Go over the answers with the class. Then play the audio program, pausing between items, and have students repeat chorally. (**3**) With the class, brainstorm other kinds of TV shows (for example: *documentaries, home-shopping programs*). Write the words on the board, and have students add the new vocabulary to the list in their books; alternatively, tell students to write at least ten new words in their vocabulary notebooks.

VARIATIONS AND EXPANSIONS: (**1**) Say or write a type of TV show, and have students point to the TV screen in the picture. (**2**) Point to a TV screen in the picture, and have students say the word or phrase. (**3**) Have students work in pairs to take turns pointing to and identifying types of TV shows in the picture.

2. MAKE A LIST!

SETUP: (**1**) Have students work in groups of three or four. (**2**) Have each group choose one person to write the list as the group brainstorms the names of TV shows. (**3**) Remind students that they don't have to agree on their favorite shows—they should compile a list of everyone's favorites. (**4**) Set a five-minute time limit for this brainstorming activity. (**5**) Invite a spokesperson from each group to tell the class the names of their group members' favorite shows.

VARIATIONS AND EXPANSIONS: (**1**) As groups tell you the names of their favorite shows, ask: "What kind of show is that? Is it (a cartoon) or (a game show)?" (**2**) Have students work in groups of three to ask and answer this question: "What is your favorite commercial?" Set a three-minute time limit. Then have students report their favorites to the class. (**3**) Have students do a survey on how often other students watch certain shows, telling pairs to list four of their favorite shows and then to interview other students in the class or in the school about how often they watch these shows. For example:

A: How often do you watch _____? Once a week? Twice a month? Once a month? Never?
B: Once a week.

Have students report their findings to the class.

3. HOW ABOUT YOU?

SETUP: (**1**) Model the questions for the class. (**2**) Have students work in pairs to take turns asking and answering the questions. (**3**) Circulate to listen in and to answer questions as necessary.

VARIATIONS AND EXPANSION: (**1**) Have students ask and answer the questions in groups of four. (**2**) Invite students to describe one thing they learned about their partners to the class. (**3**) For homework, have students write their own responses to the questions.

4. AT THE VIDEO STORE

SETUP: (**1**) Have students work individually or in pairs to look at the picture and complete the matching exercise. (**2**) Go over the answers with the class. Then play the audio program, pausing between items, and have students repeat chorally. (**3**) With the class, brainstorm other kinds of movies (for example: *war movies, thrillers, musicals*). Write the words on the board, and have students add the new vocabulary to the list in their books; alternatively, tell students to write at least eight new words in their vocabulary notebooks.

EXPANSION: Say or write a kind of movie, and have the students brainstorm titles of movies in that category. For example:

Teacher: *Horror movies.*
Student 1: *Night of the Living Dead.*
Student 2: *Halloween.*

5. WHAT KINDS OF MOVIES DO YOU LIKE?

SETUP: (**1**) Point out that this conversation uses the Conversation Tip strategy from the Preview on page 145. (**2**) Set the context: Two friends are talking about movies. (**3**) Have students close their books as they listen to the audio program for the first time. Then have students open their books and read along as they listen to the audio program again. Finally, play the audio a third time, pausing after each line for students to repeat chorally. (**4**) As students practice the conversation in pairs, circulate to give individual feedback on pronunciation

VARIATION AND EXPANSION: (**1**) Have students listen to the conversation on the audio program and place dots over the stressed words (as in the conversation chants). Review the stress marks with the class. Practice the conversation chorally, paying special attention to word stress. (**2**) Write this conversation model on the board:

A: *What kinds of movies do you like?*
B: *I like _____.*
A: *I do, too. / So do I. / Me, too.* OR *I don't! / Not me. I like _____.*

Have students work in pairs to ask and answer the question *What kinds of movies do you like?* Circulate to listen in and to answer students' questions as necessary.

Language and Culture Note: Another way to agree with someone is with the expression *Me, too.* Note this excerpt from the conversation:

A: *I like action movies.*
B: *Me, too.*

6. FIND SOMEONE WHO . . .

SETUP: (**1**) Model (or have volunteers model) the questions that students will need to ask. For example: *Do you ever watch movies? Do you like horror movies? Do you like TV reality shows? Do you watch at least three hours of TV a week? Do you like science-fiction movies? Do you like love stories?* (**2**) Have students walk around the classroom asking and answering the questions. Tell the class they have ten minutes to complete their charts. (**3**) Have students report their information to the class.

VARIATION AND EXPANSION: (**1**) Encourage students to add one more item to the list. For example: *_____ has five TVs in his home.* (**2**) Have students choose one question, survey twenty other students in the school, and then report their findings to the class. For example: *Eleven students like reality TV, and nine don't.*

USE YOUR ENGLISH!

SETUP: Have students do this activity as a homework assignment. (**1**) To prepare students for this independent conversation, model a conversation with a volunteer, using the question in the box. (**2**) Tell students to write down the information that they learn from their conversation partners. For example: *My conversation partner is from the United States. He says that reality shows are popular in his country.*

VARIATION: If all your students and their conversation partners are from the same country, have the class brainstorm other questions they can ask their conversation partners. For example: *What do you think? Are horror movies bad for children? Is TV bad for children? What are your favorite TV shows? What kinds of movies do you like?*

Lesson 4: The Park

Pages 152–153

1. AT THE PARK

SETUP: (**1**) Have students work individually or in pairs to look at the picture and complete the matching exercise. (**2**) Go over the answers with the class. Then play the audio program, pausing between items, and have students repeat chorally. (**3**) With the class, brainstorm other vocabulary in the picture (for example: *sit on a bench, visit with friends, watch the children play*). Write the phrases on the board, and have students add them to the list in their books; alternatively, tell students to write at least ten new words and phrases in their vocabulary notebooks.

VARIATIONS AND EXPANSIONS: (**1**) Say or write an action, and have students point to the item in the picture. (**2**) Point to an item in the picture, and have students say the action. (**3**) Have students work in pairs to take turns pointing to and identifying actions in the picture.

2. WHAT'S HAPPENING?

SETUP: (**1**) Call on volunteers to read each question aloud. Discuss the answers with the class. (**2**) For question 1, write students' responses on the board in the correct present progressive forms so they can see how the verbs in the list transform. (**3**) For question 3, write students' responses on the board so everyone can see the correct use of the simple present tense. If students ask why the tenses are different, explain that the present progressive describes what is happening now (in the picture) and the simple present tense describes habits, routines, and attitudes (for example: *I like _____*).

VARIATIONS AND EXPANSIONS: (**1**) Before the class discusses the questions, write on the board the

applicable present progressive forms of the verbs *jog, ride,* and *fly*. For example:

she is jogging	*she is riding*	*she is flying*
he is jogging	*he is riding*	*he is flying*
they are jogging	*they are riding*	*they are flying*

- Point out you doubled the *g* in *jogging* because the last (and only) three letters in *jog* are in the consonant-vowel-consonant pattern. The last consonant is therefore doubled to keep the vowel sound short.
- Point out that *ride* has dropped its *e* in *riding*.
- Point out that *fly* is a regular verb in the present progressive tense.

(**2**) Have students write their answers to question 1 for homework and hand in their work for correction.

3. CONVERSATION CHANT: THE BEAUTIFUL PARK

SETUP: (**1**) Play the audio program. Tell students to read along as they listen to the chant. As you play the audio program, make hand motions or clap to reinforce the stress on the dotted syllables. (**2**) Play the audio program again, pausing after each line, and have students repeat. (**3**) Have the class chant chorally.

VARIATIONS: (**1**) Once students are familiar with the chant, divide the class into two groups. The indented chant lines represent a second voice. Have one group chant the lines that start at the left margin, and have the other group chant the lines that are indented. (**2**) Have students clap or make a hand motion to indicate where the stress falls as they chant.

4. WHAT'S THE STORY?

SETUP: (**1**) Divide the class into pairs. Have students look at the pictures and answer the questions. (**2**) Write the story title "A Day Off" on the board, and have students make up their story in pairs. (**3**) Invite students to tell their stories to the class.

VARIATION AND EXPANSION: (**1**) Have students write the story, instead of telling it, and submit it to you for comment and correction. (**2**) Make false statements about the pictures, and have students correct you. For example:

Teacher: *They're eating lunch at home.*
Student: *No, that's not right. They're having a picnic in the park.*

5. HOW ABOUT YOU?

SETUP: (**1**) Model the questions for the class. (**2**) Have students work in pairs to take turns asking and answering the questions. Circulate to listen in and to answer students' questions as necessary.

VARIATION AND EXPANSION: (**1**) Invite students to report on one thing they learned about their partners. (**2**) For homework, have students write a paragraph about their partners.

USE YOUR ENGLISH!

SETUP: Have students do this activity as a homework assignment. (**1**) To prepare students for this independent conversation, model a conversation with a volunteer, using the question in the box. (**2**) Tell students to write down the information they learn from their conversation partners. For example: *Riverway Park is a popular park in my conversation partner's neighborhood. People go there to take a walk, ride their bikes, jog, play basketball, and play soccer.* (**3**) At the beginning of the next class, students can hand in their reports to you.

EXPANSION: If possible, take your class to a nearby park for conversation practice. Play Frisbee. Have a picnic. Take photos of everyone. Talk in English. At the next class, look at the photos with the class and ask questions about them. For example: "Who's in this photo?" "What are they doing?"

Lesson 5: Sports

Pages 154–155

1. INDIVIDUAL SPORTS

SETUP: (**1**) Have students work individually or in pairs to look at the pictures and complete the matching exercise. (**2**) Go over the answers with the class. Then play the audio program, pausing between items, and have students repeat chorally. (**3**) Have the class brainstorm other individual sports (for example: *bike riding, snowboarding, track and field*). Write the words on the board, and have students add the new vocabulary to the list in their books; alternatively, tell students to write at least ten new words and phrases in their vocabulary notebooks.

VARIATIONS AND EXPANSIONS: (**1**) Say or write a word, and have students point to the correct picture. (**2**) Point to a picture, and have students say the word. (**3**) Have students work in pairs to take turns pointing to and identifying sports in the pictures.

2. WHAT'S THE SPORT?

SETUP: (**1**) Model the activity of miming a sport. Ask the class: "What's the sport?" and call on a volunteer to respond. (**2**) Divide the class into groups of four or five. (**3**) Have students in each group take turns miming and identifying individual sports.

VARIATION AND EXPANSION: (**1**) Do this activity as a whole-class exercise, with one student at a time standing up to mime an individual sport. (**2**) Draw two large intersecting circles on the board. Label one circle *indoor* and the other circle *outdoor*. At the intersection of the two circles, write *both*. Ask the class: "Is skiing an indoor sport or an outdoor sport?" Write the class's response in the diagram. If students have differing opinions, write the item in both places. Continue asking questions until students have categorized all the sports according to whether they are *indoor, outdoor,* or *both*. For example: ***indoor:*** *boxing, gymnastics, wrestling, bowling;* ***outdoor:*** *hiking, skiing, golf;* ***both:*** *swimming, ice-skating, yoga, tennis.*

3. TEAM SPORTS

SETUP: (**1**) Have students work individually or in pairs to look at the pictures and complete the matching exercise. (**2**) Go over the answers with the class. Then play the audio program, pausing between items, and have students repeat chorally. (**3**) Have the class brainstorm other team sports (for example: *ice hockey, lacrosse*). Write the words on the board, and have students add the new vocabulary to the list in their books; alternatively, tell students to write at least five new words in their vocabulary notebooks.

VARIATION AND EXPANSION: (**1**) Have students work in pairs to take turns pointing to and identifying the sports in the pictures. (**2**) Play a miming game. Have pairs of students come up to the front of the class and mime playing a team sport. Have the class guess the sport.

Language and Culture Note: You may want to point out that soccer and football are very different sports.

4. PROFESSIONAL TEAMS

SETUP: (**1**) Model this activity. Call out a team sport. Have the students brainstorm all the names of professional teams playing that sport. For example:

> *Teacher: Baseball.*
> *Student 1: The Orioles. (United States)*
> *Student 2: The Red Sox. (United States)*
> *Student 3: Tigres del Licey. (Dominican Republic)*

(**2**) Have students work in groups of four to brainstorm the names of professional teams. (**3**) Call out a team sport, and have a spokesperson from each group tell the class the names of teams on their list.

VARIATIONS AND EXPANSIONS: (**1**) Students can limit their lists to local or national teams. (**2**) Have students give a brief (two-minute) presentation about a popular team in their home region. Have students tell the class the name of the team, the logo of the team, and the team's recent record. If possible, have students download a team picture from the Internet to show the class.

5. WHAT'S YOUR FAVORITE?

SETUP: (**1**) Model the questions for the class. (**2**) Have students work individually to write their answers in the first column. (**3**) Have students work in groups of three to ask and answer the questions. (**4**) Set a time limit of five minutes for this activity. (**5**) Circulate to answer students' questions as necessary. (**6**) Call on a spokesperson to report each group's answers.

VARIATION AND EXPANSION: (**1**) Have students survey other students in the school and report their findings. (**2**) Have students make a sports-related hypothesis. For example: *I think the Chicago Bulls is the most popular team in our class.* Then have students "test" their hypotheses by surveying the entire class. For example: *What is your favorite sports team?* Have students report their results. For example: *My hypothesis was that the Chicago Bulls is the most popular team in the class, but that's not true. The Indianapolis Colts is the most popular team.*

USE YOUR ENGLISH!

SETUP: Have students do this activity as a homework assignment. (**1**) To prepare students for this independent conversation, model a conversation with a volunteer, using the questions in the box. (**2**) Tell students to write down the information that they learn from their conversation partners. For example: *My conversation partner says that soccer and basketball are popular in her country. Boys play soccer and basketball. Girls play soccer.* (**3**) At the beginning of the next class, students can hand in their reports to you.

VARIATION AND EXPANSIONS: If all your students and their conversation partners are from the same country, have the class brainstorm other questions they can ask their conversation partners. For example: *What's your favorite sport to watch? What's your favorite sports team? What's your favorite sport to play?*

Lesson 6: Lifelong Learning

Pages 156–157

1. AT THE LIBRARY

SETUP: (**1**) Have students work individually or in pairs to look at the picture and complete the matching exercise. (**2**) Go over the answers with the class. Then play the audio program, pausing between items, and have students repeat chorally.

VARIATIONS AND EXPANSIONS: (**1**) Say or write a word or phrase, and have students point to the item in the picture. (**2**) Point to an item in the picture, and have students say the word or phrase.

Language and Culture Note: In the United States, anyone can get a public library card by providing a photo ID and some proof of residency (such as a stamped and posted envelope with one's address and name on it or a household bill with one's name and address on it).

2. WHAT CAN YOU BORROW FROM THE PUBLIC LIBRARY?

SETUP: (**1**) Read each question aloud, and call on volunteers to respond. For example:

> **1.** *You can borrow audio books, children's books, DVDs, fiction books, music CDs, non-fiction books, newspapers, and magazines.*

VARIATIONS AND EXPANSIONS: (**1**) Have students ask and answer the questions in pairs. Invite students to tell the class one thing they learned about their partners. (2) For homework, have students write their answers to the questions and turn them in for correction. (3) Bring in the monthly schedule for the local public library. Read through the schedule with the class so that students can see all the different events and services their local library provides. (4) Take a field trip to the nearest public library. Before you go, make sure that students have the documents they need to get a library card: photo ID and a letter or bill with their name and address. Also be sure to talk with the librarian before your class visits. Librarians often give introductory tours.

3. FIND SOMEONE WHO . . .

SETUP: (1) Model (or have volunteers model) the questions that students will need to ask. For example: *Do you go to the library often? Do you borrow books from the library? Do you go to the library with your children?* **(2)** Have students circulate around the classroom asking and answering the questions. Tell the class they have ten minutes to complete their charts. **(3)** Have students report their information to the class.

VARIATIONS AND EXPANSIONS: (1) Encourage students to add one more sentence to the list. For example: _____ *borrows English grammar books from the library.* **(2)** Have students choose one question, survey twenty other students in the school, and then report their findings to the class. For example: *Eight students borrow books from the library, and twelve don't.*

4. CONTINUING EDUCATION CLASSES

SETUP: (1) Model the questions for the class. For question 3, set the context by pointing to the picture of the cake-decorating class. **(2)** Have students work in groups of three or four to ask and answer the questions. **(3)** Circulate around the class to listen in and to answer students' questions as necessary.

VARIATIONS AND EXPANSIONS: (1) Discuss question 1 as a class. If appropriate, bring in catalogs describing other classes that your school offers. **(2)** Bring in catalogs from a local center of continuing education. Give students fifteen minutes to look through the catalog, see what is available, and select a class they find interesting. Have students meet in groups of three to share the interesting classes they found in the catalog.

(3) For homework, have students write their response to question 2 and turn in their work for comment and correction.

5. YOUR WORK/EDUCATION PLAN

SETUP: (1) Model the activity for the class, asking for a volunteer to be interviewed. For example:

Teacher: What job do you want to have in five years?
Student: I want to be a nurse's aide.
Teacher: What do you need to learn to get that job?
Student: I need to learn about biology and medicine.
Teacher: Are there classes you need to take? How much English do you need for the classes?
Student: I need to study for a nurse's aide certificate. I need more English to study in that program.
Teacher: Where can you take the classes? How much do the classes cost?
Student: I can take the classes at the Red Cross. I don't know how much they cost.
Teacher: What other ways are there to learn the job?
Student: Right now I'm working in a nursing home. I'm learning a lot, but I need the certificate to be a nurse's aide.

(2) Have students work in groups of three to ask and answer the questions. **(3)** Set a time limit of fifteen minutes for the group discussion. **(4)** Call on individual students to report their answers to questions 1 and 2.

VARIATIONS AND EXPANSION: (1) If this activity raises many questions about programs, fees, and English requirements, tell students to do some research for homework. Have them try to get as many answers as they can; alternatively, if possible, invite the school counselor to come into class to speak about training opportunities. **(2)** If possible, you may want to discuss these questions individually with students in student-teacher conferences. **(3)** For homework, have students write their responses to these questions.

6. PLANS FOR LEARNING MORE ENGLISH

SETUP: (1) Have students work in groups of three or four to brainstorm ways to learn more English. **(2)** Have each group choose one person to write the list as the group brainstorms. **(3)** Set a five-minute time limit for this brainstorming activity. **(4)** Have each group's spokesperson report the group's ideas to the class. **(5)** Write students' ideas on the board.

(6) Point to the composite list and ask individual students: "What are your plans for learning more English?"

EXPANSION: For homework, have students write their response to the question *What are your plans for learning more English?*

USE YOUR ENGLISH!

SETUP: Have students do this activity as a homework assignment. **(1)** To prepare students for this assignment, brainstorm ways that students can find the names of schools in your community that offer continuing education classes; for example, students can do an Internet search with the keywords *continuing education* and the locality. Or students can ask friends and neighbors about schools that offer continuing education. **(2)** Tell students to write down the names of the schools they find. At the beginning of the next class, students can share this information either in groups or as a whole-class activity.

Listening Practice

Page 158

1. WHAT DO THEY LIKE TO DO IN THEIR FREE TIME?

SETUP: **(1)** Tell students to read through the diagram silently. **(2)** Play the audio program. **(3)** Review the answers with the class. If there is confusion about any answers, replay the audio program.

VARIATION AND EXPANSION: To help lower-level listeners, write the answers on the board in random order. For example:

> *go to the theater*
> *go to the movies*
> *go to art museums*
> *go camping*
> *have picnics in the park*
> *play sports*
> *watch game shows*

Have students read the answers before they listen to the conversation. As students listen, they can copy the answers onto the correct lines.

2. GOING OUT

SETUP: **(1)** Have students read the questions and answers and then listen to the audio program. **(2)** If students are uncertain about their answers, play the audio program again.

VARIATION: Have students first listen and then read the answers.

3. ABOUT YOU

SETUP: **(1)** Pause the audio program after each question so that students have time to write their responses. **(2)** When students have answered all seven questions, have them share their responses in small groups.

VARIATION: Have students take dictation on the questions and then write their responses after the dictation is corrected. Write the questions on the board so students can correct their work, or have students self-correct by referring them to the Audioscript in the back of their books.

Review

Page 159

1. WHO IS IT?

SETUP: **(1)** Have students write their answers to the questions giving as many details as possible. **(2)** Circulate around the classroom to answer questions as necessary. **(3)** Collect the papers, mix them up, and then have each student select one. Make sure no student has received his or her own paper. **(4)** Have each student read a paper to the class. **(5)** Have the class guess who wrote it.

VARIATION: Collect the slips, write incomplete sentences on the board (one for every student in the class), and have students circulate to ask one another questions to find out whose name completes each sentence. For example:

> _____ *likes to go to nightclubs.*
> _____ *likes to read.*
> _____ *likes to watch news programs.*
> _____ *likes to watch tennis.*

2. WHAT AM I DOING?

SETUP: (**1**) Model the activity of miming a free-time activity, and ask: "What am I doing?" (**2**) Divide the class into groups. (**3**) Have students in each group take turns miming and identifying the action. (**4**) Then do the same activity as a class, with students coming up to the front of the room and acting out an activity and the class guessing what the activity is.

VARIATIONS: (**1**) Have the class brainstorm free-time activities (vocabulary from Lessons 1, 2, 3, 4, and 5), and write their ideas on the board. Students can refer to this list when they choose what to mime or when they are trying to guess what a student is doing. (**2**) Write free-time activities on separate slips of paper and distribute them to students. Have students come up to the front of the room and mime the action as the class tries to guess what they are doing.

3. SO DO I!

SETUP: (**1**) Model the exercise by writing the possible responses to item 1 on the board (*So do I. / I don't.*). Tell students to give true answers. Read the first line aloud, and call on a student to respond. Read the same sentence to another student, and have him or her respond as well. (**2**) Have students work individually to write their responses. (**3**) Have students compare their answers in pairs. (**4**) Circulate to answer questions as necessary.

EXPANSION: Write additional statements on the board to which students can respond on paper. For example:

I like to watch wrestling.
I like to jog.
I don't like to watch TV.
I don't like to go to nightclubs.

4. WHAT SPORTS DO YOU LIKE?

SETUP: (**1**) Give students three minutes to write their own lists of favorite sports. (**2**) Have students work in pairs to compare their lists. Set a five-minute limit for this part of the activity. (**3**) Circulate to listen in and to answer students' questions as necessary. (**4**) Call on partners to tell the class what they both like. For example: *We both like to swim.*

5. LIBRARIES

SETUP: (**1**) Divide the class into pairs. (**2**) Have students write down all the things they can do in a library. Set a ten-minute time limit for this part of the activity. (**3**) Circulate to answer students' questions as necessary. (**4**) Have students take turns reading an item from their list. Write the item on the board as students check their spelling. Have everyone check each item off as it is mentioned so that there are no duplications. Possible answers are:

read books
borrow books
read magazines and newspapers
borrow magazines and newspapers
watch movies with headphones
listen to tapes
meet with an English tutor
borrow music CDs
listen to music CDs with headphones
use the Internet
join a book group
read and write e-mail
attend a children's story hour
do a language exchange with an English speaker

Assessment

Page 160

PART 1: QUESTIONS

SETUP: Have students work individually to write the questions. Challenge students not to look at the previous lessons but to construct their questions from memory.

VARIATION: Have students write their questions on a separate sheet of paper to hand in for correction at the end of the assessment.

PART 2: SPEAKING

SETUP: (**1**) Divide the class into pairs, and have students take turns asking and answering the questions. (**2**) Circulate to listen in and to answer students' questions as necessary.

VARIATION: Have students write their partners' responses to their questions and hand them in for correction at the end of the assessment.

PART 3: LISTENING

SETUP: (**1**) Have students first read the answers silently. Then play the audio program. (**2**) Check answers with the whole class by asking volunteers to read the correct sentence aloud. If there is confusion about any of the answers, replay the audio program.

VARIATIONS AND EXPANSION: (**1**) Have students write the number of the question and the letter of their response on a separate sheet to hand in to you for correction at the end of the assessment. (**2**) As an added challenge, have students compose questions for the uncircled answers.

PART 4: WRITING

SETUP: (**1**) Ask the class: "What are the people doing in the picture?" Lead a brief brainstorming session about what the people could be saying. (**2**) Have students work individually to write their conversation. Circulate as students are writing, and answer questions as necessary.

VARIATIONS: (**1**) Have students write their conversations on a separate piece of paper to hand in to you for correction. (**2**) Have students share their conversations with a partner. Then ask volunteer pairs to perform one of their conversations for the class.

Unit Tests

UNIT 1 **TEST**

I. VOCABULARY

A. *Write the words in the correct categories. (1 point each)*

angry	desk	pen	suit
blouse	eraser	purple	white
bored	gray	sandals	worried
chalk	happy	socks	yellow
confused	map		

Feelings	Classroom Words	Clothes	Colors

B. *Name five continents. (2 points each)*

1. _____   4. _____

2. _____   5. _____

3. _____

C. *Name two oceans. (2 points each)*

1. _____

2. _____

II. CONVERSATIONS

A. *Put the conversation in order. Number the sentences from 1 to 5.*
(2 points each)

_____ Neville: Sorry. Is that Karen?

_____ Sharon: Nice to meet you, Neville. My name's Sharon.

_____ Neville: Hi. I'm Neville.

_____ Neville: Oh, sorry. Nice to meet you, too, Sharon.

_____ Sharon: No, it's Sharon.

B. *Complete the conversation with the words in the box. (2 points each)*

is that	it's	speak	what	where

A: _____ are you from?

B: I'm from Tunisia.

A: Tunisia? _____ in Europe?

B: No, _____ in Africa.

A: _____ language do you speak?

B: I _____ Arabic.

C. *Complete the conversations. (2 points each)*

1. A: How are you today?

    B: _____

    A: Oh, that's wonderful!

2. A: How are you today?

    B: _____

    A: What's the matter?

    B: _____

    A: Oh, I'm sorry.

III. QUESTIONS AND ANSWERS *(2 points each line)*

Write answers in complete sentences.

About you

1. What's your first name?

_____

2. Where is your country?

_____

3. What language do people speak in your country?

_____

4. What clothes are you wearing today?

    a. _____

    b. _____

5. What colors are your clothes today?

    a. _____

    b. _____

About your class

6. How many men are in your class?

_____

7. How many women are in your class?

_____

8. How many classmates have glasses?

_____

9. How many chairs are there in your classroom?

_____

10. How many clocks are there in your classroom?

_____

11. Where is the board?

_____

12. Where are your books?

_____

13. Where is the wastebasket?

_____

14. What are your classmates doing now?

a. _____

b. _____

c. _____

15. What are three class rules?

a. _____

b. _____

c. _____

| UNIT **2** | **TEST** |

I. VOCABULARY

A. *Write the words in the correct categories. (1 point each)*

| aunt | cousin | husband | niece | uncle |
| brother | grandparents | nephew | sister | wife |

Male	Female	Both Male and Female

B. *Write the ordinal numbers. (1 point each)*

1. first _____

2. second _____

3. third _____

4. fourth _____

5. fifth _____

6. sixth _____

C. *Write the time in words. (2 points each)*

1. 7:15 _____

2. 8:30 _____

3. 12:45 _____

4. 4:00 _____

5. 12:00 P.M. _____

6. 12:00 A.M. _____

II. CONVERSATIONS

A. *Put the conversation in order. Number the sentences from 1 to 4. (2 points each)*

_____ Just a minute, please. Susan, it's for you!

_____ Who's calling, please?

_____ It's John.

_____ Hello. May I speak to Susan?

B. *Put the conversation in order. Number the sentences from 1 to 6.*
(2 points each)

_____ A: No. It's 555-3536.

_____ A: Nina? I think you have the wrong number.

_____ A: Hello?

_____ B: Hello. Is Nina there?

_____ B: Oh. Sorry.

_____ B: Is this area code (212) 555-3538?

III. QUESTIONS AND ANSWERS

Write answers in complete sentences. (2 points each line)

1. How many hours do you sleep every night?

_____

2. Are you an early bird or a night owl?

_____

3. What housework do you do every day?

a. _____

b. _____

c. _____

4. What housework do you never do?

a. _____

b. _____

c. _____

5. What do you do before class?

a. _____

b. _____

c. _____

6. What do you do after class?

a. _____

b. _____

c. _____

IV. ABOUT YOU

A. *Write six sentences about your morning routine. (2 points each line)*

1. _____
2. _____
3. _____
4. _____
5. _____
6. _____

B. *Write six sentences about your family. (2 points each line)*

1. _____
2. _____
3. _____
4. _____
5. _____
6. _____

UNIT 3 | TEST

I. VOCABULARY

A. *Write the words in the correct categories. (1 point each)*

blanket	entertainment center	shampoo	toaster
bowl	pan	sheet	toilet
dishwasher	pillow	sofa	toothbrush
dresser	razor	stove	

Kitchen	Living Room	Bedroom	Bathroom

B. *What do you put on the table at dinnertime? (1 point each)*

1. _____   4. _____

2. _____   5. _____

3. _____

II. CONVERSATIONS

A. *Put the conversation in order. Number the sentences from 1 to 8. (2 points each)*

_____ A: Hello?

_____ A: Yes, she is. Just one minute, please.

_____ B: Fine, thanks. Listen, do you want to go to a movie?

_____ B: Hi. It's Sam. Is Katie there?

_____ B: Too bad! OK, I'll talk to you soon. Bye!

_____ C: Good-bye.

_____ C: Hi, Sam. How are you?

_____ C: Yes, but I can't. I have to do the laundry!

B. *Complete the conversation with the words in the box. (2 points each)*

address	help	name	problem
heat	may	phone	

A: Acme Plumbers. _____ I help you?

B: Hello. My _____ is Kevin Murphy.

A: What's the _____, Mr. Murphy?

B: I have no _____ in my house. Can you _____?

A: Sure. I can come today at 3:00. What's your _____?

B: 525 Pine Street.

A: And what's your _____ number?

B: It's 774–5923.

III. QUESTIONS AND ANSWERS

Write answers in complete sentences. (2 points each line)

1. What kind of home do you live in?

_____

2. What city and state do you live in?

_____

3. What's your ZIP code?

_____

4. What's your area code?

_____

5. Where do you eat dinner at home?

_____

6. Is your bedroom usually messy or neat?

_____

7. How often do you clean your bedroom?

_____

8. What brand of soap do you use?

_____

9. You have a clogged toilet. Who do you call?

_____

10. You have mice in the kitchen. Who do you call?

_____

11. What problems do you have at home?

    a. _____

    b. _____

    c. _____

12. What do you do in your kitchen?

    a. _____

    b. _____

    c. _____

    d. _____

13. What do you do in your living room?

    a. _____

    b. _____

    c. _____

    d. _____

14. What do you do in your home at night?

    a. _____

    b. _____

    c. _____

    d. _____

UNIT 4 | TEST

I. VOCABULARY

A. *Write the words in the correct categories. (1 point each)*

| celery | cucumbers | limes | onions | peppers |
| cherries | lettuce | mangos | peaches | plums |

Fruit	Vegetables

B. *Name five breakfast foods. (1 point each)*

1. _____   4. _____

2. _____   5. _____

3. _____

II. CONVERSATIONS

A. *Put the conversation in order. Number the sentences from 1 to 6.*
(2 points each)

At the vegetable and fruit stand

_____ A: All right. Anything else?

_____ A: OK.

_____ A: May I help you?

_____ B: I'd also like three pears.

_____ B: No, thanks. I'm all set.

_____ B: Yes. I'd like five pounds of potatoes.

B. *Complete the conversation with the words in the box. (2 points each)*

| 'd | please | right | soup | special |

At the cafeteria

A: What's your _____ today?

B: A chicken sandwich and a bowl of _____.

A: What's the soup today?

B: Potato.

A: I _____ like the lunch special, _____.

B: Coming _____ up!

C. *Complete the conversations. (3 points each)*

1. At the table:

A: _____ the bread.

B: Here you are.

A: _____.

A: _____ more orange juice?

B: No, thanks. I'm all set.

2. At the supermarket:

A: _____, where can I find the butter?

B: In the _____ section.

A: And where can I find the ice cream?

B: In the _____ section.

A: _____.

3. Talking about foods:

a. A: I like strawberries.

B: So _____ she.

b. A: He's hungry.

B: So _____ we.

III. QUESTIONS AND ANSWERS *(2 points each line)*

Write answers in complete sentences.

1. You want to make vegetable soup. What do you need?

   a. _____

   b. _____

   c. _____

   d. _____

   e. _____

   f. _____

2. What's your favorite fruit?

   _____

3. What supermarket do you recommend?

   _____

4. How often do you go out for dinner?

   _____

5. What does *lb* mean?

   _____

6. What fast food do you like?

   a. _____

   b. _____

7. What do you usually eat for breakfast?

   a. _____

   b. _____

8. What do you usually eat for lunch?

   a. _____

   b. _____

9. What do you usually eat for dinner?

   a. _____

   b. _____

UNIT 5 TEST

I. VOCABULARY

Draw a map of your school neighborhood. List ten things and places on the map. (20 points)

II. CONVERSATIONS

A. *Put the conversation in order. Number the sentences from 1 to 7. (2 points each)*

_____ A: Thank you!

_____ A: Excuse me. Where's National Bank?

_____ A: Go straight; go past the coffee shop and the bakery. National Bank is on the right?

_____ A: How do I get there?

_____ B: Go straight; go past the coffee shop and the bakery. National Bank is on the right.

_____ B: Yes. That's right.

_____ B: National Bank? It's on Central Street.

B. *Complete the conversation with the words in the box. (2 points each)*

about	can	long	package	priority	send

At the post office

A: _____ I help you?

B: Yes. I'd like to mail this _____ to Chicago.

A: How do you want to _____ it?

B: _____ mail. How _____ does it take to get there?

A: _____ three days.

C. Complete the conversation with the words in the box. (2 points each)

check	'd	deposit	identification	may	slip

At the bank

A: _____ I help you?

B: Yes. I _____ like to make a _____. Here's my

deposit _____ and the _____.

A: May I see some _____?

B: Of course.

D. Complete the conversation. (2 points each line)

Calling 911

A: 911. This call is being recorded. What's the emergency?

B: _____

A: Where are you calling from? What's the address?

B: _____

A: What's your name and phone number?

B: _____

A: What's happening now?

B: _____

A: Is anyone hurt?

B: _____

A: _____ are on the way.

III. QUESTIONS AND ANSWERS *(2 points each line)*

Write answers in complete sentences.

1. How do you like your neighborhood?

   a. _____

   b. _____

2. What can you buy at the post office?

   a. _____

   b. _____

3. How often do you write letters?

   _____

4. How often do you go to the post office?

   _____

5. Where is your drugstore?

_____

6. What bank do you use?

_____

7. Where is your bank?

_____

8. What do you do at the bank?

    a. _____

    b. _____

9. What should you do if there is a fire in your home?

    a. _____

    b. _____

10. List two real emergencies to call 911.

    a. _____

    b. _____

UNIT 6 TEST

I. VOCABULARY

A. *Name seven different types of stores you can find in a mall. (2 points each)*

1. _____   5. _____

2. _____   6. _____

3. _____   7. _____

4. _____

B. *Name three different ways to shop. (2 points each)*

1. _____   3. _____

2. _____

C. *Complete the sentences with the words in the box. (2 points each)*

ads	credit card	order form	toll-free number	Web sites

1. The newspaper has many _____ for store sales.

2. To buy something online, you complete a(n) _____.

3. You call a(n) _____ to make an order from a catalog.

4. You can pay with a(n) _____.

5. There are many good _____ on the Internet.

II. CONVERSATIONS

A. *Put the conversation in order. Number the sentences from 1 to 10. (2 points each)*

_____ A: How would you like to pay?

_____ A: Can I help you?

_____ A: What's the credit card number and expiration date?

_____ A: What's the item number?

_____ A: What color do you want?

_____ B: With a credit card.

_____ B: 1029-1928-0299-0014, 11/09.

_____ B: Green.

_____ B: Yes, I'd like to place an order.

_____ B: 23-887-01.

B. *Complete the conversations with the words in the box. (2 points each)*

fill out	level	sold out	stationery	where

1. At the shopping mall:

    A: Where can I get a notebook?

    B: Try Sandy's _____ Store.

    A: Excuse me. _____?

    B: Sandy's. It's on the second _____ next to the toy store.

2. At a store sale:

    A: The sheets are _____. Can I get a raincheck?

    B: Yes. Please _____ this form.

III. QUESTIONS AND ANSWERS *(2 points each line)*

Write answers in complete sentences.

1. How often do you use a credit card online?

    _____

2. How often do you compare prices before you buy something?

    _____

3. What time of year are there good sales?

    _____

4. What's a raincheck?

    _____

5. What's your favorite piece of jewelry?

    _____

6. Where do you shop for shoes?

    _____

7. What clothing stores do you recommend?

    _____

8. What kinds of shoes do you wear?

    _____

9. What can you get at a hardware store?

_____

10. What can you get at a coffee shop?

_____

11. What kinds of things can you buy at yard sales?

    a. _____

    b. _____

    c. _____

12. What can you get at a sporting goods store?

    a. _____

    b. _____

13. What can you get at a department store?

    a. _____

    b. _____

    c. _____

14. What can you get at an electronics store?

    a. _____

    b. _____

UNIT 7 ▮TEST

I. VOCABULARY

A. *What are the months of the year? (2 points each)*

1. January
2. _____
3. _____
4. _____
5. _____
6. _____

7. _____
8. August
9. _____
10. _____
11. _____
12. _____

B. *Match the words with the temperatures. (1 point each)*

_____ 1. warm   a. 90°F

_____ 2. cool   b. 32°F

_____ 3. cold   c. 50°F

_____ 4. hot   d. 70°F

C. *Match the seasons with the activities. (1 point each)*

_____ 1. winter   a. rake leaves

_____ 2. spring   b. shovel snow

_____ 3. summer   c. go to the beach

_____ 4. fall   d. plant a garden

D. *Match the holidays with the activities. (1 point each)*

_____ 1. Christmas   a. turkey dinner

_____ 2. Valentine's Day   b. Santa Claus

_____ 3. Thanksgiving   c. parades and fireworks

_____ 4. 4th of July   d. noisemakers

_____ 5. Halloween   e. hearts and chocolates

_____ 6. New Year's Eve   f. children in costumes

E. *Name three things you find at a birthday party. (2 points each)*

1. _____   3. _____

2. _____

III. QUESTIONS AND ANSWERS *(2 points each line)*

Write answers in complete sentences.

1. How many seasons are there where you live?

   _____

2. What is the weather like in each season?

   a. _____

   b. _____

   c. _____

   d. _____

3. What is your favorite weather? Why?

   a. _____

   b. _____

4. What weather don't you like? Why?

   a. _____

   b. _____

5. What was the weather like yesterday?

   a. _____

   b. _____

6. Write a weather report for tomorrow.

   a. _____

   b. _____

   c. _____

   d. _____

7. When were you born?

   _____

8. When's your birthday?

   _____

9. What do you do on your birthday?

   a. _____

   b. _____

   c. _____

10. What's your favorite holiday?

   _____

11. What's your favorite holiday food?

_____

12. What's your favorite holiday activity?

_____

13. What greeting do Americans say on Halloween?

_____

14. What greeting do Americans say on New Year's Eve?

_____

15. What greeting do Americans say on a person's birthday?

_____

16. You can go anywhere in the world! Where do you want to go on a trip?

_____

17. You are going to Tahiti! What do you pack in your suitcase?

   a. _____

   b. _____

   c. _____

UNIT **8** **TEST**

I. VOCABULARY

A. *Name eight parts of the body. (2 points each)*

1. _____   5. _____

2. _____   6. _____

3. _____   7. _____

4. _____   8. _____

B. *Name two different kinds of doctors. (2 points each)*

1. _____   2. _____

C. *Name four things you can buy in a drugstore. (2 points each)*

1. _____   3. _____

2. _____   4. _____

II. CONVERSATIONS

A. *Put the conversation in order. Number the sentences from 1 to 10.*
(2 points each)

_____ A: How about this afternoon at 3:45?

_____ A: Doctor Mayer's office. May I help you?

_____ A: Can I have your name, please?

_____ A: Do you have a fever?

_____ A: What's the reason for the appointment?

_____ B: Yes. I'd like to make an appointment with Doctor Mayer.

_____ B: I have an earache.

_____ B: That sounds good.

_____ B: Yes. It's 102.

_____ B: Paul Gomez.

B. *Put the conversation in order. Number the sentences from 1 to 10.*
   (2 points each)

   _____ A: I have an appointment with Doctor Strucker.

   _____ A: Gina Sanders.

   _____ A: Here you are.

   _____ A: 10:30.

   _____ B: Can I have your name, please?

   _____ B: Can I see your insurance card?

   _____ B: OK. You're all set. Doctor Strucker's office is Room 114.

   _____ B: What time is your appointment?

C. *Complete the conversations. (2 points each line)*

   1. A: How are you doing?

      B: _____

      A: Oh? What's the matter?

      B: _____

      A: I'm sorry to hear that. I hope you feel better soon.

      B: _____

   2. A: How are you feeling?

      B: _____

      A: I'm glad to hear that.

      B: _____

D. *Complete the conversation with the words in the box. (2 points each)*

cough	help	recommend	try	works

At the drugstore

   A: May I _____ you?

   B: Yes. I have a bad _____. What do you _____?

   A: _____ Tussin Ease. It really _____.

   B: Thanks.

III. QUESTIONS AND ANSWERS *(2 points each line)*

Write answers in complete sentences.

1. What are some healthy habits? Give three examples:

   a. _____

   b. _____

   c. _____

2. How often do you sleep eight hours a night?

   _____

3. What medicine do you recommend for a stomachache?

   _____

4. What medicine do you recommend for a headache?

   _____

UNIT 9   TEST

I. VOCABULARY

A. *Answer the questions. (2 points each)*

1. What does a bank teller do?

_____

2. What does a nurse do?

_____

3. What does a barber do?

_____

4. What does a carpenter do?

_____

5. What does an auto mechanic do?

_____

6. What does a fisherman do?

_____

7. What does a mail carrier do?

_____

B. *Name five jobs that require a uniform. (2 points each)*

1. _____ **4.** _____

2. _____ **5.** _____

3. _____

C. *Name three safety signs. (2 points each)*

1. _____ **3.** _____

2. _____

II. CONVERSATIONS

Complete the conversation with the words in the box. (2 points each)

ad	afternoon	experience	looking for	newspaper
address	come in	fill out	name	thank you

Applicant: Hello. My _____ is Arif Benizar. I'm calling about

your _____ in the _____ for

a lab technician.

Employer: Yes. We're _____ two lab technicians. Do you

have any _____?

Applicant: Yes, I do.

Employer: Can you come in and _____ an application?

Applicant: Yes, I can _____ this afternoon.

Employer: Fine. The _____ is 1058 Broadway.

Applicant: _____. I'll see you this _____.

III. GETTING A NEW JOB

A. *Read the help wanted ads and answer the questions. (2 points each)*

Waitress Wanted
p/t
bilingual pref. (Spanish/English)
exp. req'd
Apply in person at Café Guadalajara.

Security Guard
3rd shift
refs. req'd.
pay DOE
Call (781) 555-6252.

1. Which job is part-time? _____

2. Which job requires references? _____

3. Which job is at night? _____

4. Which job pays depending on experience? _____

5. Which job prefers a bilingual applicant? _____

B. *Complete the application.*

Work Experience *(4 points each line)*

(job)	(employer)	(address)	(date)
(job)	(employer)	(address)	(date)

Education *(3 points each line)*

(school/college)	(degree/diploma/certificate)	(date)
(school/college)	(degree/diploma/certificate)	(date)

References *(3 points each line)*

(name)	(position)	(phone number)
(name)	(position)	(phone number)

IV. QUESTIONS AND ANSWERS *(2 points each line)*

Write answers in complete sentences.

1. What's your job?

_____

2. What do you do at work?

a. _____

b. _____

3. What do you wear at work?

_____

4. What job would you like to have in the future?

_____

5. What hours do you work?

_____

6. What are two good reasons to leave a job?

a. _____

b. _____

7. What are two good reasons to fire an employee?

a. _____

b. _____

UNIT 10 TEST

I. VOCABULARY

A. *Name six kinds of TV shows. (2 points each)*

1. _____   4. _____

2. _____   5. _____

3. _____   6. _____

B. *Name five kinds of movies. (2 points each)*

1. _____   4. _____

2. _____   5. _____

3. _____

C. *Name four sports. (2 points each)*

1. _____   3. _____

2. _____   4. _____

II. CONVERSATIONS

A. *Complete the conversation with the words in the box. (2 points each)*

love	maybe	plans	sorry	would

A: _____ you like to go to a Lynx concert with me on Friday?

B: Sure. I'd _____ to!

A: Can you go to the art museum with me on Sunday?

B: Oh, I'm _____ . I already have _____ .

A: That's OK. _____ some other time.

B. *Agree or disagree with the statements. (2 points each)*

1. I like to watch game shows.

   _____

2. I don't like to watch TV.

   _____

3. I like horror movies.

   _____

4. I like golf.

   _____

5. I like to watch basketball.

   _____

III. QUESTIONS AND ANSWERS *(2 points each line)*

Write answers in complete sentences.

1. What do you like to do in your free time?

   a. _____

   b. _____

   c. _____

   d. _____

2. What's the name of a museum in your town?

   _____

3. What's the name of a nightclub in your town?

   _____

4. What's the name of a theater in your town?

   _____

5. How often do you go to an amusement park?

   _____

6. How often do you go camping?

   _____

7. What kinds of movies do you like?

   a. _____

   b. _____

8. What are your favorite TV shows?

    a. _____

    b. _____

9. What do people do in parks?

    a. _____

    b. _____

    c. _____

10. What's your favorite sport to watch?

_____

11. What's your favorite sport to play?

_____

12. What's your favorite sports team?

_____

13. What do you like to read?

_____

14. What can you borrow from the public library?

    a. _____

    b. _____

    c. _____

15. What job do you want to have in five years?

_____

16. What do you need to learn to get that job?

_____